Raccoon Sixty

The Writer formerly known as 

One Printers Way
Altona, MB R0G 0B0
Canada

www.friesenpress.com

First Edition — 2023

ISBN
978-1-03-917723-9 (Hardcover)
978-1-03-917722-2 (Paperback)
978-1-03-917724-6 (eBook)

1. TRV010000 TRAVEL, ESSAYS & TRAVELOGUES

Distributed to the trade by The Ingram Book Company

MORE OF WHAT PEOPLE ARE NOT SAYING ABOUT THIS BOOK

"A great many people writing now would be better employed keeping rabbits." Dame Edith Stilwell

"A must for all travellers of the road and soul." *St. Petersburg Times*

"Irresistible. . . Immensely readable . . . a saga that is part myth, part Shakespeare, part Jackie Collins . . . a whirlwind . . . that reads honest and true." *The Wall Street Journal*

"A rarity that comes along perhaps half a dozen times per decade." Stephen King

"These epic events brilliantly described . . . warn of the dangers that arise when we fail to anticipate the consequences of our actions. This is one of the finest books I have ever read." Madeleine Albright

"Thank you, thank you, thank you, thank you, thank you." Joe Biden (president)

"What I do object to is a pedestrian, ungrammatical prose style which has left me with a headache and a sense of wasted opportunity." *The Guardian*

"Wann immer ich mit Hillary Clinton zusammenarbeiten konnte, war es mir ein großes Vergnügen." Angela Merkel

"A keeper thanks to the decadent recipes, including zingy biscotti and ethereal orange puff cake." *Christian Science Monitor*

"Raccoon Sixty lives up to his reputation as travel writing's answer to Banksy." Rufus T. Driftwood

"Funny, poignant, occasionally breathtaking." *Financial Times*

"Replete with literary allusions as diverse as haiku master Basho, James Michener, and Franz Kafka. . ." *The Rocky Mountain News*.

"It was written after I died and I haven't read it, but I am hearing good things." Elvis

"This book should be must reading for US foreign policy makers." *Forbes*

"What fresh hell is this?" Dorothy Parker

"This is deep thinking slimmed down for people who aren't totally sure whether Socrates was the toga guy or the gyro guy." Cathal Kelly

"Sidesplitting essays . . . a delightful compilation circling the theme of death and dying with nods to the French countryside, art collecting, and feces." *New York Times Book Review*

"A treat for Nabokov admirers." Kirkus

"Intoxicating. . . Like the best of Dickens." *New York Times Book Review*

"The year's greatest literary escape." *People*

"It was so great you're gonna love it." Donald Trump

"Combines uncommon storytelling with rare wisdom, worth the wait." *LA Times*

"A saga filled with joy and pain, humour and bitterness, and an array of characters who live, breathe, and illuminate the world." *Publishers Weekly*

"It isn't a whodunnit, or even a whydunit, but it may be the first work of a new, very Amsian, and post-modern genre—the whynotdoit." *The New Yorker*

"Not since Harry Potter has a book caught fire in this way." *The Economist*

"I never thought that I'd relate to a story about trying mindfulness in a Mormon survivalist household. If you are thinking about trying mindfulness, this is the perfect introduction." Bill Gates

"A book that you can curl up with and easily finish on a weekend, with or without a glass of wine." *The Miami Herald*

"Hilarious, often wonderfully perceptive, uncompromisingly ambitious, and written by a master of the English language." *The Financial Times*

DEDICATION

To my twelfth grade English teacher, Miss "Rosie" Robinson, without whose unflagging criticism, exasperation, and, ultimately, despair I may never have become an accountant.

Table of Contents

It's all because of the Virgin

Twisted Tales From the East

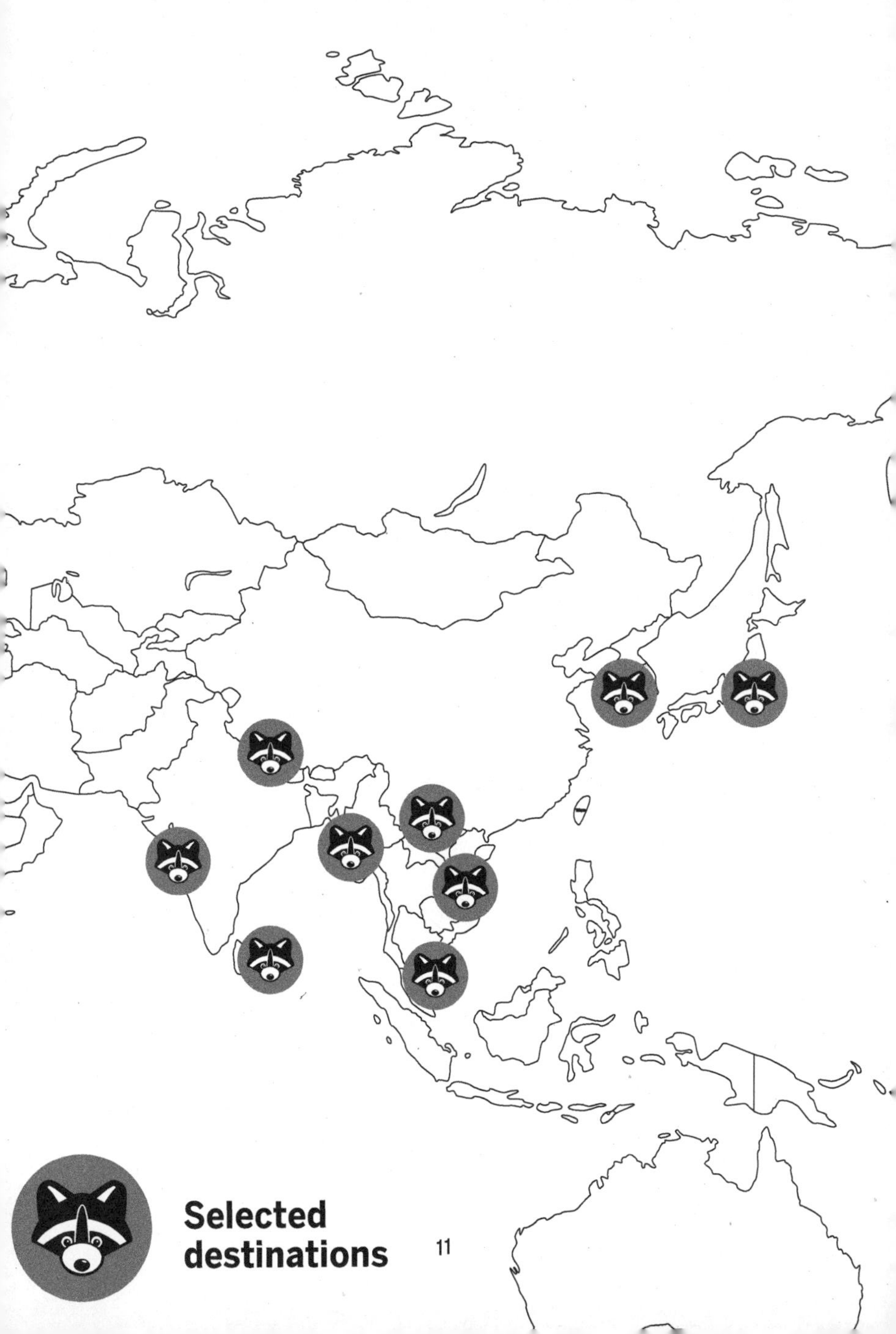

A WORD FROM THE AUTHOR

This book uses only raccoon-friendly paper sourced from raccoon-friendly forests.

No taxpayer support of any kind was wasted in bringing this resource to market.

A portion, maybe just a little bit, of the net profit from the sales of this book might go to some of the impressive front-line charities the author had the privilege of visiting. Or, heck, maybe all of the profits, depending on how we feel on the day. But we absolutely promise we won't ask them to pay for any of the losses we might rack up if you are stupid enough not to buy this book.

Any similarity to any creature or humans, living or dead, is purely good luck rather than as a result of good writing.

Boon Doggle Publishing is a division of Boon Doggle Corporation.

Our mission: "To change the world one garbage can at a time."

PREFACE

"Travelling - it leaves you speechless, then turns you into a storyteller."
—Ibn Battutah

So why do we travel?

It is a question that we seldom ask ourselves and yet it seems like a reasonable question to get out of the way when starting a travel book. Is it just to get away, escape, be moving? Do we go for culture in all its component parts (food, music, sport, architecture, history, religion, etc.) and nature in all its components (the weather, geography, flora, fauna, etc.)? Of course it is usually a combination of all of these attractions, underlaid by a need to fulfil a desire perhaps unknown even to ourselves. There is no one simple universal answer to this question; it is an intensely unique and personal set of preferences and circumstances that gives us the itch.

As for myself, my renewed love affair with travel was prompted by my job. To be more specific: the opportunity to escape my job. In the latter part of my working life I spent twenty-five years as a civil servant—more accurately described as a bureaucrat, a moniker that garners about the same level of social status that a mass murderer or banker might expect. I have long been envious of the respect enjoyed by used car salesmen and telemarketers.

My mind began to wander and explore the possibilities of what life might be like without the constraints of daily employment. Travel was an irresistible option, but how might that choice unfold? As a Clark Griswald farce or an Indiana Jones adventure? Which one would be me? A tourist or a traveller? Someone who goes somewhere to see something awe-inspiring that he already knows about, or someone who goes somewhere to be surprised by something new? We all fit somewhere on that continuum and, like most of you, I am guessing, like to sample a bit of everything on that range; it's all good fun. Within these covers you may join us climbing the walls of Angkor Wat, sleeping with strangers in a loft in the Burmese backcountry, being helivaced off a mountain in the Himalayas or feeding stray dogs in the back streets of Kathmandu. Whether it's for adventure or a relaxing family vacation, the desire to travel seems to be in our DNA.

Things really got rolling in fourth-century Mesopotamia when the wheel was invented. Back in antiquity on the busy Easter and Christmas holidays, the wealthy Romans would head to their villas and spas in the country to escape the crowds of last-minute shoppers at the forum. More recently, leisure travel, the precursor to tourism, also has a long history. In the Middle Ages, recreational travel came into being. The spread of organized religions gave rise to the traditions of pilgrimages, some of which, like the family trip to Disneyland and the honeymoon by the Eiffel Tower, continue to this day. By the 1600s, the intelligentsia saw it as an educational rite of passage to go on grand tours and connect with others of similar social and educational standing on their gap year.

For example, Lord Byron didn't miss the chance to sow a few oats at the same time. Although a learned man, he may have been oblivious to the fact that he might have been the first sex tourist, the word tourist having entered the English vocabulary for the first time in 1772. He had taken up with the recently married eighteen-year-old Countess Guiccioli, whose nubile charms inspired him to dash off the first few verses of his masterwork *Don Juan* while visiting Italy in 1818. Naughty postcards not coming into general use until the 1840s.

Entrepreneurs, always on the lookout for evolving trends, took note of all of this, and savvy startups morphed into nascent travel agencies in the 1840s. The first mass-market package tours were introduced by Thomas Cook in 1855, and a mere forty years later, 20,000 customers had taken trips with his company.

It was the beginning of a boom that has lasted to this day. As of 2016, we had one and a quarter billion (that's 1,250,000,000) international arrivals the world over, those arrivals spending US$1.2 trillion on their excursions. The whole endeavour to that point contributing 8 percent of the world's annual GHG emissions. Thomas as much as anyone would be stunned to see how that fledgling industry has burgeoned. His first tour was a twenty-four-mile railway excursion from Leicester to Loughborough and back, costing each of his 500 customers one shilling. Things have come a long way since then.

What would have motivated those first package tourists? A twenty-four-mile trip down the tracks, one would assume, wouldn't promise anything dramatically different in culture or nature. So there must be another element at play here—the subconscious craving for escape and the experience of the unknown, which can only be satiated by just being away.

Travel allows you freedom—freedom from the day-to-day responsibilities of home life: doing the dishes, cutting the grass, and all the rest. Freedom to be anonymous and reinvent yourself for a few days, weeks, or months. Freedom to simplify your life down to the core essentials, a reductive process that focuses the mind on life's biggest questions. Wine or beer, left or right, today or tomorrow, or maybe not at all?

Problems seem less urgent. The answers to life's complexities might not be revealed, but time and distance can put them into better perspective. I am hoping that, as you hitch a ride with me on planes, trains, rickshaws, buses, hot air balloons, barges, and cabs, you will be reminded of that liberation and it will inspire you to get up and go rather than click and be carried. Unaccustomed as I am to writing a book (this is the first for me in my current identity), I feel the need to clarify how some of the chronology or content may vary from traditional publications.

As well as being a first for me, I am hoping that it will be a book of firsts for you, the reader, too. This is not some presumptuous master plan cooked up while high on cheesies and Red Bull to revolutionize the literary experience, but a recognition that, now, for better or worse, we are changing how we digest and or now more commonly absorb information.

How, you ask, will this be a book of firsts? Let me tell you what I am hoping for. These stories chronicle the travel adventures of my wife, Trixie, and me and span a period of about ten years, and touch on nine countries on the Asian continent, along with a transformative experience in the Swiss Alps. How to organize this scattershot sampling of experiences becomes a problem: by date, by country, by entertainment value? Any good marketer will advise you to "hook 'em early, get your best, glitziest, most eye-catching product out there first."

Having abandoned that idea, I have decided on a roughly chronological, but not necessarily a numerically sequential presentation. I had better explain. Here as I sit typing out this preface in February of 2021, I think back to some of the first drafts of these chapters scratched out on location. As the memories refresh themselves, I recall that many of the destinations had their own local conventions for keeping track of the years. I was in Myanmar in 1383, Japan in Heisei 31, Nepal in 2073, 2550 in Buddhist Sri Lanka, or the year 41 if Pol Pot had had his way in Cambodia. But, no, better that I stick with what I know—the Gregorian calendar, even if it does mean hoping that you don't notice that George Bush isn't president (did it ever dawn on us that we would miss him one day?) anymore.

This book also is the first in the new literary genre—Coonlit. The first by a cisgendered trans-species who identifies as a raccoon. My orientation not yet having achieved mainstream acceptance, I have been reticent to enlist any luminary to pen this preface. Lacking the blink bait celebrity endorsement, I have filled the cachet void by quoting liberally from everyone from Anonymous to Zappa. All of this should have no relevance to the reader; we are all creation's creatures, after all. I am just trying to fill out the list of firsts here.

Another first, how to cater to the distracted reader? We are all living distracted lives now. How far is your electronic device from you right now? If I listen hard enough, I am certain that I will hear it ping.

With this in mind, I am writing this as a Book E, not an ebook, although it will also be issued as an ebook. Confusing? Yes, well, you may as well get used to it now. So, yes, a Book E. Included in the text of my stories you will find internet addresses to all kinds of interesting (at least to me) links. My hope is that these curated references will spare you from being inundated by the internet's data tsunami. With any luck these selections will lead you to some higher ground where you may dip your toes into some relatively benevolent pools of information. All you have to do is take a picture of the web link with your device and click on it.

Before you know it, you could find yourself right beside us learning the etiquette to using a squat toilet in India; find yourself parasailing with hawks and biting our nails together while landing at the most dangerous airport in the world.

Now, after more than ten years of full retirement, I offer you another first: a superannuated guide to adventure tourism. There is a section for the memory-challenged at the back of the book titled "What Did We Learn?" Here, you can safely test the robustness of your grey matter in a risk-free environment.

So, after all that, how did we make out answering the question about why we travel? Not very conclusively, I guess. But maybe we could conclude that it's the same sort of conundrum as asking people why they climb mountains. The answer may be just as glib and simple as "because we can." And "we can" in ever-increasing numbers, so why not let "have pension, will travel" be your motto?

It is a wonderful big planet that we have out there—enjoy it and be safe. On second thought, it's a scientific fact that you are safer alone and indoors, so don't go out at all; better stay in bed with a good book.

Part I

FIRST STEPS

Chapter 1

The Yolk Was on Me

Egg for Eight

"THE FIRST CONDITION OF UNDERSTANDING A FOREIGN COUNTRY IS TO SMELL IT."

– Kipling

"TRAVEL FAR ENOUGH AND YOU WILL MEET YOURSELF."

– David Mitchell

Backpacks. Backpacks? What is it with the backpacks?

We have been suitcase people since 1996. That was when we took the kids out of school and drove around Australia in a van for nine months.

Since leaving those free-range travel days behind, travel and wheeled luggage had become synonymous. It was now 2006 and things were about to change.

By this time, my wife and I had found ourselves in a more adventurous frame of mind. Our children had reached the phase where parental input was considered no more than harassment, the mortgage was at a non-threatening level, we had good health, and a secure income that was never quite enough, but whose is? So taking full advantage of the best perk available to a civil servant—vacation time—I took a three-month leave of absence from my job—unpaid, I hasten to add, lest you feel aggrieved enough to start an online bullying campaign (good luck finding me) or dispatch a hitman.

We figured that we should try a gentle, peaceful introduction to independent travel, starting in Asia. We had been musing about how ideal Nepal would be, a little trekking, a trip to an ashram, some cultural exploration, all that later kiboshed due to the Nepali civil war, a tragic 17,000 dead by its cessation. We recalibrated our plans and headed for Southern India instead. My first impression was that India is full, full of everything. If you are looking for anything more insightful than that, read on at your peril.

With trembling hands and a deep breath, we handed the keys to the car and the house to our kids and off we went. Twelve weeks with no fixed address, our worldly possessions in our backpacks, our feet to take us where only your feet can take you, and no cell phone to drag us back to the life that we had suspended at home, the future beckoned. The promise of the unknown was the major pull. When does an adventure morph into an ordeal, or a humdrum event blossom into a delight? You will never know until you go.

Our great adventure starts somewhat unconventionally as my wife Trixie and I head off in opposite directions. Trixie flies to Germany for a short visit with her sister while I travel west toward Asia. As usual, she is ahead of me, leaving a couple of days before me and stretching her lead by an hour for every fifteen degrees of longitude that she travelled east while I would surrender an additional hour for every fifteen degrees that I flew toward the Orient. By the time we are reunited, I will have crossed the International Date Line and somehow a whole day of my life will have evaporated. Apparently my travel insurance doesn't cover such losses.

My flight plan is not, as you would say, a straight shot. It is wrought with layovers. My first leg takes me from Victoria to LA for a seven-hour stopover. Too chicken to head into the city in case I miss my connection, I hang out at the international food court, a multi-ethnic collection of grim faces assembling grimmer looking food. It's hard to imagine taking one of life's true pleasures, eating, and devaluing it more. If it gets any more efficient, it'll be "tap card, insert nozzle in mouth, pull trigger, ease up when nearing the uvula in order to avoid spillage." For a change of scenery, I decide to visit the space-age-looking building in the middle of the complex that is home to an actual restaurant, only to be confronted with the same problem that I'd had on my last visit, twenty-five years earlier. It seems the only way to approach it on foot is through car parks and across a four-lane highway. The clientele seems to have changed from my previous trip. I recall corpulent white businessmen wearing stunted neck ties accompanied by athletic-looking Black girls who probably didn't earn their living from athletics, at least from none of the Olympic disciplines. What they have now are obese youths with sideways baseball caps and baggy-arsed trousers—oh, for the good old days.

LA to KL (Kuala Lumpur) with Malaysian Airlines was around twenty hours of uneventful boredom. The 747 was recently refitted with personal LED screens, but I don't watch much—the sound quality is still dismal, like trying to decipher Shakespeare with a blow dryer going full blast in both ears. Naturally, we have the usual in-flight info—the world map with the plane the size of Australia imperceptibly inching its way toward our destination. We have an additional feature every half hour or so: a rendering of a plane appears on an otherwise blank screen with an arrow and a distance emanating from mid fuselage, with the word *Mekkah* at the top of the screen. It takes me ages to figure out that it is telling us the direction and distance to Mecca.

Duh. . . . Malaysia is a Muslim country, and, naturally enough, this is a flight comprised of mostly Muslim passengers. I think if they could synchronize the Mecca alert with the fasten seatbelt signs, they'd really be onto something. Might be enough to convert a few infidels.

Arrive in KL airport to another seven-hour layover. This hub of aviation is super modern, built with expansion in mind. At first glance I think that the multi-storey car parks are apartments with balconies, spectacular bougainvillea plants trailing down their sides. The airline provided a free day room at one of the airport hotels. I am to rendez-vous with Trixie there; she was to arrive six hours prior to me from Frankfurt after visiting her sister. Before the twenty-hour flight took its toll, the concept felt vaguely naughty. Married twenty-four years and this our first tryst in a hotel day room!

I get to hotel registration, looking forward to a cozy reunion . . . not for long.

"My wife Trixie has checked us in. Can you tell me the room number?"

I get a puzzled response. "No, she's not here, sir. She has a reservation for tomorrow. We have one for you though."

"Tomorrow? No, our flight to Mumbai leaves tonight in six hours!"

Half in a daze, half seething, I trudge to my room armed with the airline phone number. I dial the number and although the English at the other end isn't BBC, it's better than my Malay. After several false leads, we finally determine that Trix wasn't on today's flight but tomorrow's. Those bozos at the travel agent must have fouled up somehow due to the dateline being a factor.

So what to do next? I ask if I can move my flight to the next day. This is when the fun really starts. I get some Malay version of "Sorry not my department."

"You try this number nin tree fi seum fi eckeckeckeck."

"Sorry, I think I got most of that. Nine-three-five-seven-five. Was that last bit eight?"

"Noh, eckeckeckeck."

"Eight?"

"Noh, Eck, eck, eck, eck."

"Egg?" I venture. As soon as I say it, I realize that we are plumbing new depths in Canadian-Malaysian relations. I can almost feel the disbelief coming through the phone lines—this twit doesn't know the difference between booking a flight and ordering breakfast. We are importing cretins now.

"Noh, Noh, Noh EGG! ECK, ECK, ECK, ECK!" this time with real feeling.

I try "X . . . X," this time feeling that I am making real progress, having progressed from foodstuffs to letters—before you know it, we will be on to integers.

"NOH, NOH. . . ." You know the drill.

Oh, Buddha. Finally, the light goes on in my jet-lagged (that's my excuse) brain.

"Eight, eight, eight, eight." How thick can a Scottish accent be? Or maybe how thick can a Scotsman be?

"YES, YES, eck, eck, eck, eck!"

Much embarrassed laughter and apologies on both sides. I don't think we could have been happier if we had won the lottery. After many thanks, I hang up the phone then punch in the numbers that will lead me to the solution to all of my problems and get . . . voicemail! @$#%

I have a brain wave, head down to the lobby and log onto email. I see an email from Trixie in my inbox entitled "Sorry." It turns out that she was late and missed her flight—not a foiled stuck-in-a-traffic-jam-missed-the-flight-by-minutes sort of late, not even a bad-luck-slept-through-the-alarm-by-the-time-I-woke-the-flight-was-gone kind of late, but a carefree spectacularly oblivious sort of a late—an oops-got-the-day-wrong kind of a late.

Anyhow, by the time I read this Trixie is now in transit, having been able to shunt all the bookings out by a day with a promise to meet up with me in Mumbai. With some fancy footwork (no more phone calls) back at the airport, which include me retrieving my bags from the bowels of baggage handling and the help of sympathetic ticketing staff, I too am able to book for the following day.

The next day I decide to surprise Trixie at arrivals. The temptation for merciless ribbing and sarcasm is huge, but this is an event to treasure and put in the bank, an ace up the sleeve, like a get-out-of-jail-free card to be used on a very special occasion. Like some serious misdemeanour, such as forgetting the wedding anniversary or leaving the toilet seat up.

As she saunters unsuspectingly into arrivals I allow myself to voice a casual "nice of you to drop by" over her shoulder. A big reunion, hugs, kisses, everything hunky dory.

Finally, at 10 p.m., mighty hot and humid, we arrive in the Mumbai airport, a very rundown facility that would make a Greyhound bus depot look palatial. We link up perfectly with the driver from our hotel. Thank God at last in India (you are probably thinking the same thing). The drive to the hotel is something else. We ask Manjit, the driver, to leave the windows down so that we can better experience the sights and sounds and smells of Asia. We pepper him with questions. What chaos, what an assault on the senses, what fun! For a while—until we pass through an area at least a couple of kilometres long, shanty after shanty lining the side of the street, thick smog, wood smoke, row upon row of rag-clad bodies asleep on the "sidewalk," a scene from *The Fog*. We cross a bridge; the air is thick with the smell of something human, definitely human, but in inhuman quantities. We are forced to close the windows or vomit.

Traffic is a stop-start affair. At one intersection, a toddler, no more than three years old, totters around in the barely lit road in the midst of trucks, cars, and buses. He is just a decoy so that his mother, baby on hip, can beg from the vehicles stuck in the traffic snarl that the tot has created. At the next intersection, a spindly, rag-clad old woman with crippled hands looms out of the gloom and scratches her nails down the car window—it's a scene straight out of *The Walking Dead*.

I find the experience intimidating. But why? Do I think that poverty is contagious? Am I afraid that they are violent? Does guilt increase with proximity?[1]

We arrive at the hotel in virtual silence; equal parts jet lag and culture shock are to blame. The room is adequate, a refuge. Of course, things will be different tomorrow thanks to the usual travellers' tonics of sleep, breakfast, a shower and above all, the daylight that curbs the terrors of the imagination.

It is why we travel, there is no up without the down. The sense of anticipation about arriving in a new place is a rush, the anonymity of darkness heightens that feeling of being alien. Some of the most powerful memories and impressions are indelibly formed in those first few hours.

We didn't know the half of it.

1 http://worldpopulationreview.com/world-cities/mumbai-population/

Chapter 2

Champagne and Orange

Qu'ils mangent de la brioche

"POVERTY IS LIKE PUNISHMENT FOR A CRIME YOU DIDN'T COMMIT."

– Eli Khamarov

"IS IT POSSIBLE THAT MY PEOPLE LIVE IN SUCH AWFUL CONDITIONS? I TELL YOU, MR. WHEATLEY, THAT IF I HAD TO LIVE IN CONDITIONS LIKE THAT I WOULD BE A REVOLUTIONARY MYSELF."

– King George V

Up early the next day, well rested, fed, and refreshed, we are impatient to get outside and experience our new surroundings at street level. Mumbai, as you might expect, is chaotic, but what surprises me is how grand many of the buildings in the old quarter are. Courthouse, boulevards, museums, universities—you name it. All seem to have been built around the 1860s, imposing and ornate and on a scale more in keeping with Paris or London than a provincial outpost. That was in the heyday of the "Empire" ,150 years ago, and it looks like nothing in the way of maintenance has been done since. Although it's all in very sad shape indeed, you can see that it must have been magnificent in its day. Obviously nothing was done on the cheap. For example, when King George V of Britain visited in 1911, the raj had decided to commemorate the event. The welcome wasn't a few balloons and a sign saying "Welcome to India, Georgie." They built a monument called "The Gateway to India." If you visualize a portico the shape and roughly half the size of the Arc de Triomphe, you get the idea. Nothing like omnipotence and unlimited manpower to get things done.

We get our first up-close experience with the beggars—they are everywhere. What hasn't been said about the poor of India? I think having spent a couple of years working in Africa in the '70s did take some of the element of shock out of it for me (although I had never seen anything on a scale such as this). Probably being an insensitive bastard was a bigger factor. We can't all be Mother Teresa

. . . . but why not?

There are many ways of dealing with the tragic cases that you encounter, a few being:

The rational accountant's approach. Me to beggar: "Sorry you've lost your arms/legs/family/hope/skin/eyes/parents/home (as appropriate), but I gave at the office, don't you know. Payroll deduction. The money should be working its way through to you anytime now. If you are not getting your share, take it up with the United Way."

Nah—rationalization is not going to work.

The oblivious approach: A trance-like state, a brisk pace, eyes straight ahead. This can work, but if you flinch you are sunk. Case in point, while walking along the shore of the Mumbai harbour I hear the dreaded plaintive "Please, sah," and make the beginner's mistake of turning to see where the voice is coming from. It has been years since I've seen the movie *Top Gun*, but the lingo sprang instantly to mind.

"Ice Man to Maverick—bogey at seven o'clock," I crackle to Trixie. I look again. Shit. *"He's got a lock on me."* A pitiful, one-legged wretch on crutches. Our dignified sauntering gait isn't working—he is gaining on us. We pick up the pace. What a bizarre spectacle it must have made. Two speed-walking Caucasians with a one-legged beggar in hot pursuit.

Ludicrous/heartless/pitiful/darkly comic and shameful all at the same time.

"Ice man to Maverick . . . break right . . . break right . . . head for cover." It isn't until we reach the sidewalk that we finally shake him. A dirty trick, I guess, but the sidewalks are a near-impassable obstacle course for the able bodied at the best of times. Bricks, chunks of paving, broken tile, pot-holed earth, with the curb being the only clue as to its intended use. Poor guy didn't stand a chance. I will fry in hell, there is no doubt about it.

Sometimes even when you intend to be charitable, the circumstances confound you. One fellow appears out of nowhere in front of me, blocking my route. Poor soul has no arms, no begging bowl that I could see, but is pleading for rupees. My rational mind at work again: "How do I actually give an armless man money? Stuff it in his pockets, put it between his teeth?" That's as far as I let my thinking go.

There is a moral argument too that you would actually be filling the pockets of unscrupulous parasites more than the needy. Many of the handicapped and children only see a portion of the money that they collect. Their protectors/handlers take the lion's share for their own addictions.

So, what to do? One night on the way back to our hotel we happen upon a little girl, four or so, curled up under a lamp post. Trixie gives her a couple of oranges we had bought at the corner stall. The child's face lights up. A plan is hatched.

The next night we buy a bag of oranges on our way back from dinner in a pretty affluent district, which consequently is popular with street kids. Trixie sees a young boy in a doorway and gives him an orange. As we weave our way through the throngs of evening merrymakers, she hands out another to a little one we encounter. Before we have gone another twenty yards we are practically mobbed—insistent tapping, prodding, tugging, poking little fingers demanding attention. After the oranges are gone, which takes about a minute, the kids still aren't. They trail us—it is like a scene from the pied piper of Hamelin. We are forced to deke into an up-market, air-conditioned ladies' shoe shop complete with security guard in order to shake them. After half an hour perusing pairs of shoes that cost more money than these children would see in a year, it is finally safe to venture out.

So how should we navigate this predicament? Some days we do nothing, some days a lot, but with a feeling that it doesn't make much difference either way.

The next evening we celebrate Trixie's birthday, stay in and dine at the hotel's rooftop restaurant. A fine meal washed down with a bottle of champagne courtesy of Kuala Lumpur duty free, cost about forty dollars—or, to put it another way, about a monthly income for half of India's one billion plus people. Shades of Marie Antionette's "let them eat cake." I guess history will be the judge of how civilized the West was in the twenty-first century.

Well, that was a bit more of a downer than I intended, so what else did we get up to? We made a few odd type of excursions, banal and yet peculiar because I could—but hadn't—done them in my own town.

We visit the university library, bump into a fellow who turns out to be a CA (chartered accountant) and commiserate with him about year ends and tax returns—some things are indeed universal.

Drop into the Supreme Court and sit in on a civil case. It is a scene from Dickens.

Watch a hundred or more overlapping cricket matches being played simultaneously in one of the maidens (public parks). Like everything else there, it is chaotic and indecipherable but seems somehow to work and the people have fun making it work.

City traffic is a perfect example of said chaos. We have a great aerial view from the balcony of the university library. There seems to be no order to it, it is like peering down into a roiling petri dish. There are no lines or lanes involved, it appears more like a moving river of mosaic tiles complete with back eddies, tributaries joining in or branching off, the majority of the tiles being yellow Fiat taxis, circa 1960. I don't know who baksheeshed (bribed) who for that contract but it must have been a whopper. There are easily tens of thousands of these beaters.

At street level, the perspective is quite different. The sensation is of elbowing your way through a crowd rather than actually driving. Congestion is everywhere and the distances between the vehicles are inches or less on all four sides, but thankfully, speeds are slow. The logic of the taxi drivers, however, escapes me. They pester you mercilessly for your custom and when you finally succumb to using their services and you do succeed in getting them to use the meter, they seem hell bent on either:

a) minimizing the fare by getting the trip over with as soon as possible, or

b) eliminating the fare altogether by trying to kill you in the process.

One particular driver, clearly more than a few raisins short of the full fruit cake, must have seen too many Dukes of Hazzard episodes. He floors it to catch the traffic light, already red, without factoring in that there is a traffic roundabout immediately after the light. We careen around the traffic circle on two screaming bald tires, Trixie and I in the back seat squished to the windward side trying to keep the heap from capsizing like a dinghy in a storm. His reward was an earful and no tip at the end of the trip.

Mumbai being India's Bollywood, naturally we go to the movies. The movie is a bit of disappointment, a "thirty -something" sort of a show, the crowd mostly well-to-do Mumbai yuppies dressed in the boring jeans and T-shirts of the West. The previews are the best part of the experience. A sign flashes on the screen. I am sure that it's a transparency on a projector: "Please stand for the playing of the national anthem."

We all dutifully rise. It is a poignant moment. A hush fills the theatre. Then silence . . . too long a silence, thirty seconds, then a minute.

A few titters start to be heard followed by louder shushes from the patriots in the crowd. The atmosphere is charged, the silence interspersed by the growing number of snickers from the audience. The knockout punch comes when a wag standing behind me blurts out,

"Vee urr playing git in the silent mode."

Mercifully, the last few bars of the anthem blare out at the same time as the patrons erupt in gales of laughter. This alone is worth the price of admission. One more formality has to be dealt with before the show starts - the censors' certificate.

Again with the projector, this document looks for all the world like a microfiche copy of one of our old government travel vouchers I had to complete back in the eighties. A hodgepodge of arcane columns, serial numbers, measurements and signatures. Bureaucracy is one of the ingrained pieces of culture left by the British. Heaven help India if they ever have a "cut-the-red-tape initiative"; they would put millions out of work.

The movie itself proves to be a challenge, a truly bilingual mix. Hindi and English used interchangeably, sometimes both languages in the same sentence. Neither the actors nor the audience bat an eye, as far as I can tell in the dark, as they effortlessly switch from one to the other. We bail at the intermission: a smoke break.

One thing that quickly becomes apparent in India is that there are people everywhere and layers and layers of activity. Our hotel, for example, is one of three occupying the same building, with a separately owned restaurant on the roof. It takes me a while to figure out who all the folk are who are loitering on the landing of each floor. Well, doormen, of course. Each hotel has a doorman for its own guests and somehow they know which tourist to open the door for. Obviously "shared services" and contracting out aren't high on the agenda here.

On the last day in Mumbai we visit Mahatma Gandhi's residence from the 1920s and '30s, now a museum. It couldn't be less grand but the impact is all the more powerful because of it. A very special place. A few framed letters that he had written (to everyone from Tolstoy to Hitler, it begins "Dear friend"[2], a few simple dioramas (the sort of thing your kids made in Grade 3) of key events, and a restoration of his bedroom, a mat, spinning wheel, a few books, a walking stick,

2 https://www.mkgandhi.org/Selected%20Letters/letter.htm)

reading glasses, and writing material all on the floor. I've got more clobber than that in my backpack.

It's amazing to think on all that he accomplished.

After our sampling of a few slices of Mumbai city life, I am no wiser as to whether our experiences are in any way representative of the whole chapati, a mega feast comprising some seventeen million souls and five main languages if you include English.

We would happily stay longer and sample more delights, but a massive sub-continent stretches out below us, waiting to be discovered.

Chapter 3

Riding the Volvo U-Boat

A Goan Hamster

"YOUR BODY IS NOT A TEMPLE, IT'S AN AMUSEMENT PARK. ENJOY THE RIDE."
—*Anthony Bourdain*

"OF THE SEVEN DWARFS, THE ONLY ONE WHO SHAVED WAS DOPEY. THAT SHOULD TELL US SOMETHING ABOUT THE WISDOM OF SHAVING."
—*Tom Robbins*

It's dark, claustrophobic, and teeth-chatteringly cold as I wearily squint through my half-shut eyes for the umpteenth time. We have left at night and taken the overnight sleeper bus to the state of Goa, a small (about the size of Liechtenstein) former colony of Portugal on the Arabian Sea coast.

I quickly realize that I would never have made it as a submariner. Our transport is a retrofitted Volvo bus with two tiers of bunks with two bunks per tier on either side of the aisle. We are on the bottom bunks, so essentially at floor level, shivering next to the air-conditioning duct. If we incline ourselves to the full height of the berth, about two feet, we can see out of the bottom six inches of the original bus window. This is to be our crypt for the next ten hours.

Before turning in we chat to an English couple across the aisle. Wow, have these people ever had adventures up north. Their taxi driver beaten up, swarmed outside a Muslim mosque, etc. Gee, I am overcome with the travellers' equivalent of "keeping up with the Joneses." Not to be outdone, I decide to go hog wild and visit one of the local barber shops tomorrow. Yes, I know. I am a daredevil.

The motion of the bus makes for a pretty good sleep, punctuated only by the occasional alarming narcoleptic dream. On waking in a cold sweat, I take no chances and reconfirm with Trixie my wishes to be cremated.

We spend a couple of days in Panjim, the state capital, at a quaint hotel that is a conversion of an old colonial home. The atmosphere in general is much more relaxed than Mumbai; the Goans and non-Goans are only too happy to say that this isn't really India. Four hundred and fifty years as a Portuguese colony until the Indian liberation/ invasion (take your pick) in 1961 will do that to a place. Lots of centuries-old Catholic churches. Everything from small chapels to huge cathedrals. It is clear that the folk here take their religion very seriously, although despite that the buildings are in serious need of repair. The only new "temple" in town is the bank building, similarly imposing and ostentatious. It will be interesting to see whether the coming of the new religion, money, proves to be as sustaining as the old. It may be just a rose-tinted perspective of the people, but the few locals that we talk to are saddened by the loss of the innocence and hospitality of the people and the development/exploitation (take your pick) that has come with progress.

Despite the changes, we find the people friendly and patient. As everywhere in India, language is a challenge. We are swept up into a throng of streetside cricket fans watching a test match on a TV store window. They are typically eager to share their excitement and explain the finer points of the game in a selection of Konkani, Marathi, Hindi, and even some Portuguese. They would have been wasting their time even in English, but their enthusiasm trumps all barriers.

Ordering food in the restaurants should be easier if you are OK with the element of surprise—just point to a few items on the menu and cross your fingers. We think we are doing pretty well except on one occasion when we notice the Indian family at the table next to us, the mother trying to shush her guffawing sons. So what's the joke? It feels awfully like it is us. We nod to them, smile sheepishly.

"I am so sorry," she says, leaning over, whispering conspiratorially. "We didn't mean to listen, but do you know you have just ordered six different types of bread?"

Pretty hard to bluff your way out of that one. "Well, yes, of course we knew. We are researching for our new diet book, *Man Does Live by Bread Alone*." Tourists being regarded as a bit odd, you never know: it might have flown. Anyway, we fess up and those lovely folks are only too happy to practise their English, flag down our waiter to cancel the bun bonanza, and order us some delicious rava fried fish.

Time for us to move on. As we check out of our hotel, we listen to the owner complain to everyone and no one in particular: "Two years ago they are wanting air con, last year they want TV. This year, the TV not the right angle for watching from the bed! This isn't the bloody Marriott, isn't it?!"

He is locked into the spiralling equation—improved amenities plus increased room prices equals increased expectations, which leads in turn to increased complaints. Of course the growing profits give the whole cycle momentum.

We take up residence in a little resort on one of the less developed Goan beaches. The drive down is interesting on the NH (national highway) 17, a road paved for the most part and nearly a full two lanes plus the invisible third lane running down the centre, which is reserved for whoever is driving the biggest vehicle at the time. A couple of other features not normally found on the autobahn are bullock carts and speed bumps. The "resort" is nice. It's easy to see how idyllic it must have been, but it is changing fast. You get the feeling that India hasn't had much practice in dealing with garbage. In the past, things had a purpose, were used, broken, fixed, and reused ad infinitum. Now that the disposable age has arrived, trash (plastics, in particular) is everywhere and it is ugly.

No complaints though—good food, warm weather (32C), cooling ocean (31C), and eternal sunshine. The day's big event is setting the time on my digital camera—the days are just packed. The next day (a weekend) will be a day of rest.

People have been very friendly although a little difficult to read at times (unless they are trying to sell you something). They have this peculiar mannerism, "the head wobble." The best way I can describe it is if you have seen a bobble head doll that mounts on the dashboard of a car, go over a bump in the road and the head kind of wobbles in a circular motion, not a nod, not a shake. Similarly with the head wobble, when there is a bump in the conversation (a pause, a question, an observation), you insert the head wobble. It seems to be a multipurpose gesture implying yes/no/maybe/I agree, etc., allowing you to carry on without addressing the issue at hand. I kind of like it, but doubt if I could get away with adopting it.[3]

We pay a visit to the local town to get cash from an ATM. The cash machines here are housed in phone-booth-sized air conditioned palaces and come with an armed security guard. This particular sentry figures he has a bigger role to play. He follows me into the booth, leans over my shoulder, and starts giving me directions. He seems to be a frustrated financial planner: "No, no, this is a very expensive town, you are going to need more than 5,000 rupees, cancel the transaction and start again. I will do it for you."

Next stop is to be pampered at the beauty salon. It is actually a barber shop with more of a Speedy-Muffler-workshop vibe to it. Bare concrete walls with steel shuttered rollers fronting onto the sidewalk of a busy street. I take my seat in a classic '50s barber chair, all chrome and weathered leather, footrests, neck rests, and levers. I let him know that I want a shave. I don't haggle or even ask the price—best to keep on good terms with anyone holding an open razor to your throat.

He adjusts the headrest and lathers me up, tilts my head back. I catch a glimpse of the razor out of the corner of my eye—my first experience on the receiving end of a cut-throat razor. I redirect my eyes heavenward to gaze at the peeling paint, cracked plaster, flecks of daylight glinting through the holes in the roof and the inactive ceiling fan that clearly hasn't worked in decades. The dust is so thick on it that it has taken on an organic quality, like moss. The barber clamps my nose between his thumb and forefinger—gulp, here he goes. He swoops in, notches around the sideburns, uses my schnozz to steer my head around like it's a gamer's joystick. Effortless backhand and forehand strokes—this is going very well.

---

3 https://www.youtube.com/watch?v=EoJ4Bvsq7gQ

Then an acquaintance lurches in from the sidewalk, and he and my barber engage in conversation. The discussion becomes more heated, my nose is still in the vice-like grip. My stylist is waving the blade around over my exposed gullet. He's like some sort of crazed orchestra conductor cranking out a piece by Stravinsky (I'd prefer something by Brahms). My eyes follow the razor like I am watching Federer versus Nadal on centre court. Despite the pressure on my nose I am involuntarily pulling back from the action. Then, "kerthunk," the headrest collapses under me. My head continues to dangle daintily from his fingertips like he's holding onto some sort of grotty rag. With a final flourish of the razor he dismisses the intruder and gets back to business. He reassembles the headrest and carries on, it's all in a day's work.

Before he is half-finished though, a beggar turns up at the side of the chair. The barber wipes the razor on a sheet of newspaper then puts it down, whacks me on the knee as he pulls out the drawer in the counter in front of me, rummages around in a box of grubby notes and coins and sees the scrounger off with a rupee. He wipes his hands on his pants and gets ready again. I try to reassure myself that he's only clumsy when he doesn't have a razor in his hands. The rest of the shave goes uneventfully. Hallelujah, it is over! But, wait, me being a neophyte, I don't realize that a good shave should be done twice. I had no idea that he would repeat the process—this time, thankfully, without the interruptions. First, the close shave then the closer one. Best I have ever had although part of it may be the relief at having escaped unscathed.

All that remains to be done is to settle up. He asks for fifteen rupees—about forty cents. I give him a twenty and say that he can keep the change. His only response is an expressionless stare and the inscrutable head wobble. It could mean "Aw, shucks, thanks," or "No, we don't do that here," or "Cheap bastard." I have a ways to go in the head wobble deciphering front, and, likewise, the tipping practices.

After a few more simple days spent beachside, we decide to say goodbye to our little family of pets—Kermit, the frog that lives in the toilet roll holder; Gordon, our roving gecko; and Basil, the "eeezno rat." He appeared one afternoon when we were ending a meditation session. I don't know who got the bigger fright, him or us. Anyhow, our reaction was "that wasn't a rat, was it?" Thanks to the meditation I was instantly channelling a Fawlty Towers episode in my synapses. Manuel's plea "Eezno rat, Mr. Fawlty, eez hamster, I call him Basil." Naming him after that was a piece of cake.

On reflection, I think Basil was no rat, having seen a creature a couple of days later, no kidding here, the size of a rabbit on steroids; the only cat that would have been a match for it would have been a tiger.

Chapter 4

Crampi in Hampi

Whiskey Marketing Board Representative

"I THINK THAT TOILETS ARE MORE IMPORTANT THAN TEMPLES."

—Narendra Modi

"IT WAS LUXURIES LIKE AIR CONDITIONING THAT BROUGHT DOWN THE ROMAN EMPIRE. WITH AIR CONDITIONING THE WINDOWS WERE SHUT, THEY COULDN'T HEAR THE BARBARIANS COMING."

—Garrison Keillor

Tilted back in my reclining seat, sweltering in the dead heat of an Indian night, I stare above my head. The corpses of squished mosquitos are speckled randomly on the white metal of the overhead luggage shelves, dimly illuminated by the few functioning cabin lights. I could try and imagine myself in some inverse universe where the constellations are black and the night sky is white, but no. I can't escape reality that easily. We are on another overnight ride in a sleeper bus. I wonder what do they use these buses for during the day.

In any event, the farther you get from the cities, the less salubrious the transport. This rattler is non air conditioned and comes with a driver not quite so skilled at anticipating the speed bumps scattered along the route. This results in a kind of double-negative effect on your attempts at sleeping. As you are rudely awakened at the jarring impact of thundering into one of these berms, you are launched out of your bunk then pounded back into the berth as the coach returns to earth. Sleep doesn't return easily as your mind goes into overdrive contemplating all manner of potential perils. Everything from are there cows on the road? Has the sluggish driver been partaking of Idukki gold (the legendary hash of Kerala, the final destination of the bus)? And perhaps more pertinently, is my backpack, which is tied onto the roof with some string, still there or not?

We arrive sleep-deprived but with luggage in the town of Hampi at dawn. The town abuts the historic ruins of Vijayanagar. The site is a bewitching fusion that stirs the senses. Hints of Death Valley, bold granite forward flavours of Stonehenge, with an intense finish reminiscent of Rome, a blend of intriguing complexity tinged with regret. You probably have guessed by this time I am ready to murder a bottle of plonk, not having seen as much as a glass of vino since leaving Mumbai. That isn't going to change here as meat and alcohol are both taboo.

The city was the centre of one of the largest Hindu empires about 600 years ago. It was huge in its time, roughly forty-three square kilometres and home to half a million citizens, now mostly in ruins (sultanate invaders in the 1500s to blame). Aqueducts, baths, elephant stables, arenas, plazas, palaces and temples, a metropolis rivalling anything in the world at that time (London only a village of about 50,000 peasants). The carving on the stonework is incredible. They say one door frame may have taken ten man years to finish.

"What did you do at work today, dear?"

"Same old, same old."

Well, maybe we shouldn't be too smug—what are we producing that will be admired 600 years from now?

Hampi itself is making a bit of a comeback as a destination and, boy, do you get service. The fastest town in the West. Got a pair of pants made, a load of clothes laundered, and a pair of shoes resoled all in the same couple of hours. We cap off the day watching the sun set over the ruins. It seems that the monkeys have the same ritual, or maybe they come to watch the tourists; we can see the silhouettes of dozens of them on the ridge behind us.

As we start back for our guest house, the call of nature catches Trixie short, so she is forced to consider the facilities at the bus depot. She tries unsuccessfully to convince me that I also need to go. I am no fan of what passes for plumbing in India. The squat version is typical, simple, easy to use and hygienic, **IF IT IS MAINTAINED!**

Now you should know that although Trix is German and speaks flawless English, she does still fall victim to the odd mistimed metaphor. She finally gives up trying to convince me that I have a sympathetic bladder and blurts out in exasperation "Why is it always me that has to take the plunge first?"

We look at each other, blanch, and shudder. After the deed she returns ashen faced. It will be some hours before she smiles again. She is still in therapy. I dare not admit that my back teeth are floating and try to make a nonchalant bee line for our hotel. For those of you unfamiliar with the intricacies of spending a penny in India, please refer to this excellent tutorial:[4]

The city's governance model might best be described as capitalist socialism. People were free to set up home at the side of the street or set up stalls amongst the ruins (a UNESCO heritage site). It was five rupees to gain entry to the archeological site (India is not immune to the evolution of travel into a gentrified marketable commodity; I gather the "squatters" have been "relocated" and the entry fee raised to 500 rupees), and ten rupees to park. Parking seems to be available on any random undemarcated patch of dusty road. As soon as you stop, an "attendant" will miraculously appear and our tuk-tuk driver will complete the transaction, no haggling. No one is in the mood to spend any longer than necessary out in the dusty, throat-parching forty-degree heat.

Contented with the sights and sounds of Hampi, we take our leave. Having had our fill of sleeper buses, we decide to try an overnight sleeper train. As we sit on the platform waiting for our carriage to arrive, a Sadhu (travelling wise man) approaches. It is a calling not for the faint of heart where one's existence relies solely on the charity of others. He makes an impressive sight—long orange robes, head scarf, long beard, spindle shanked, and sporting a staff. There follows as eccentric a conversation as I can recall, it takes a couple of minutes before he gets around to his pitch. He needs train fare to get back to his guru. It isn't until he leans in close to show me a crumpled photo of his swami that I become aware of his breath. It's evident that he is currently getting his spiritual guidance from Johnny Walker—or, more likely, some cheaper local equivalent—phew. The parley goes nowhere, but the tone gets testy. He turns his attention to my right. Well, he picked the wrong Catholic, German anthroposophist to take on.

4 https://www.youtube.com/watch?v=dKkryfdtMNQ

Uh oh, when Trix's opening line is "I need you to UNDERSTAND why I'm not going to give you any money," I know he is in trouble. I almost feel sorry for him, almost. Several minutes later, ears burning, he reels off down the platform, probably none the wiser but certainly none the richer. There must be easier ways to earn a living!

The train ride itself is no picnic, not helped by the fact I have developed a dose of the crampies in Hampi. The passengers are a mix of tourists and Indians in typically gregarious humour. The latter have no reticence about satisfying their curiosity on any topic, they cut straight to the chase and any subject is fair game—country of origin? Marital status? Inside leg measurement? You name it.

An affable sports coach on his way back to his college asks me, "How much do you earn in a year?" I do the math in my head converting to rupees—yikes, that's a lot of rupees. I tell him anyway and by way of atonement try to explain that the government takes nearly half in taxes, pensions, etcetera. He laughs and tells me that I have miscalculated (I haven't), he knocks a zero off my number and pronounces that "it is still a good salary, but not quite as much as I earn." I leave it at that.

Our destination is Mysore, a regional capital and home of the magnificent Maharaja's royal residence. The Mysore dynasty dates back to the fourteenth century. This current opulent palace, having been built less than 100 years ago, is newer than the Eiffel Tower. The royals of course had a taste for fine clothing too and the city is also famous for its fine silks. We visit one of these magic-making operations. Stunning, delicate, intricate creations produced on clattering, oily, antique machinery, not a computer in sight. Work Safe agencies would no doubt have a fit if they were to do an inspection. It's one of those curious situations where tourism dollars may actually preserve the skills and craftsmanship. Textile tourism could be the next big thing, if only it can compete with the profits from a switch to mass production.

The results are pieces of art, really. The energetic foreman guides us as we weave our way through the maze of equipment. It's a labour-intensive process to set up the unique patterns and load the multitude of coloured silk bobbins. Proud staff positively glow as they explain the processes and showcase their handiwork.

After a strenuous day watching other people work we return appropriately enough to our own palace. The Chittaranjan palace was originally built for Mysore princesses and has been restored and repurposed as a hotel. Now unimaginatively renamed the Green Hotel, it provides very pleasant accommodation and room service, which we take advantage of.

When we finish eating we foolishly leave the tray outside our room. Regrettably, no one had warned us that the ecofriendly practices also appeal to a troop of mischievous local monkeys. During the night they arrived on the scene expecting some leftovers only to be disappointed. These eco-terrorists demonstrate their displeasure by tossing plates and cups off the balcony.

Fleeing from the resident hooligans, we head back to the coast for some relaxation. Out for a stroll we meet an Indian family on the beach and get talking. It turns out the parents are both teachers. They insist we come with them to the wife's school, some two hours away, where she is the headmistress. It is two classrooms and a canteen for the seventy students. They are determined to go over their accounts with me; by this time it is dark and the school has no power after regular school hours. Unfazed, she has us huddle around her table, poring over the books (an exercise pad) and their bank statements, auditing by flashlight.

The school's annual budget is about 50,000 rupees, or $1,500. The government funds the headmistress's salary of about 1,500 rupees a month and one rupee per child per day (school meal program, I guess), enough for 100 grams of rice each.

The second teacher is provided 1,000 rupees per month and the cooker (cook) 700 rupees per month (they must have CUPE here too). Everything else has to be funded by the community or donations.

At the end of the evening the father finds us a driver to take us back to our hotel, which is a relief as he is just learning to drive himself and we don't fancy him practising on us on the pot-holed, unlit country roads. The driver, actually two fellows, don't speak any English and get directions from Mr. Nayak as he bundles us off into the car. A bit spooky bouncing along the backroads listening to our pilot/copilot chattering/scheming in their local language. We try to communicate using gestures and place names to confirm our destination to no effect.

About half an hour into the trip we see the headlights of a car in the distance, heading in our direction. As they draw near, they flash their lights, we toot our horn. Our car brakes to a screeching halt, as do they, the vehicles, having passed each other, are about twenty-five yards apart. Our copilot jumps out of the car and runs back to the other car. It's a pitch-black stretch of road in the middle of nowhere. We hear voices, our driver waves and shouts back, both cars restart their engines and reverse back to each other at top speed and come to a stop abreast of one another. We are jostled out of our vehicle, my imagination working overtime. Will Canada Post be delivering our kids a letter with my severed ear and a ransom note inside? You guessed it—no.

Bodies pile out of the other car—a family, always a reassuring sign. The passengers do a vehicle swap, the cars do U turns, all conducted without the benefit of English. We all continue, hopefully, on our way with changed cars and drivers. Hmm, maybe a cell phone would come in handy now and again. A half hour later we are dropped safely at our hotel gate. We conclude the transaction at the agreed-upon rate and exchange friendly good nights. Whether planned or not, this Indian version of the Pony Express works like a charm.

The next day we cross into the communist state of Kerala, the first democratically elected communist government state in the world. Who needs Google when there are taxi drivers around? The employment equity set-up is a bit hard to figure out, though. Women do a lot of jobs that would be male dominated in the West. The majority of labourers are female, and not the lollipop-holding type of labourer, but the rock-crushing and cement-bags-on-top-of-the-head type. Conversely, the sales staff in the sari and silk shops are men. And despite the prevalence of the hammer and sickle, a female gas station attendant only gets two thirds of what her male counterpart earns.

For a change of pace we charter a converted rice barge, the good ship *Crocodile*, for a three-day cruise of the Keralan backwaters, a little holiday from the holiday. Just us and our crew of three.

Our captain, Shiva is a tubercular septuagenarian with a rib cage that supermodels would kill for. His choppers consist of a handful of tombstone teeth dotted around his gums. Normally as mum as an oyster and yet any time he opens his mouth his stoic expression is transformed into a beaming Jack-O' Lantern smile.

Engineer Alij, outboard operator who also doubles as our translator, which is a bit of a stretch because he, like the rest of the crew, doesn't speak any English, only the local language, Malalyan. I am guessing, like with everything else on this voyage, that he got the job because he is better at charades than everyone else. In any event, we observe protocols and go through channels.

Ranjeesh, sporting the same Clark Gable moustache as every other Indian (men, certainly, women, occasionally) rounds out the crew as cook and steward. A fine job he does too.

It is all very relaxing motoring/poling along peaceful canals and waterways viewing village life and looking down into the adjoining paddies—a kind of Indian version of Holland. We occasionally stop for miming sessions with rice paddy workers—friendly, dignified folk.

Relatively, it is quite an affluent area. Cinderblock houses, people are well dressed and fed. It is for the most part tranquil except for one narrow channel. It must have been a main thoroughfare or tourist stop. As we pass each house the kids rush out to the banks of the canal, demanding:

"One pen!"

"Sorry, we don't have one," we reply.

"One coin!"

"Sorry, don't have one."

"One chocolate."

"Nope."

"Gimme hat!"

One pain in the neck. By the end of it I am ready to give them one finger, but, hey, we are supposed to be ambassadors, so we just smile and wave back. Some well-intentioned individuals don't know what they have started with their selfie bait. Begging aside, it is an enjoyable interlude.

As satisfying as the corporeal pleasures have been, we figure that it is about time to sample some of India's famed mysticism. Better empty your mind for the next ethereal episode.

Chapter 5

From the Frying Pan into the Ashram

To Each Their Own Ashram

"YOU ARE NOT ONE PERSON BUT THREE. THE ONE YOU THINK YOU ARE, THE ONE OTHERS THINK YOU ARE, AND THE ONE YOU REALLY ARE."

—*Sai Baba*

"LOOK DOWN AT ME YOU SEE A FOOL, LOOK UP AT ME AND YOU SEE A GOD, LOOK STRAIGHT AT ME AND YOU SEE YOURSELF."

—*Charles Manson*

Now we arrive at the ashram (I never thought I would hear myself say that). This is Prasanthi Nilayam or, in banal English "Abode of the Highest Peace," the headquarters of Sathya Sai Baba, or Swami or Baba, as his devotees refer to him. It is located next to the town of Puttaparthi, which itself is 160 kilometres north of Bangalore.

A hot tip from a friend in Victoria who had recently visited this guru/philanthropist brings us to the gates of the community. A prophet with a grassroots following in the tens of millions who welcomes all faiths, who was a complete unknown to us provides an intriguing attraction to Trixie. The fact that it doesn't bring in the leisured classes with nothing better to do than light some incense, put on some yoga music, and find themselves attracts me. Oh, yeah, and the fact that it is cheap.

This operation is to ashrams what Vegas is to gambling and mass shootings. Everything is on a grand scale and no photographs allowed.[5] I estimate that there must be about 4,000 rooms for the followers and scores more dormitories for those less well off. We one percenters spare no expense and are rewarded with a deluxe room (married quarters), which has white-washed walls, bare black vinyl floor tiles, two steel cots circa 1950s English hospital ward, and an indoor toilet. The bars on the windows lend a *One Flew Over the Cuckoo's Nest* ambiance. Not that we are incarcerated—it's to keep the monkeys resident in the tree by our window from coming in and visiting. What more could you want for five dollars per night?

An average of 50,000 believers stay on the grounds every night. He had one million actual living, breathing, walking, talking human beings (not Twitter followers) show up to wish him well on his seventy-fifth birthday in 2000. It must have been quite a cake.

The main worship hall, and Baba is worshipped as a god, is an open-air roofed plaza, about 600 feet by 800 feet. Marble floored

5 http://www.sathyasai.org/

with Byzantine columns of pink and gold supporting a turquoise and gold Rococo ceiling with huge chandeliers that look like they are straight out of Versailles (Louis the fourteenth, another dude with an affinity for fancy lamp shades, who also tellingly regarded himself as having divine lineage). The stage at the front of the hall looks like it is made from icing sugar that you would find on a ten-year-old girl's birthday cake: multiple layers of lemon, pink, and powder blue plaster, with liberal gold highlights.

Swami rolls in twice a day, or not, as his whim takes him, to be worshipped. We the assembled masses sit bare foot, cross legged on the marble. He is driven into the temple in a brand new Toyota car, which cruises at a slow walking pace across the front of the auditorium before parking behind his chair on the stage. There is no denying that there is a certain gravitas, but I have a hard time buying that this little eighty-year-old guy with the afro haircut is God. And yet the reverence emanating from the people around me shows their conviction that they have just received a drive-by blessing from God seated in the Yogi Buggy. I guess that it isn't every day that you can say that you were six feet away from God and that he looked right at you! And when you talk to the devotees, and they come across as perfectly rational, they do believe that he is God (and not in the Clapton sense, but the genuine, heal the sick, vomit up golden eggs, raise the dead article).

This is a travel book that brings you brushes with greatness.

I do try to keep an open mind; I even buy a set of the duds. All white, a kind of Ku Klux Klan ensemble but without the pointy hood. There are things here that are undeniably impressive. There is no doubt that this is big business and a lot of good has been achieved in terms of hospitals, schools, colleges, shelters, irrigation projects, and the like being established in many parts of the world. So in that regard not much different than our Western gurus, the Gateses and the

Zuckerbergs. We give them our money in return for a better life and hope—trust? assume? —that they will spend it wisely.

The accommodation and food are basic, but what we are charged is very modest and there is virtually no "sales pitch." All denominations and races are welcome and are all here and amicably interacting—yet Baba is no elitist "export" guru. He has the support of millions of locals, including many in positions of power. I don't get the sense that there is any mind manipulation going on—certainly nothing of the scale or sophistication of the torrent of conditioning constantly coming out of our TVs, computers, and social media.

Our second day in the ashram coincides with the state New Year (India is a great place for party animals—you can pack in a half dozen or more New Years' parties, sprinkled through the calendar in different parts of the country). All the stops are pulled out—a regular jamboree. Bright silk parasols form a fence around the temple, colourful flower garlands strung everywhere, silk turbaned musicians—a scene from *The Arabian Nights*. To add to the hodge-podge, incongruously, there is a brass band that could have stepped right off a US college football field that belts out, amongst other songs, "La Bamba." Alas, not a sitar in sight.

Swami swans in, in his car, resplendent in his yellow robes, and takes his seat at the front to loving applause. The thousands in the crowd are packed in pretty tight, all sitting cross legged on the cool marble floor. I've seen wilder New Year's celebrations, but in fairness my people are Scottish. Alcohol or not, things are about to take a turn for the unexpected.

An Indian fellow not far from me can't contain his excitement and stands up to get a better view. A ponytailed Westerner disguised as a scarecrow gets up, puts his hands on the rogue's shoulders, and gets him to sit down. Much merriment ensues. Dance and music played by various bands, different tunes played simultaneously in some cases. Trixie hears bagpipes—it is New Year's, after all. Swami stands up, so again does the Indian, so again does Mr. Ponytail, who delivers a swift kick up the backside of the unsuspecting follower. This worship is a competitive business. They glare at each other for a few moments, then "peace and light" prevail. Baba drives off to more rapturous cheers, not having said a word. Admittedly, he is eighty, but still he has predicted that he has another sixteen years in human form to go. He will have to up the interaction level a bit if he is going to add to his millions of followers.

There is a definite institutional vibe to the place, which I feel most in the canteen, lined up with my steel tray, dressed in the same white as all the other "inmates." I often get the urge to ask "What are you in for?" This is all a bit of a cheap shot given that there is no set agenda for the day, and no restrictions other than to be in your room by 9 p.m. You are totally free to walk through the gates any time and eat/ shop or do whatever you like in the adjacent town.

The weirdest experience was hearing folk recounting the miracles that they have seen Swami perform, all done in a dispassionate manner as if comparing the merits of different lasagna recipes—most bizarre. But then again, maybe not, as I have my own revelation one day while sitting alone in the canteen. I have a visitation from Swami. As I am eating, a fly keeps buzzing at the corner of my eye. Every time I glance in its direction the fly disappears and I find myself looking at one of Swami's many inspirational sayings posted on the wall: "Love all, serve all."

Is Baba, the fly, drawing my attention to this message? I guess it depends on your capacity for belief or maybe on just how impressionable you are. Whatever it is, this place makes you think. Or it might just be the heat and the ban on beer.

Forecasting the future is a tricky business, even for a god. Sai Baba would die in 2011 from respiratory problems at the age of eighty-four, some twelve years short of his prediction. Some devotees have explained the shortfall by saying that Swami was talking about lunar years rather than solar years. This combined with the fact that there is disagreement about when he was actually born provides ample room for debate about the accuracy of his prediction. His funeral was attended by half a million mourners, including India's then-prime minister, Manmohan Singh, and future prime minister, Narendra Modi.

It is an interesting four days of reflective life, but any lasting impact, if there is one, must be on the subliminal self, which is where I suppose it counts the most.

On a more practical level, the Swami Mobile does inspire us to hire a car and driver for our retreat to the wilderness. As usual, we audition the part. There are often entrepreneurial freelancers who hang out at popular tourist destinations. It is worth investing a couple of bucks for a ride back to your hotel to check out a prospective Ben Hur. The criteria are: i) does it feel like the car will make it? ii) does he understand "I need to go pee" (in English)? iii) does he know how the crow flies? iv) does he hope to retire on the proceeds of this trip?

Sanjay ticks all the boxes. Our successful candidate will take us inland to one of the wildlife reserves high in the Western Ghats. The vehicle is one of the classic Ambassador cars common throughout India. It looks a bit like an enlarged Morris 1000. The design hasn't changed in the forty odd years that it has been in production. This particular model looks like it was one of the first off the production line. It must have been a luxury model in its day. In-dash eight track player (broken), sun-bleached plastic roses on the back window shelf, speedometer that threateningly tops out at 140 KPH (God forbid). As soon as you hit 70 KPH the back wheels judder and shake so much you would swear that you have snow chains on.

We set out, pass a truck with an elephant on its flatbed, then a typical Indian family of four out for their Sunday drive: Dad on his cell phone, other hand on the throttle, junior between his knees astride the fuel tank holding onto the wing mirrors, Mum side saddle on the back, a beautiful silk sari streaming out behind her, cradling a baby in her arms. Eight slitted eyes half shut squinting against the wind and dust. Helmets? You have to be kidding.

We are on the usual two-lane "highway," We pass a truck, which is passing an auto rickshaw, which is passing a bicycle, which is pulling out to avoid an old lady who is spreading a sheet out on the shoulder of the road to dry her crop of red chilies. Ho hum, another day on India's roads.

Our driver is good, he is about a fifteen-HPM man in rural areas. HPMs are honks per minute, my algorithm for determining how conscientious drivers are in making their presence known. Tooting is a good thing and to be encouraged. The approach to driving doesn't change between rural and urban. Speed—the same: as fast as possible. Overtaking—the same: whenever you feel like it. The only thing that changes is that you increase the HPMs.

I clock Sanjay doing twenty-eight HPMs along one built-up stretch—very diligent. With every vehicle in on the act though you can imagine the racket, and how they figure out who is honking for what and why is just one more of the unsolved mysteries of India. We continue up the winding hill roads, dodging all animals, potholes, vehicles, etcetera, but one. As we are passing a bus parked at its stop, its driver decides to make a ninety-degree turn right in front of us. No signal, no horn, nothing. Sanjay does his best to take evasive action, with much skidding and squealing of tires we collide with the bus and narrowly avoid being sandwiched into a wall on the other side of the road. Fortunately no one is hurt as it is more of a glancing blow, just the front fender is bashed in so it is still drivable.

Not a life-flashing-in-front-of-your-eyes sort of experience, but still shaken up enough to find myself wondering if I'd remembered to put on clean underwear that morning. We check the damage (to the car) and decide to continue although I am not too happy about the dent on the rim of the front wheel. I lean out the window to check on it as we are driving, it looks wobbly to me. Despite Sanjay's protests, I get him to stop. We get out and I show him the problem. He thinks that it is pretty funny, I finally get the joke. He shows me the other three wheels and they are all in worse shape than the one that I am fretting about. So we carry on. I don't know whether to be reassured or more worried. It's hard to maintain a blasé attitude when passing the all-too-common car wrecks at the side of the road.

We reach Periyar National Park without further misfortune. The villages at the entrance to the sanctuary are touristy and a bit frantic. We have been lucky enough to get reservations at "The Lake Palace" for three nights and it is actually inside the park. Access to it is by boat across an artificial lake created by the Brits in the late 1800s. It is a charming six-room restored former game lodge, kind of a cross between the raj era (fine china and waiters in bow ties and waistcoats) and *Jurassic Park* (there's a moat around the hotel despite being on an island and a six o'clock curfew; critters abound).

It is much cooler being here up in the hills (1,400 metres), civilized and relaxing, miles from the usual hubbub of India. Dressed for dinner in a clean T-shirt specially saved for the occasion, sitting on the veranda peering out into the pitch black with its incessant insect soundtrack, it is easy to conjure up visions of monocled Englishmen sipping G and Ts and blathering things like "I say, smashing shot this aft, Julian. Dropped that kitty faster than a housemaid's knickers. Let's bag a couple more of the blighters before tiffin tomorrow."

Of course in those days there were estimated to be more than 100,000 tigers in the country; now, sadly there are a mere 2,000, about thirty-five in this sanctuary. There is, however, still thriving fauna in the park. We are entertained with sightings of monkeys, elephants, deer, and wild boar, but, alas, no tigers or T Rex.

We pass through tea plantations, strangely located in the Cardamom Hills, en route back to the heat and tumult of the lowlands. They are very picturesque—I don't think Ireland could be greener. Every so often when you think that you are miles from civilization a woman will pop out of the thick jungle of infinite hues of green lining the side of the road as a dazzling splash of colour with a pot on her head. The effect is like seeing a man in a suit carrying a briefcase stepping out of a forest: odd. After meandering around the backwaters of southern India for the last two and a half months, it is time to start heading for the exit. But before we do it's time to have a look at India's chin.

Chapter 6

Spittin' Image

Bangalore Carpet Shop

"I DISLIKE FEELING AT HOME WHEN I AM ABROAD."

—George Bernard Shaw

"WE HAVE A FINITE ENVIRONMENT—THE PLANET. ANYONE WHO THINKS THAT YOU CAN HAVE INFINITE GROWTH IN A FINITE ENVIRONMENT IS EITHER A MADMAN OR AN ECONOMIST."

—David Attenborough

We venture into the Tamil Nadu state for a visit to Kanyakumari, population 29,761, at the very tip of the subcontinent. It's where the nub of India in the shape of Ryan Gosling's chin protrudes into the frothy convergence of three large bodies of water: the Indian Ocean, the Bay of Bengal, and the Gulf of Arabia. It's a low-key pilgrimage town where devotees come to visit temples and bathe in the sacred waters. To do something symbolic I get my chin shaved.

We find a shoreside hotel room with a balcony virtually hanging over the top of the fishing village, a perfect spot to watch the everyday activity, including all the perfectly natural human digestive functions that are performed at the tide line; you won't see any of this on reality TV.

It is getting hotter—fortyish—and the time for our Indian departure is getting close. We elect to save the train trip from Kanyakumari to Kashmir (India's longest, at sixty-six hours and 3,734 kilometres) for another visit and so we fly to Bangalore for good food and the shopping that we have been putting off. There is a trend developing—we started using buses then progressed to trains, tried a barge, switched then to private cars, and now planes. We must be getting tired.

After arriving in the Bangalore airport, the little shuttle bus takes us from the plane to the terminal, passing a couple of dogs trotting across the runway. Dogs chasing cats, sure, and, yes, the occasional mailman, the odd car, uh huh . . . but a DC 10? That's gotta be an Indian thing. The local buzz is about George WB's visit to India. Better keep quiet about the commies in Kerala or Georgie's promise of radioactive material for India's peaceful nuclear power program will be toast.

The population was nearly a billion in 2006—did I mention that already? Well, it has increased by over 300 million since then, and another 100 since I started this sentence. They reckon about thirty-five births every minute. . . . I can't get the image of a sausage factory out of my head. Seems to me there are more obvious choices for Indo/

US collaboration. There are little vans that drive around Indian towns blaring out ads for free vasectomies. There's got to be a synergy there for an exchange program with the US considering how much that they spend on Viagra advertising. I can just imagine a photo op for the two great leaders symbolically—ahem—shaking on it. Headlines could be interesting too. How about "An Indian in the hand is worth two from the Bush" or some such?

India is the place to be if you like being the centre of attention. For a start, it is nowhere nearly as multiracial as the West. Sure, they have their own continental differences (which were much more noticeable than I expected, from north to south it can be like contrasting a Swede and an Italian), but tourist hot spots notwithstanding, you are often the only white face around. Mix that with the naturally curious nature of the people and you can imagine what little personal space you get. Even when you don't think that you are on display, you are. Walk into a seemingly deserted shop and, eerily, the lights go on and the fan starts (they certainly know how to minimize overhead. Unless there is a customer the staff sit in the heat and the dark). Walk down the street a few yards without your sunglasses on and the Rayban man will be upon you in a flash.[6]

Trixie walks into a jeweller's shop (there are a ton of them, India's love affair with gold. And who can blame them? Matched with their skin tones it's a combination made in nirvana and heaven) and has a look at a few display cases of pendants, about half a dozen trays, fifty or so items on each tray. The owner, indifferent, sitting passively gazing out into the street. Trixie asks to see one.

"You will be wanting the middle one from the second row on the fourth tray. Am I right?"

---

6 https://www.cbc.ca/radio/undertheinfluence/how-a-pants-free-tom-cruise-rescued-ray-ban-1.4625924

He of course knows he is right and is just asking out of graciousness. Geez, these guys are good. Mental note: never play poker with an Indian jeweller.

And that's pretty much the way it is wherever you go. It must be what it is like to be a film star. It can get wearing at times, in certain spots the "touts" hound you mercilessly, these chancers have developed many catch phrases to hook the gullible. For example:

"Where are you coming from?"

I've learned not to name my hometown of Victoria or country Canada—their knowledge of geography is just too good. And before you know it you will be into some nonsense story about "I have a letter from my auntie in Toronto in my shop that I need you to translate for me."

My new stock response to the "where are you from?" question became, without breaking stride, "Lasqueti—it is a small island in the Pacific."

If the reply to that is of the "do they take Euros there?" variety, that is the cue to avoid eye contact and turn on the afterburners. If the reaction is a blank stare and an "I am never hearing of this place," chances are that it is just one of the many friendly curious people we met who are trying to make conversation. You don't want to miss out on the hospitality of a genuine Indian invitation if you get the opportunity.

The climate shapes the culture and cultural norms, which brings me to India's "war on phlegm." It is clearly a national commitment, as minister of defense, Raj Rumsfeld, puts it "We don't negotiate with phlegm, we put it out of our bodies."

And how is this done? Well, there are a variety of stages in the process.

Stage 1: "the inhale," which, while fairly innocuous, still requires the bystander to take precautions. Hold onto something solid so that you aren't sucked into the vortex and swallow repeatedly to compensate for the localized change in air pressure.

Stage 2: "the dislodging of the payload," ear protection strongly recommended. The volume of the resulting sub-tracheal grinding can churn out decibels equivalent to a jet engine during takeoff. The tone, however, is more akin to a fully laden 1975 British Leyland double-decker bus (I used to ride the 11A from Glasgow to Bearsden, so I should know) going uphill unsuccessfully trying to snatch up from second to third gear: "Ooooaccchhgghhh."

Stage 3: "the discharge." A stream rather than a splat—a jet-like a squirt from a detergent bottle. The big finish, glorious release, ejaculation in a public place.

These guys are unparalleled—sultans of snot, maharajahs of mucus, exemplars of excellence in expectoration—in short, la crème de la phlegm. I've seen guys target a garbage can from ten feet away while running across a busy street without even breaking stride. These are no furtive emissions but audacious demonstrations of their full artistry and hours of practice. I am reminded of Wayne Gretzky in his heyday threading no-look passes between bewildered defensemen.

And don't get me wrong: I am all for it and think it's something we should consider adopting for the West. I figure if the one billion-plus Indians ever can afford the Kleenex option, the world's forests will be a goner in no time.

See, I told you it was hot—hot enough to fry a mad dog's brain

Bangalore is a fun city, with a booming economy, 1,200 new high-tech companies in the last five years (more cabbie stats). Power is still a challenge, maybe even more than other areas of the country. We had four power outages in one morning, which apparently isn't uncommon.

But we didn't come to India to find tech but to escape it, so we do the tourist thing and look to buy a carpet. Because of the odd dimensions of our dining room back home, we need an odd-sized carpet. Naturally, this size is in short supply so the salesman puts the price up. Well, I will show him. I had spotted another shop, "Rugs and Riches," not far from our hotel. Next day I set off to refind it. Finally, success after navigating the maze of alleys and streets. Not the selection that I had hoped for—in fact, not a carpet in sight. The only inventory is racks and racks of women's clothes.

"So where are the carpets?" I ask.

"Carpets? No carpets," comes the bewildered reply.

"Yes, you know rugs, carpets. Your shop is called Rugs and Riches." It is hard to get good help these days so I am being patient.

"Yes, yes, Rugs and Riches. Used clothing from the ladies."

Damn it—Indian/English spelling strikes again, what they were trying to get at was "Rags to Riches." Ah, well, it brought back fond memories of my breakfasts in Goa—my favourite "serf service scrabbled eggs 7days a week" at Henrees restoreant.

And so the great carpet caper continued. I try another shop, same problem with the measurements, the trader is more resourceful though and calls his warehouse. The carpet duly arrives. It is unrolled with a flourish. It is the same one as we looked at in the first shop. The same not as in the spitting image of, but as in the identical self-same article. They had actually brought the original carpet from the other shop. We act dumb and start to bargain, but we can't even get the price down to the original price negotiated in shop number one. So, changing tactics, we let him know that we know the carpet hasn't come from his "warehouse." We are treated to all kinds of explanations and excuses—pure fabrication, of course, but great entertainment.

To shorten an already longish story, we now have a carpet. If it arrives is one thing; if it is the right dimensions is another!

We go out for an excellent last Indian dinner, another tip from a local, and a last tuk tuk (auto rickshaw) ride back to the hotel. We pull up at the traffic lights, about another eight vehicles of varying types abreast of us (Bangalore's one-way system). The motorcyclist next to us is lost; he and our driver start discussing directions. The lights change and we all roar off like it is the start of a Grand Prix. Our cabbie and the biker continue their discussion as we weave in and out of traffic. All the details finally communicated, he waves and swerves away in a cloud of blue smoke.

As much as anything, that moment seemed to sum up India for me. Competitive, frantic, no clear discernable direction in mind, but with an unshakeable confidence that things will work out fine and that there is always time to help out others along the way.

So, after a healthy dose of culture shock, or maybe "awakening of the senses" is a better description, we must take our leave, well pleased with our potpourri of experiences from just this small corner of the subcontinent. Happy in the knowledge that there are so many more untapped adventures to be had when we return. I can understand it if you are leery about a trip to India. It is overcrowded. It is volatile, chaotic , incessant, and can be shockingly harsh. There are at times scenes that are hard to watch so we turn away.

But I tell you this: the loss would be entirely yours. You see, India is an interesting place. It truly is.

Chapter 7

A Trip to Serendip

Where is Waldo?

"I LIKE A MAN WHO CAN RUN FASTER THAN I CAN."

—Jane Russell

"IN A TIME OF DECEIT TELLING THE TRUTH IS A REVOLUTIONARY ACT."

—George Orwell

After leaving India with four security checks in the space of about fifty yards, we travel to Serendip, otherwise known as Sri Lanka (or if you want to go back to 1948 and Britain's colonial days, Ceylon) for the third month of our southern Asia sojourn. First impressions are favourable: some spectacular scenery and generally fewer signs of abject poverty than India. I thought that I had broken the habit of comparing everything to India, but you can't visit India and not leave without a deep, lasting feeling about the place. For me, the extremes of visual and social sensations add up to a mixed emotion: part awe and part bewilderment. If someone were to ask me if I would go back again, my answer could just as easily be "In a heartbeat!" as "Never again!" It is that kind of place.

At the time of our arrival in Colombo, in the late aughts, the political situation is dicey. The government's clashes with the Tamil Tigers in the north verge on degenerating into civil war and yet remarkably here in the capital of Colombo it all appears to be business as usual. The attitude to the strife is blasé. And yet the armed troops and sand-bagged gun emplacements dotted around the downtown look pretty permanent rather than a reaction to recent bombings. The nonchalance of the Sri Lankans is contagious and, after a couple of days, we adopt a similar indifference to the military presence. That's not to say that if a car had backfired you wouldn't have found me hiding under a bush.

It isn't the only strange vibe to the city. It also feels like there is some curious type of time warp going on. The hotels and restaurants have dim, twenty-watt lightbulbs out of the 1940s, the women all wear Jane Russell-type brassieres from the 1950s (the effect more dramatic than silicone any day), the cars all seem to be from 1960s Britain—Morris 1000s and Ford Zephyrs. The fact we are staying at the venerable Galle Face hotel complements the theme. The likes of Maggie Thatcher and Winnie have stayed there (fake news alert), hopefully not in the same room or at least at the same time.

Getting around the charming teardrop-shaped island, 800 kilometres tip to tip, is not as easy as, yes, you've guessed it, India. India, where you could virtually shake a tree and find a driver. No such luck here. I even resort to trying a few numbers off the internet. But it is all about keeping your eyes open. One day when stopping in at the internet café I notice the name plate "Lanka Travel" on the entranceway to the building next door. Bingo, that ought to be the answer. So I climb the stairs to their second-floor offices.

Hmm, I enter into a dimly lit room, chockablock with Sri Lankans all busily filling out forms, then shuffling forward to a couple of reception desks for processing. Not a jaunty travel poster in sight. Being white, of course means I get the VIP treatment—one of the clerks comes over and leads me to the manager's office. I am greeted with a warm handshake and offered a chair.

It doesn't take much discussion to figure out that I am barking up the wrong stairwell. Lanka Travel is an employment agency that arranges jobs for Sri Lankans overseas. If I'd fancied being a plumber in Dubai or a carpenter in Qatar, I could have been on the next flight out, but as far as hiring a driver to take us 200 kilometres up the road, no dice. Tellingly, after the export of tea, earnings sent home by expat Sri Lankans are the next biggest source of foreign currency for the country. Lumber is another money earner, but to call it an industry would be a stretch. Trucks just seem to pull up at the side of someone's house, spill their load of tropical hardwoods, and the owners go to it with clapped-out chainsaws.

We move to less salubrious digs to stretch our budget and consult with the owner of the guest house, who duly sets us up with a driver. A more taciturn fellow you would be hard pressed to find. We dub him "Slim." I have seen snakes with bigger hips. He was not big on chit chat; in fact, in his own passive-aggressive way, he actually actively discouraged it.

Being of a certain age, I am not impressed by our society's trend toward distractedness. For example, say if I am in a store at the counter and the phone rings, the caller who didn't so much as get off their butt to come down here immediately becomes the centre of the universe while I on the other hand am relegated to the status of chopped liver. The tyrannies of technology continue to multiply faster than I can do them justice here.

Slim may have been waging his own secret war on technology's assault on meaningful social interaction. Nah, I think that he just didn't like to talk.

In any event, whenever you spoke to him, he would stop the car no matter where he was—in the middle of an intersection, on a roundabout, driving down the highway (fortunately I never did try to talk to him when he was overtaking anyone). He was oblivious to blaring horns, swerving vehicles, comments about his parents' status, etc. But to be fair, he was giving us his undivided, undistracted attention, fully engaged and in the moment; the mayhem in the immediate vicinity simply didn't exist for him.

Understandably, his shock tactics worked: he had us trained in no time, Trixie and I took to riding in the back seats. Slim's relationship with us morphed into a chauffeurial arrangement where communication would be limited to us informing him of our destination before we set off. This arrangement seemed to suit him just fine. Shades of *Driving Miss Daisy*— "Take me to the Piggly Wiggly, Slim."

After a long drive, silence broken by only our two voices, Slim dropped us off on the east coast of the island, where the most amazing beaches are. This was also where the 2004 tsunami hit the hardest. There were still some pretty grim reminders of the catastrophe. Houses with side walls and roofs on, but front and back walls obliterated, like a tank had rumbled right through the building. Fishing boats wedged high up in trees, like some bizarre modern artwork. The folks at the resort where we stayed modest by Western standards, home of the three-quarter length bed sheet, a shower that was more of a light drizzle, and the standard-issue lightbulb, one of had some incredible stories to tell.

The tragedy is not over for many. The fisher families that lived here and survived face an uncertain future. This area being prime tourism real estate, many "investors" are taking an interest. Despite relief aid having been raised, the fishermen's homes have not been rebuilt. There is speculation that the land will be expropriated and the survivors relocated far from their original settlements, which would mean that they will add the loss of their way of life and their livelihood to the loss of their homes and loved ones. Government is presumably looking at this as a way to create jobs and growth; the developers who are all too willing to help, with maybe less altruistic motives, are overly willing to ingratiate themselves with whomever gets to make the call. One wonders what say the fisher folk will have in making this decision.

Sri Lanka is also rich in history and culture so we decide to take in the ancient cities up north, the golden triangle, including Anuradhapura (these names just roll off the tongue), first founded in 380 BC and capital of the country for nearly 1,400 years.

This area is quite close to the contested lands between the Tamils (predominantly Hindu) and the majority-elected government (Buddhist). The latest round of the seven-year peace talks (Hey, don't knock it, the Afghan War, started in 2001, still shows no signs of finding a peaceful conclusion), planned to take place in Geneva, had just been cancelled because the two sides couldn't even agree on how to get there; our timing is impeccable. This is the first country we have been to where it isn't a good idea to let folks know that you are Canadian. Apparently there are around 300,000 Canadians of Tamil descent in Canada (about .1 percent of the population) and as far as raising funds for the rebels is concerned, Toronto is to the Tigers what Boston was to the IRA. Who knew?

There was talk in town about reports of car bombings in Vavuniya, a town about seventy kilometres from where we were staying, so we decided that it was time to leave.

It wasn't until we returned to Colombo that we could get some better information on the situation. Although even there, there was pretty intense news laundering going on in the media. At one point as we were walking through a mall we heard reports of a significant battle going on in the north of the island. For a couple of days we read the papers, listened to the radio, watched the news, talked to people, and could find no trace of the story. It was as if it never had happened, like somehow we had both dreamt the same dream. Only by visiting the internet café and logging onto the BBC World Service could we confirm that our ears hadn't deceived us.

As the end of our first epic backpacking adventure looms my wife and I choose to spend the last three weeks in a more pampered fashion. Our flight home connects through Kuala Lumpur, so spending our remaining days in Malaysia shopping and lounging on sun-kissed beaches will be the perfect acclimatization.

Kuala Lumpur is a very upmarket, modern city—clean, great transit systems, very organized, in total contrast to . . . you know. The more traditional markets are more fun to visit than the shiny malls as much for the banter and audacity of the merchants as the goods.

They stock all the high-end names too. Trixie barters for a "genuine" leather Louis Vuitton handbag, which is obviously synthetic. When she calls the seller's bluff on this, he replies without missing a beat, "Yes, you are right, it's only a leather blend."

How can you resist this kind of shopping, I ask you?

Our adult daughter,Scara, and son, Rocky, join us there as planned and we make for some of the offshore islands so that they can do some diving. Unfortunately, because of a local holiday, all of the smaller resorts are full. Instead we find ourselves in a kind of Butlins camp for Asian package holidaymakers, mostly Chinese. We certainly don't fit any of the prerequisites—no black hair, not shorter than five feet three inches, no Nike or Billabong logos on our clothing, no ability to write in anything other than Arabic script. Four tall, skinny, round eyes whose pale epidermises are primed, ready to roll out the red carpet for the hot tropical sun.

What to do? Well, the setting is beautiful, the accommodation civilized, the people all very friendly and the entertainment perpetual. The camp—sorry, resort, commandant—sorry, entertainment director, was a regular Tokyo Rose blaring propaganda over the PA system at all hours of the day.

"We're going to party, all night long . . . until 12 o'clock . . . come on . . . get high, get drunk!"

We pass, but are up for . . .

"It's snorkelling time! We will see you at the beach in five minutes." This was to be an unforgettable experience.

Holidaymakers stream down the sands of the beach to the shore like it is the evacuation of Dunkirk. We are carried along by the tide of Jacques Cousteau wannabees. I swear that I could have lifted up my feet and I would still have been wafted to my craft. We pile into boats fifty people to a load, are handed lifejackets, and set off with another half a dozen similarly loaded vessels for our common destination.

We are heading for a nearby island marine park which has a sheltered bay with a fringing reef just off shore. It is not exactly a National Geographic experience with the crush of aspiring aquanauts itching to go deep. As we round the point of our desert island and the bay comes into view, a spectacular sight greets us . . . more bloody boats! Probably another six or so, blockading the bay in a semicircle, creating a reef beyond the reef, if you will. That isn't the most astonishing part of it though.

Within the perimeter created by the boats is a seething mass of orange, body after body. A jumble of life-jacketed torsos, limbs, and heads. Head to head, flipper to mouth, elbow to ear, butt to knee—every contortion the Kama Sutra ever dreamt of[7] and then some. A flailing mass of anatomy, all face down, enthralled by the sights below. Of the hundreds of people here in the water, not more than a handful, it transpires, know how to swim! So tightly are they packed that I could have run across the bay on the backs of these game vacationers and reached the other side without getting my feet wet.

One by one the crew lower us passengers into the water. The skipper looks perplexed when we take off our lifejackets. He gives us the full safety drill: "Stay inside the rope."

And off we go, bumping into snorkels, fending off limbs, swimming away in a vain attempt to escape the thrashing hordes.

I do find a clearish spot and dip below the bedlam, it is tranquil down here, the fish are beautiful and abundant. The reef is a mesmerizing changing kaleidoscope of colours as the amount of light coming down from the surface varies according to how thick the carpet of bodies above me is at any given time. Ain't nature wonderful?

As I look up, a mild panic sets in. Not to anthropomorphize, but I think this must be how a seal feels when he's below the pack ice and can't find a way through. The anxiety is only fleeting. I point my arms above my head, steeple my fingers, give full throttle to the flippers, and head for the surface like a surging Polaris missile. As I breach the surface a strange thought crosses my mind . . .

"Could James Cameron be filming a remake of *Titanic*—for the Asian market?"

---

7 https://en.wikipedia.org/wiki/Kama_Sutra

No, but the IMAX-worthy Himalayas of Nepal will provide the backdrop for our next jaunt.

Part II

A LITTLE BIT UP A LITTLE BIT DOWN

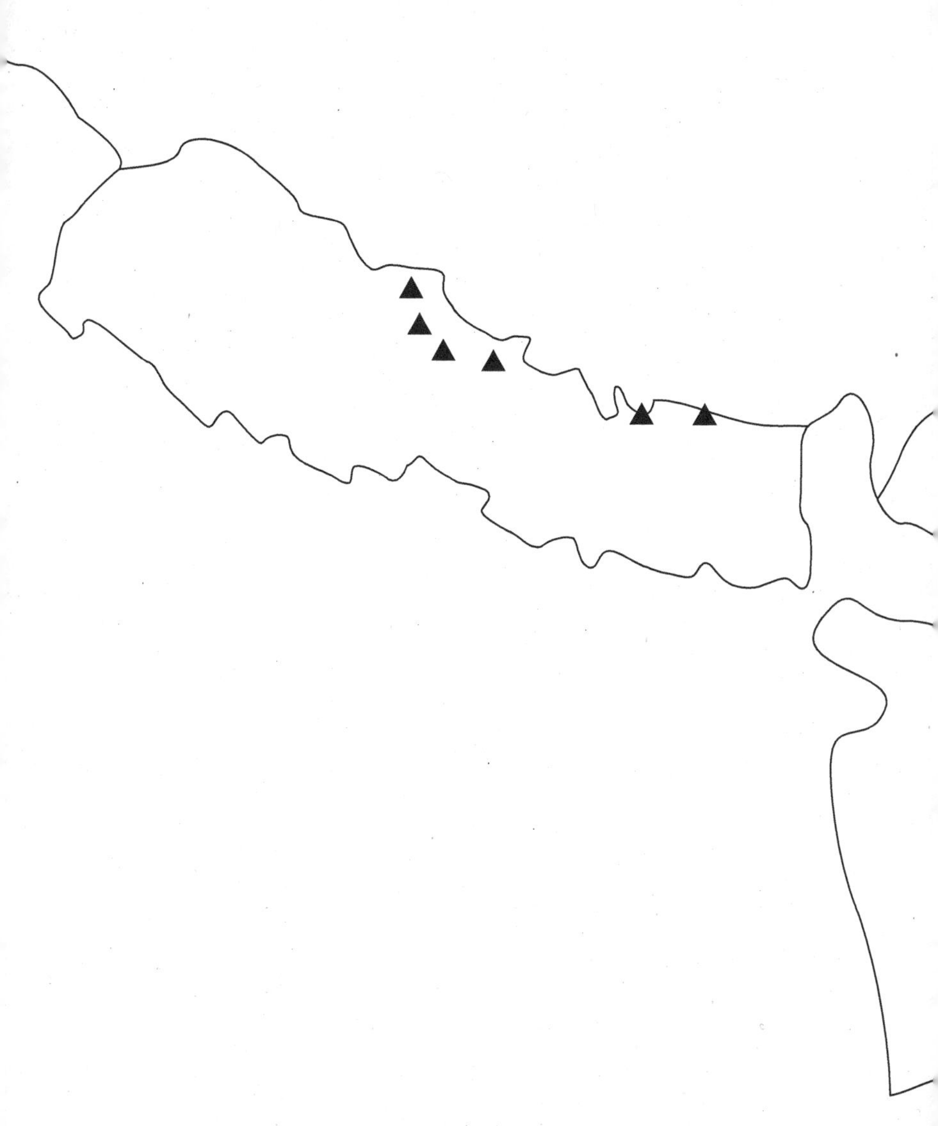

Chapter 8

Climb Every Mountain - Or at Least One Hill

The doctor will see you now.

"THE WIDTH OF NECK AND SHOULDERS SUGGESTED A RUGBY PLAYER, THE BROKEN NOSE CONFIRMED IT. WHICH GOES TO SHOW HOW WRONG THAT YOU CAN BE, AS HE HAD NEVER PLAYED THE GAME IN HIS LIFE."

—*Spike Milligan*

"AFTER CLIMBING A GREAT HILL ONE ONLY FINDS THAT THERE ARE MANY MORE HILLS TO CLIMB."

—*Nelson Mandela*

So you might be wondering how does a recently pensioned bureaucrat and his retired business owner wife end up wandering around on the roof of the world. Well, let me explain.

Up until 2010, our enjoyment from the mountains came from contemplating them at a distance or sliding down our local ski hills, which top out at roughly 1,600 metres; it was a beginning.

The real momentous step forward in our appreciation for living the high life happened in Europe in the year 2009. As part of our transition to non-work life, we decided to take an extended driving holiday in Europe. The trip included a week in Switzerland, a week that would cement the lure of the mountains in our minds.

Hiking in the Bernese Oberland is the clincher. With its scenery like no other, its beauty defies all description other than to say it gives me a crick in the neck. That can happen to anyone when you are repeatedly striking a statue-like motionless pose, head at 135 degrees, jaw slack, and the hairs on the back of your neck standing straight up.

The cause of this trance-like state? A triple crown of 4,000-metre snowy peaks dominating the vista: Eiger, Jungfrau, and Monch. The three translate into English and lumped together as the Ogre, the Virgin, and the Monk, they have me thinking that we have the ingredients for an old time music hall joke—maybe

A virgin walks into an auberge and says to the ogre behind the bar,

"Does the monk have a Toblerone in his cassock? Or is he just happy to see me?"

The nice lady at the Swiss tourism board office in the town of Klein Scheidegg at the bottom of the mountain seems lukewarm about using my joke in their next advertising blitz. At any rate, she does suggest that we could just make the last train of the day up the mountain. Only the Swiss would think of constructing a railway up to a 3,500-metre saddle between two peaks called the *Jungfraujoch* on the side of a mountain of 4,100 metres. A gain in elevation of nearly 1.4 kilometres mostly tunneled inside the mountain, and, oh, yeah, built in 1912!

As luck would have it, there is also space for Trixie and me in the climbers' hut for the night. The train is empty except for one other guy (the fact that it would have been cheaper to buy a ticket to Rome than going up the Alp may have had something to do with it). Once off the train and out of the station there is still a bit of a hike across a slightly inclining glacier to the hut, a gain in altitude of only another 150 metres or so. The sun is beginning to set behind the Alps and we are the only two out on the ice. It's strangely eerie, quiet, moonlike, and bloody hard work. I feel like Neil Armstrong but with lead boots on. We head across the ice field—wheeze, plod, gasp, repeat for about an hour until we reach our destination.

It more resembles a space station than a hut. All metal sheeting, steel beams, catwalks, and girders bolted to the side of the mountain. I stumble into the bunk room, exchange pleasantries with an American climber who gives me the advice that at this altitude it makes sense to do things a little slower. I tell him that if I do things any slower I'll be stationary. He laughs, thinking that I am joking!

After a short nap we join our fellow Alponauts for dinner—only six folk, including us. The American and his Italian buddy and a Swiss duo—they will be heading off on the morrow for the summits. Another 500 steep metres of actual climbing. One of the Swiss is a cocky whipper snapper in his twenties. The other fellow is much older, brown, weather-beaten skin, bristly silver-grey hair, steely gaze. A pocket-sized Dirty Harry in his prime. Over supper it becomes apparent that Dirty Harry, real name Werner, is sixty-nine and is a guide who will take the young fella to the summit.

We all turn in early. I summit my bunk, which adds another six feet to my personal altitude best that I'd set earlier in the day. Trixie and I both spend very uncomfortable nights due to the combination of the altitude and the knowledge that if nature calls the bathroom block is across an outdoor catwalk in a minus-five-degree howling wind.

After a restless night on top of the Virgin (sorry, *Jungfraujoch*), the next morning we have the glacier to ourselves. Our bunkmates left for their climbs at 5:00 a.m., by the light of their flashlights. We are treated to a spectacular sunrise, clear and crisp. What better introduction to being in the high of the mountains could there be?

Our appetites whetted by our Alpine experience, we contemplate the idea of doubling our delight. "Why not go walk about among the 8,000-metre peaks of the Himalaya?".

We have been beguiled.

With those prophetic words from across the breakfast dishes on the 18th of September 2010, the die was cast. A trip to Nepal will happen, then another, then another, then another.

The on-and-off Nepali civil war had pretty much ground to a halt by 2006, although a few of the Maoist rebels holed up in the mountains hadn't gotten "the memo" in a timely fashion and were still occasionally collecting "taxes" from unsuspecting hikers for the next couple of years or so. Figuring that there is no such thing as the perfect time, we decide that the fall of 2011 is as good as any, and off we go.

Having spent a couple of days getting somewhat culturally acclimatized, we swap the craziness of Kathmandu for the craziness of Nepal's roads. Riding the bus 200 kilometres east to Pokhara takes six hours. Speed doesn't kill here, it's the drop that'll get you. We get the last two seats on the bus, pretty deluxe, numbered seats, no bags or children on the roof, had air conditioning at one time—obviously a tourist bus. My seat is not the best though: middle seat at the back. All five in the back row are permanently in the recline position. This is going to be great: six hours at the dentist. Maybe it's for the best: when I do get up I see through the panorama of the driver's window three vehicles abreast approaching us on a two-lane road. Pass the Novocaine!

As for Pokhara, think of a Nepalese version of a Banff or Queenstown, all manner of adventure activities available and stores enough that the tourists can shop until the cows come home, which, on Main Street, is about 8:45 at night. We book a six-day trek in the nearby Annapurna area. We meet DB, our guide/porter, a little powerhouse, a member of the Gurung tribe from the Mustang area. He's our encyclopedic Kit Carson by day and our Jeeves by night. "Another pot of tea, madam? Another blanket?"

The trek will be a good workout and a test for us even though it is a beginners' hike and we carry only light day packs.

Our taxi ride takes us as far as the township of Naya Pul, little more than a roadside bazaar. The stalls and shops carry all manner of equipment and goodies. DB, knowing that whatever we buy he has to carry, keeps us moving. Thwarted, the shopkeepers turn their attention to easier prey.

As we approach the entrance to the park we are greeted by swarms of butterflies as thick as the candy wrappers on the ground. We register at the checkpoint and commit to abide by all the park rules, which include "Please saving the caressings for the private moments."

Our first day is through farmland of rice/millet/buckwheat. The second day we are up into the jungle belt with its continuous deafening buzz of insects and roar of waterfalls. It's a busy route, like a walk on Victoria's waterfront; the trail is frequently a staircase built out of rocks, maybe the 5,000 steps to enlightenment. Traffic seems to be made up of three kinds of walkers. Roughly a third suppliers of the villages (T-shirted, sports uniforms), a third villagers (a clutch of mothers and babies making their way home after getting their "shots" in the valley below), a third trekkers, all nationalities, shapes and sizes. We are passed by a beefy quartet of fellows—muscle shirts and clunky boots, look more like soccer hooligans, but there's no Watney's Red Barrel or Spam to be had[8] —you never know who you are going to meet!

Every so often there will be a spell of fifteen minutes or so when you meet no one. The rhythm of the walk takes over, you find yourself whistling "Colonel Bogey" and fancying yourself as Maurice Herzog in 1951 on his way to be the first person to conquer an 8,000-metre peak, Annapurna.

Then you turn a corner and find yourself face to back with Beckham and his donkey train strung out in a twenty-yard string. "Becks" is still deadly from the set play, he hurls a rock at his lead donkey, gets the team back on track. Becks is worth every penny of his 40,000 rupees a year (if he earns the national average of about $2 per day).

Each night we stay at the local tea houses, which provide all the value you'd expect for 300 rupees a night ($4). Tonight's suite is elegant in its simplicity. It is a corner suite, the exterior sheathing is of quarter-inch plywood. The interior is chic retro—vinyl flooring on the floor but also on the ceiling and walls. Elegantly appointed with a light switch, inside the room no less, and a nail to hang your belongings on. All built to the highest Nepali earthquake standards—i.e., none.

It is all still very tropical and warm at this elevation, so a little bit of privacy and a half-decent cot is all that is needed.

The bathroom facilities generally could be said to be rustic and functional, the ones in our guest house in our current hamlet Ulleri being of the common outdoor thunderbox variety, nothing daunting, in the daylight. A night mission is another kettle of fish.

---

8 https://www.google.com/search?q=spam+sketch+youtube&rlz=1C1CHBF_enCA888CA888&oq=Spam+sketch&aqs=chrome.1.0l8.10126j0j7&sourceid=chrome&ie=UTF-8

Sometime after midnight, feeling the need for a visit to the loo, I make my way to the privy, a typical ceramic keyhole in the ground affair. Enter the chamber and switch on the light. Big mistake. In seconds I am being swarmed by insects, swirling and buzzing around my head like WWII fighters going in for the kill. I turn off the light, pronto.

I am plunged into darkness, my night vision ruined because of glare on the light when I switched it on, blind and paralyzed for fear of touching or bumping into who knows what in the inky pitch black. Gradually, feeble sight returns. It is a bright moonlit night and the light of the moon penetrates some way into the hut through the glassless window on the side wall. Certain features, however, are lost in the shadows.

Really needing to go now, I have to take matters into my own hands. Ready, aim, but where? Oh, well . . . fire!

From somewhere in the vicinity of my feet I hear splatter splatter then splish splish splish as I find the target hole in the floor. I have a targeting system now. The moonlight lights up my pee like tracer bullets and as long as I can maintain constant pressure and elevation and keep my eye trained on the tracers, I have a lock on the target. "Shack" as they say in USAF.

Mission accomplished, I return to base, the sortie a success. It's all a learning experience.

On the third day we check out of the lino-tel and get back on the StairMaster, steeper yet, it's plekking, more plodding than trekking and, gad, it's hot. Field of vision gets a strange sort of workout too—it's either the fifteen feet directly in front of your boots or the 15,000 feet immediately above your head, not much in between. Thankfully, DB keeps us posted on the highlights in the intermediate zone, e.g., languor monkeys playing in the trees.

Apart from the obvious benefits of not having to lug our own pack, hiring a porter guide provides local employment, and gives you the opportunity to learn about the local nature. But perhaps best of all is the chance to exchange stories about day-to-day life in our respective countries. I guess it should come as no surprise that we have a lot in common. DB's major concerns are about his children's future and how he will be able to afford putting kids through school,. Some things are just universal.

On the third evening we arrive at the "Ghorepani" checkpoint, which is the jumping-off point for Poon Hill, the high altitude point of our trek, at 3,210 metres. I ask the park administrator how many have signed in today.

"A hundred and ninety-five," the answer.

I expect to see them all and then some at sunrise tomorrow morning.

DB wakes us at 5:00 a.m. I look out the window—a few hundred headlight beams are already sweeping their way up the hill. We join the tousle-haired convoy. Get up to the summit by around 6:00 a.m., in time for the sunrise. It's a pretty tense atmosphere, a lot of effort has been expended to get here, there's jostling to find a spot to take that perfect photo that shows that you were the only one here.

Here it comes, the sun; the effect is spectacular as it lights up the mountains in pinks, oranges, peaches, and, finally, sparkling white. A few thousand photographs later the mood relaxes—the day's major assignment has been completed successfully. Folk start to loosen up—drink tea, strike funny poses, offer to take photos for their neighbours, have a laugh.

We wander down a little goat track off to the side, to a lesser hill about a half a kilometre away, stretch out, warm the bones as the sun gains height and heat, snooze for a while: bliss. A couple of hours later we head back down; by now the village of Poon Hill is deserted, the vista of the Annapurnas as special as ever.

Mesmerizing really, easy to get carried away, with those views and names like Namche Bazaar, Dhaulughiri, Cachenchunga, wouldn't it be cool to climb one? Then you come to Earth with a bump when you remember that you are only at a little over a third of the height of one of these giants and that it would take another five days just to reach the snow. Oh, well, time to become a Buddhist—some other lifetime.

We continue on our way, dip down into Rhodo forests, huge gnarly stands of Tolkienesque proportions, which must be even more amazing in spring blossom. Tonight's accommodation is an oversized tin box (all sides except the floor) with a gobsmack view of Annapurna 1. Dine with the rest of the trekkers on the al fresco stone patio. These invariably enjoyable social events and an opportunity to trade invaluable scoop: "Where you from?", "Where are you going?" "Where have you been?"

It is always scramble seating, there are a few empty chairs at our table. Uh oh—there's the four bruisers again and heading our way. One of them has a bottle of whiskey in one hand and a big kielbasa sausage in the other—this could be interesting. Turns out the four yobos are actually Russian. One cardiologist, two anesthesiologists, and one Budweiser salesman (I'm not making this up). We spend a fun evening with them enjoying their hospitality. You never do know who you are going to meet. We say our good nights to the Muscovites and leave them to close the place down as we retire to our favela.

On our second last day DB takes us on a path through Alpine scenery connecting small villages. Serene. The local village kids eye us on the way by. We know that they know that we are just dying to take their photos. Then candy, balloons, or—even worse—cash will be exchanged and we'll be on the ugly slippery panhandling slope together. Says a lot for the character of these poor folk that they haven't resorted to hassling already.

The last night on the trail provides us with a fitting finale. A group of female Nepali and Indian army officers is staying at our guest house. They are on a trek to promote team-building and cooperation between the countries. The hotel owner invites us to attend a cultural show that he has arranged in their honour. We get to sit with the VIPs and are presented with garlands of marigolds and seats to sit on!

I'd forgotten the quaint Indian way of blending politeness and directness. The young woman next to me, "Mini," leads off with:

"What is the purpose of your visit and your age, if you don't mind me asking?"

Me (feeling like I'm going through immigration): "Fifty-eight, and just doing some touristy things like trekking, rafting, sightseeing."

She: "Oh, and still so handsome and adventurous too."

Me—swooning: "I could take any amount of this. There's no fool like an old fool!"

I should also mention that these women, twenty-four to thirty-eight years of age, as well as clearly being of discerning good taste, are amazingly well accomplished—a regimental doctor just back from Darfur, a colonel in charge of the presidential bodyguard, the chief psychologist at the Mumbai base, etc., etc., etc.—but above all drop-dead gorgeous.

Kind of bears out the old Nepali folk legend about a group of beautiful women warriors that were sent to turn back Tibetan invaders in 705. Apparently when the Tibetans saw the beautiful faces of their enemy, their hearts dissolved into yak milk, which flowed into the Himalayan rivers, giving them their milky colour (so nothing to do with glacial runoff).

Well, OK, so I took a few liberties with the stuff in the last paragraph, but like any folklore, there's a couple of real facts in there.

The cultural event was enchanting: dancing village women, aged seven to seventy. But the fun was just beginning as the event evolved into a take-no-prisoners sort of an ethno-Bollywood mosh pit knees up—much fun.

In the morning we say goodbye to our sisters in arms—you really never do know who you are going to meet.

We head back down to the lowlands satisfied with our first sojourn in the Himalayas, but aware that bunking on top of the virgin can't stand as my record altitude forever. We get set to go higher.

Onward to the Langtang Himal.

PS If you like to do your mountaineering like me, in bed with hot cocoa and a book, you can't go far wrong with Jon Krakauer's *Into Thin Air* for sheer size of calamity. But Maurice Hertzog's *Annapurna* is hard to beat in terms of feats of endurance and compassion. Took them another five weeks overland after getting down to base camp, to get to something resembling a hospital in Kathmandu, 1951.

Chapter 9

Satisfaction

Did anyone remember to pack the yak turds?

"THERE ARE SOME DAYS WHEN I FEEL LIKE I AM GOING TO DIE OF AN OVERDOSE OF SATISFACTION."

—Salvador Dali

"WITH NO DIRECTION HOME
LIKE A COMPLETE UNKNOWN
LIKE A ROLLING STONE"

—Bob Dylan

Accessing the trail heads is an adventure in itself for the most part made by bus. Generally, these trips will take six hours or more on roads that have more in common with the Coney Island roller coaster than with a highway. More about those experiences later. After a few days of R and R in Kathmandu and one of those bus rides we find ourselves in the Langtang Himal mountain range. The range is one of many that comprise the Himalayas as a whole.

The Langtang trek is a joy shrouded in mountain mist, bleak and windswept, eerily atmospheric like *Wuthering Heights* in IMAX. There is lots of varied scenery, nice tea houses, fewer trekkers, and the villagers are too poor to afford garbage. After six days of leisurely hiking on the Autoroute, as I have dubbed the trail due to the large Gallic contingent here, we reach the upper Langtang Valley, late in the afternoon. On the way, we encounter scores of tumbled-down yak herders' houses, kilometres of stone-walled corrals, and hundreds of metres of stupas. Not in the style that we are familiar with. These look more like four-foot-wide-by-seven-foot-tall highway medians and also go by the name of Mani (which translates into "the one who will stay forever") walls. Placed end to end in the wall of the "median" are stone tablets approximately two by three feet, all with the same carving in Sanskrit: "*Om mani padme hum*" the same refrain, carved by hand out of the rock, hundreds of thousands of times by the Buddhist monks who used to live in this high altitude valley. As this labour of love clearly took decades of work to complete, I feel justified in at least taking a couple of keystrokes and a few moments of your time to shine a light on the gist of it.

". . . . the six syllables, *om mani padme hum*, mean that in dependence on the practice of a path, which is an indivisible union of method and wisdom, you can transform your impure body, speech, and mind into the pure exalted body, speech, and mind of a Buddha. . . ."

Well, that isn't actually my explanation, but the Dalai Lama's. Chew on it for a while, but don't despair if the *ah ha* moment doesn't come to you immediately. His holiness is on his fourteenth incarnation.

We reach Kangyn Gompa (3,900 metres), the last tea house destination/settlement. There's a bit of a Rolling Stones feel to the place. Old ladies lean on their gate posts. Is it my imagination or do they all look like Keith Richards? Anyway, they're finished being "beasts of burden" for the day, they could be just "waiting for a friend," but I suspect they want to "gimme shelter." Charlie Watts isn't here but the yaks "kerklank kerklonk" out their introduction to "Honky Tonk Women" on their bells. We make our way to our chosen guest house, bless the Lonely Planet (they have a tip for everything, including best cappuccino bar on Mars). You can't always get what you want, it's full. Damn that Lonely Planet.

We revise our plans and stay at a house adjacent to an abandoned monastery that sits like a citadel above the village, cool. Bloody freezing. Actually, it is minus-five Celsius overnight, no joke, when the tea house is essentially a glorified shed. Quite swish in other ways, it has an attached bathroom—i.e., it's inside the house—which, alas, froze solid during the night.

Rather than shiver in our sleeping bags under cover of the night for another hour until daylight, we head outside at 5:30 a.m., to walk a moonlight mile and enjoy the clear skies. We startle ourselves and some slumbering yaks as we nearly walk into them. They slowly stretch, get up, and lumber off, the moonlight creating sparkles on their frost-covered wool. Don't even go there with the "Jumpin' yak frost on the grass, grass, grass."

And there she is standing in the shadows, "Dorgie . . . Dorgie."[9] Dorje Lapka, a 6,966-metre peak, dominates the valley. She's so cold but then the sun begins to rise and we are treated to a spectrum of

9 https://www.youtube.com/watch?v=RcZn2-bGXqQ

colour, starting with every shade of steely blue transitioning ever so gradually into dazzling white. An image that doesn't fade away and was starring in my dreams for months.

Body and soul defrosted, we head back to the kitchen, eat a healthy breakfast, and prepare for our hike up to the viewpoints on Kyanjin Ri, 900 metres above us. After five hours of doing my best Herman Munster shuffle we reach the lower viewpoint. The wind is beginning to pick up noticeably, so Trixie decides to stop here and drink in the spectacle. Gahljan, our Tibetan guide, and I continue up the knife-edge ridge that connects the lower viewpoint to the peak. It takes us another hour to reach our 4,774-metre goal. We are the only ones there. We might as well be 2,000 light years from home. Glistening peaks all around, crystal clear, there's no white like snow white—heaven. The Tibetan peaks in the background are only a trekker's cough away (about five kilometres). A small avalanche rumbles down the face of Langtang Lirung (7,996 metres) directly opposite us. Breathtaking—if the altitude hadn't already taken my breath away.

Ghaljan erects one of the prayer flag poles that had blown down. I can't imagine why, but the scene reminds me of the iconic photograph of the raising of the torn and frayed US flag on Iwo Jima. Struggling to come up with anything remotely similar about the two events, I will just throw out a few random contrasts instead.

Elevation
Iwo Jima - Mount Suribachi 545 feet
Kyanjin Ri - 4,733 metres

Human toll
Iwo Jima - 7,000 US dead, 22,000 Japanese dead
Kyanjin Ri - 1 smiling (always) Tibetan, 1 shattered Canadian

Ordinance deployed
Iwo Jima - US naval barrage 8,000 tons of explosive
Kyanjin Ri - 4 yak turds

The yak turd reference might not sound that pertinent, but just think: firstly, they are commonly used as fuel for fire, secondly, there aren't that many around at this elevation, thirdly, the turds are actually more like dried cow pats and the trick is to let it loose and try to roll them down the mountain like a Frisbee on its rim. I must say I turned out to be a bit of a natural at the sport. A couple was still bounding down the mountainside when they disappeared from view. I hear that it is going to be a demonstration sport at the next Olympics and if all goes well, will replace that gymnastics with the ball thingy.

Formalities completed, we head back down, which in some ways is harder than coming up. The last thing I expected was to find sand up here, but I guess I shouldn't have been so surprised given that this area was a sea that separated the Indian subcontinent from Asia long, long ago. Being as surefooted as a giraffe on an ice rink at the best of times, I slide down on my keister more often than I would like to admit—it is still a small price to pay for the experience.

I can't help it but I do find it hard to go on a trip and not measure up the experience against some sort of pre-existing picture in my mind's eye. But I must say that this particular part of the trip far surpassed what my expectations of Nepal would offer.

SATISFACTION.

"Dorgie, Dorgie, when will those clouds all disappear?
Dorgie, Dorgie, where will it lead us from here?
Dorgie, you're beautiful, but ain't it time we said goodbye?"

With apologies to Jagger and Richards.

This, of course, isn't the end of the story. As is always the case in Nepal, the oft-heard mantra "a little bit up . . . a little bit down" applies. Having spent another chilly, restless night in our fridge, we bulk up on another of our landlady's breakfasts. Its a family affair and mother's little helper prepares the local specialty for us, *tsampa*, a stick-to-your-ribs porridge-style dish made from roasted barley. Our hostesses' cooking wasn't the best we had sampled on our trip, but you are pretty much obliged to eat where you sleep. When you are paying as little as five dollars a night (hot water for a wash is available for an extra fee), it is seriously frowned upon to eat at the neighbour's and deprive your host of a few additional rupees from the meals.

And we are off, back down the trail heading with trepidation for Surabesi and the dreaded return bus trip to Kathmandu. Trixie would rather have a root canal than go through that experience again. I am not without reservations myself. Going downhill this time, in a rickety Nepali bus with sketchy brakes, in one of the inauspiciously named "Kry Brothers" fleet is enough to make a grown man cry.

I shouldn't have worried. When Trixie is between a rock and a hard place, fate has met its match. As luck would have it we had been leapfrogging another group on our ascent. We had become friendly with a Californian couple, Jeff and Julie, and by extension their entourage of five Nepalis, porters, guide, and Sirdar. They are using the Langtang trek as a warmup acclimatization hike for their trek to EBC (Everest Base Camp) the following week. Having successfully completed the "little bit up" without any adverse altitude effects, they had arranged to make the "little bit down" portion as short as possible. I think there was a little of BTS (brown trouser syndrome) about the drive back going on too though.

The shortcut that they had organized involved being picked up by helicopter from halfway down the trail at Langtang village. Trixie decides to give it one more shot and her sleuthing and negotiating skills with the Sirdar bear fruit—there are a couple of seats still available at a price. The price miraculously ends up being exactly the amount of USD we have in our wallet. It's cash only up here. Luckily for Ghaljan we had already given him his tip before he set off with our backpack for a rendezvous with us in the city the next day.

The guest house manager then appears and takes centrestage in the production. I assume because he can contact the helicopter company he has the final say on the manifest. We sheepishly hand over the last of our greenbacks expecting or maybe just hoping that we will get a boarding pass or at least a receipt in exchange. Nope, just a "be at the helipad by two o'clock."

We arrive at the helipad at the appointed time—it is just a clearing of flat ground on the side of the valley, a near-vertical drop of hundreds of feet on one side and a massive steep rock bluff towering above us on the other. There must be thirty or more people here. This better be a big helicopter. We are all standing in a circle just behind the row of white rocks that demarcate the landing zone. A mixed bag of human cargo, young and old, poor and well-to-do, and our American friends.

A young Nepali woman runs up to me, her tiny daughter in tow, and blurts out in desperation, "My daughter is going to Kathmandu to go to kindergarten school, but they are telling me that they don't have a ticket for me anymore. Please take her with you."

I hadn't bargained on being conscripted into some sort of emotional rescue mission. Flummoxed and clutching at the nearest straws, I utter something like,

"But she doesn't have a ticket either, right? And what do I do when I get to Kathmandu?"

Not to be denied she counters with, "Oh, small children are not needing tickets and my sister is waiting for me at the airport."

With that, she thrusts her daughter's hand into mine. The kid looks up at me with wide, trusting eyes and that is that. Her mother, whatever her name might be, vanishes as suddenly as she appeared without so much as a "miss you." To make things worse, I start to get that sinking guilty feeling in my stomach that the last-minute tickets probably had been sold off at a premium to the highest bidder—gulp, me? And that we may unintentionally have even been the cause of the mother's reservation disappearing. The hand of fate works in mysterious ways.

Before long the chopper comes into view, a small speck down the valley, as it nears us it grows in size—not much, not nearly enough! I grip the child's hand firmly, give her a reassuring smile, and promise myself to try and make the whole experience as relaxed and normal as possible and calmly coax her over to the helicopter when my name is called.

In no time the chopper looms overhead and as it slowly descends towards the pad, throws up clouds of dust, pebbles, and sand. Heads bowed and eyes closed, we stand buffeted in the downdraft. As soon as the bird settles on the pad, the pilot cuts the engine. It is the signal for a stampede and, to my disbelief, my little girl is leading the charge, dragging me along in her wake. Wild, wild horses couldn't have broken her grip.

We jostle forward with the swarm of passengers hunched forward, fearful of the decelerating rotors above our heads. The copilot hauls me in, the kid with me, our grip is as unshakeable as iron. She beams up at me with wide brown eyes full of awe and gratefulness. I get a fleeting insight into the heady elixir of adulation. I can get a sense of how our heroes can get addicted to the drug.

Somehow we are one of the first on board, bags and passengers follow, all thrown inside the cabin like bales of hay. Julie is on and I spot Trixie seated by the door on the opposite side from me.

It is mayhem. As more of the mob attempts to clamber aboard, the copilot sticks his boot out the door, clears a space and slams the door shut. It's like a scene from the fall of Saigon. Before we know it the rotors are picking up speed again. Seconds later we are airborne—time waits for no one. I glance out the window and see

Jeff still on the ground shrouded in a cloud of dust. He stands slack jawed, mouth agape, clutching his hat, his combover hair whipped vertical in some sort of forlorn cockatoo farewell salute, watching in bewilderment as we leave him in our wake, its rough justice.

Something isn't right. We are airborne but going down. No sooner had we got off the ground than the pilot banked off to the left and down, down into the gorge of the valley below. I felt like I could reach out and touch the treetops as they rushed up to meet us. I have the feeling in the pit of my stomach that it's all over now. Prophetic words from past conversations echo in my head "Next trip, let's do something adventurous for a change?" Who said that!?

Are we in serious danger? I don't know. I doubt that the copilot could have counted the number of passengers that piled into the aircraft or even had a rough idea of the weight of the baggage on board, but there are way more passengers than seats, you couldn't find a seatbelt even if you wanted to. There isn't an empty lap amongst the tangle of bodies. Nepal has a reputation of having some of the best and worst pilots anywhere. Pay for pilots in this part of the world isn't competitive so it often attracts castoffs from other countries or frustrated young go-getters who can't find a job at home. With the weather, geography, and dated air fleets, these new arrivals either become very, very good very, very quickly or they . . . er, um they were wise not to go long in the stock market.

Slowly, the rate of descent levels off and we bottom out and then begin the gradual climb up to the valley rim. We spot another helicopter heading toward Langtang village; Jeff will get a ride on that one.

It isn't until we eventually crest over the mountain ridge that I finally start to relax. My little girl with no name must sense this as she eases her vice-like grip on my hand and stares me in the face with eyes the size of saucers. For the first time since we've been thrust together we have a chance to talk. Nepali and English isn't a great combination for communication, but at least we think that we have somehow made a connection by the time we touch down in Kathmandu.

Safely back on the ground, the girl with faraway eyes spots her auntie, drops my hand for the first time since we took off from Langtang, and scampers into her arms. Hugs and kisses completed, Auntie comes over to me, shakes my hand, overwhelms me with gushing waves of appreciation, offers of meals and undying gratitude.

I feel like a bit of a fraud given that I hadn't really done anything. The pleasure had been all mine and to top it off I get to feel what it must be like to be Superman for a day. We say our farewells to Julie and wish her the best with her trek to EBC.

Everest, hmm. Everest . . .

Postscript

At 11:56 am on April 25, 2015, a massive 7.8 earthquake hit Nepal, its epicentre only a few kilometres from Langtang village. In seconds, an estimated 40 million tons of rock and rubble tumbled down from the overhanging mountains above onto the hamlet below. There were no Supermen that day—all were lost, buried for eternity.

A hundred and seventy-five villagers, twenty-seven guides and seasonal workers, and forty-one trekkers gone, vanished from the face of the earth as if they had never existed.

And the girl with the faraway eyes . . . ?

Chapter 10

Lightning Strikes on the Gokyo Trek

Who was that masked man?

"IT DOESN'T HAVE TO BE FUN TO BE FUN."

—Barry Blanchard

"HE WHO REMAINS CALM WHEN THOSE AROUND HIM PANIC PROBABLY DOESN'T KNOW WHAT IS GOING ON."

—Anonymous

Our appetites for the Himalayas merely tantalized by our 2011 trip, it isn't long before we are back. This time we try the spring hiking season. It is late February when we make another hair-raising bus trip into the mountains. The next morning after a restless night's sleep, we depart the trailhead town of Bhandar; it is cool, misty, and lightly drizzling. It's early in the trekking season and we won't meet many travellers on our hike to Namche Bazaar. It feels good to be walking after another predictably uncomfortable bus ride and to be master of your own risk management. The clouds obscure the high mountain vistas, but there is plenty to see to keep us engaged.

We meet an elderly man on the trail oddly decked out. All in white, shirt, V-neck sweater, slacks, and shoes, he looks like he stepped off the cricket pitch, which seems unlikely. Even though we are only at 500 metres there isn't much in the way of flat ground and if you hit a six it would be game over. As it turns out he is actually in mourning—not for a lost ball, but a family member and is all in white as is the Hindu custom. We settle into our stride, have occasional stops for a brew at the tea houses along the route. Trudge along with romanticized notions of following in Edmund Hillary's footsteps. This used to be the route that expeditions took to get to Everest before the airport was built at Lukla. It is much less used now and feels a bit like the world has passed it by. We see several vacated homes, which will soon be occupied when the farming season starts, and too frequently burned-out shells of buildings, the unfortunate result of *rakshi* (the local moonshine), boredom, wood fires, and timber construction.

Fuel is in short supply, and if a trekker wants a boiled egg it means using propane brought up by mule from Bandhar. The authorities are doing their best to discourage deforestation, better late than never. Still, it's common to see tall rhododendron bushes pruned to within an inch of their lives in a weird poodle's tail-like topiary topped off with blossoms of woodpecker red.

After six hours of walking, which is our rough average for a day, we settle in for our first night. It is a clear night, but there is no moon. The blackness in the valley is total, the valley ridge and the sky blend into each other anonymously. The twinkling lights of the homesteads perched on the valley walls form their own constellations and merge seamlessly with the heavens. The next day is no less scintillating as the sun illuminates the frost and snow crystals and the mica in the Himalayan sand glitters like the sequins on a figure skater's tutu.

The following night is Losar, the celebration of the Tibetan New Year. The hosts and Nepali only guests at the tea house are enthusiastically downing mugs of *rakshi*. Before long, the scene reminds me of the rowdy Hogmanays of my youth, complete with hollering matches and glassy-eyed Nepalis standing toe to toe jabbing index fingers in the direction of their disbelievers, feet rooted to the ground while their upper body sways in that peculiar slow circular motion a bit like hula hoop in hyper slo-mo. Surprise, surprise, the results of too much of a good thing are pretty much the same whether you are a Buddhist, Hindu, Protestant, Catholic, etc.

We figure that it is time to beat a hasty retreat before one of those fingers inevitably ends up pointing in our direction. The party rocks on until the wee hours—unfortunately not loud enough to drown out the scrabbling of the critters in the wall of our room. Bizarrely there is a poster of the Empress Hotel on the wall. It's a grand old Victorian luxury hotel that stands imposingly on the inner harbour of my home town. I nod off staring up at the garrets of the Empress, a treat usually reserved for yacht owners and Victoria's homeless people.

The next day we set out in spectacular sunshine—shorts, hats, and sunscreen the order of the day. We climb higher to the Lamjura La pass at 3,500 metres, which will take us over into the next valley. The melt is full on, the trail is clear but the surrounding land is still snow covered and glitters and sparkles as brightly as ever. The silence is occasionally made mysterious by eerie singing in the phone lines, which we discover is caused by the bells on the pack mules resonating with wires as they lug their supplies up to Namche Bazaar, the trailhead for the Everest region.

We stop at villages, often no more than a cluster of houses, for meals, they are always communal events. Being as it is springtime, there are puppies, kid goats, and chicks everywhere. A mother's work is never done, so the little children are free range too. The villagers can also be naïve to some of the perils that the outside world can bring. A mother blithely watches her child, two or so, chewing on a AAA battery. We frantically explain to her through our guide the danger, she fishes the battery out of the kid's mouth, and throws it in the fire.

The kid, in search of some new mischief, walks over to one of the puppies and good-naturedly kicks it a few times. The mother smiles. So what should we do? What's advice, what's interference? Should we tell them to be nice to puppies? Is there any point to "advice" like this if we aren't starting from some sort of common values?

The best that we can come up with is to pick up the dog and make nice with it in the hopes that demonstrating love and affection will rub off. Nah, the kid wanders off and kicks one of the other dogs. The mom beams proudly, as if to say, "That's my boy, ain't he cute?" And of course, he is.

The trek is not a piece of cake. Long days, lots of up and down—you learn to curse the downhill because you know you will have to recoup the altitude you have lost and more. Our progress is steady but slow and we begin to wonder if we have allotted enough time to reach our goal of the Gokyo Lakes.

To make matters worse, on the sixth day, I get sick and we are laid up for two days in Nunthala, fortunately at one of the nicer inns. Nevertheless, I can't help feeling sorry for myself. I spend a couple of days propped up in bed in my sleeping bag wearing my toque and glove liners, charting our progress, or lack thereof, on the map.

Nothing to do but dream up fanciful comparisons to Captain Scott of the Antarctic. "I hope that England will not think ill of us, the lads have given their all, blah blah blah. . . ."

Of course as is usual with these intestinal ailments all is not inaction all of the time. Eye-popping, toe-curling moments of blind panic tend to spring on you without notice. I try to be more philosophical about it all. The Buddhists have their eightfold path to enlightenment, number one being the cheery "Life is suffering." I have the urge to drop a line to the Dalai Lama and suggest it's time for a new 2.0 version of the "Buddha." Surely after 2,000 years a new edition is due. In any event I'm thinking the new number one ought to be "Lack of bowel control far from home is suffering." That would be more on the money.

On day three I start to feel well enough to do a little reading, Peter Mathiessen's *The Snow Leopard*. It's a combination intro to adventure in the Himalaya and Eastern mysticism. My appetite is also beginning to return. Still being skeptical of the local food, I resort to the good old Western stomach flu comfort food standbys, which are all readily available, although as it turns out, a bit long in the tooth.

Flat Coke, expiry date 2012 (what the heck, it probably has the half-life of Uranium 235 anyway), Mars bar, and crackers, expiry date 2011—a little squishy, but sugar and salt never go off, do they? Local boiled potatoes, hold the half-empty bottle of ketchup, expiry date 2010.

Energy somewhat recharged, we head back on the trail. As we head higher, we encounter fewer mule trains. Ten or twelve of these creatures are the usual number in a train. The mule herder seems to keep the show moving but the mules themselves seem to establish leading rights by a kind of push and shove "after you Claude" sort of a jostling. The yak trains, on the other hand, you definitely want to show some respect to. We follow the locals' lead and clamber up the embankments on the high side of the trail when the yaks lumber by.

If I'd wanted the Pamplona experience I would have gone to Spain. Each beast is a ton of hairy, horned bad attitude. There's usually only four of these headstrong animals to a group and even then they will often hold up proceedings by cracking skulls together to sort out whos on first.

North of Lukla the trail gets busier as the trickle of local traffic is joined by the throngs of trekkers who have flown into the highest airstrip in the Nepal Himal. The villagers and porters demonstrate human ingenuity in all its individuality and creativity manifested in geraniums poking out of backpacks, four sheets of plywood tied onto a stooping back, two backpacks lashed together with a duffle bag on top. What you can say is that it's probably one of the most environmentally friendly "highways" on the planet.

The trekking season brings employment but it isn't easy work; everything that goes into the mountains goes on foot. If it is not four-legged it is on small men with big loads towering above their heads, so heavy that when they take a breather they have to keep their pack on and wedge a stick under it to ease the weight or else they won't be able to get started again. We pass a group of porters on lunch break; they lay sprawled at the side of the trail like some defeated retreating army, glazed, dull, dead eyes gazing into the middle of nowhere.

A few kilometres north of Lukla we come to Namche Bazaar. It is another good workout. At this altitude (3,400 metres) and above, altitude sickness (AMS) can occur. We stay for two nights in order to acclimatize and reduce the risks. It isn't a hardship: this township is a hub for the Everest region and has bakeries, equipment shops, and restaurants aplenty. Trixie takes the opportunity to add a little Nepali couture to her wardrobe.

Her retail therapy scores a puffy down suit that adds a certain Pillsbury doughboy allure not to mention two thick inches of fluffy warming insulation all round. Given the right imaginative circumstances I could maybe see a 6'6" anorexic supermodel carry this off as haute couture. A super sexy rib tickler au bouffant combined with divine cushioned flood pant pantaloons accessorized with to-die-for hand-woven yak wool mitts avec les chausseurs de Doc Marten and topped off with une woolly chapeau avec les oreilles flaps—très jolie.

It's the ideal getup for Namche, whether going out for a night on the town or promenading on main street tip toeing through yak and mule droppings during the day. Main Street is also the thoroughfare for the animals carting supplies up to the camps and villages north of here.

But I digress . . . do I ever . . . must be the altitude. Get some advice re Diamox, the latest altitude sickness prophylactic.[10] Diamox is, as with many things medical, no sure thing. We end up lost in the Bermuda Triangle of experience, science, or faith in our search for the source of the cure. The choices are to go with the experience of the old-school trekking guides who simply recommend just drink water, take your time, and go down if you feel unwell. These guys' livelihood and tips depend on happy, delivered trekkers. Or we could opt for the scientific solution, often overhyped by drug companies more worried about bottom lines than integrity. Or go with faith and old wives' tales and smear your throat with charcoal from a virgin's fireplace and put the feather of a black chicken under your pillow. I have a feeling that option A is the least dependent on the placebo effect.

Blood vessels hopefully now used to a reduced complement of oxygen, we continue on our way, veering northwest at the magnificent monastery at Tengboche. After Tengboche the trails become quiet again. We may walk for two hours or more without encountering a mule train or other trekkers. At this altitude the snow still blankets the ground. With the days lengthening, the sun slowly warming, and

10 https://my.clevelandclinic.org/health/diseases/15111-altitude-sickness

the modest traffic it means that the pathway has begun to thaw into a slightly slushy, muddy strip about a foot wide. Our route will take us to the Gokyo Lakes area, which has spectacular views of Everest. We have decided to give a miss to the more travelled easterly route that goes to EBC, which has great views of pilgrims ticking off boxes on their bucket lists.

The hours hiked each day become much shorter; the trail is steep switchback up and down. The conventional wisdom is not to sleep more than 300 metres higher than the previous night, drink lots of water, and if you have AMS symptoms, don't delay, to go down, down, down, and in a hurry.

We are now at day seventeen of our walk and only a day away from our destination and turnaround point of the Gokyo village, which we hear is no more than a cluster of inns, or tea houses, as they are called in Nepal. The trail is really just a little strip of commerce existing to service the trekking trade and the few yak herders eking out a living. The trail is only starting to come back to life after the winter shutdown. The tea house owners winter down in the valleys, or the Sherpa region, where many of them were born.

This last stretch is short, only nine kilometres, but strenuous due to the altitude and rugged terrain involved. The beautiful scenery and sun peeking in and out to light up the sparkles in the snow make it all worthwhile.

More than once we stop at the rustic inns for a rest break where we are regaled by their owners. Over mugs of tepid tea we listen to tales of their mountaineering youth and check out their photographs on the wall. There, they beam arm in arm with famous mountaineers or stand atop the world's biggest one, variously known as Sagarmatha ("Forehead in the Sky"- Nepalese), Chomolongua ("Mother Goddess of the Universe"- Tibetan), or Everest (some Welsh bloke's name – English). These innkeepers, now mostly retired from Sherpa and guiding duties, have literally set up shop in the shadow of their former workplace, and very nice it is too.

Finally we are up on the plateau surrounded by the desolate tundra of the high mountains. There is a bleak, windswept beauty to the place—no vegetation, a few largish boulders and a shrinking layer of last winter's snow carpeting the ground with the peaks all around us. We stroll past the first two of the five lakes of this, the highest freshwater lake system in the world.

We are pretty pleased with ourselves after seventeen days on the trail. Min, our Nepali guide and porter, figures that we are only a half hour from our goal. It is definitely a Kodak moment (this was in 2013 so Instagram wasn't "a thing" then, OK?).

I pause to get my camera out and call for Trix and Min to strike a triumphant pose. Trix isn't up for it; in fact, she doesn't look so good at all. Before we know it she grimaces, and is bent double, holding her head and stomach. Nausea, headaches, and vomiting are all signs of AMS.

She wants some privacy, not knowing whether she is either going to need to throw up or defecate. The only shelter available is behind a rock about the size of a loveseat. After the deed, a horrendous episode of diarrhea, she emerges, ashen faced, still in agony, and weak as a kitten. So now what?

Carry on to the village and gain another 100 metres in altitude, the last thing you should do if you are suffering from altitude sickness, or go down to the little inn where we'd stopped for tea half an hour earlier and try to get help? Staying put isn't an option. It is mid-afternoon and there isn't a building or a soul in sight. It is quite possible that no one will come this way for the rest of the day.

Down we go, Trixie strung between Min and me, barely able to walk. Exhausted, we reach the tea house. The owner isn't really open for the season yet but opens up a room for us. We get Trixie onto the bed and fish our sleeping bags out of our cold backpack. The room is freezing and unheated. Luckily, Trixie is kitted out in her Michelin man outfit, but she isn't feeling any better and is still shaking uncontrollably. I climb onto the bed and under the sleeping bags with her, hoping to heat up her and the bags simultaneously.

The elderly owner isn't going to be much help to us. Min must go down to Machermo, the village that we'd set out from this morning to get help. They will have a satellite phone and contact with Kathmandu. It will soon start to get dark so even if we get through it's doubtful that they will send in a helicopter today. Min heads off back down the trail at the trot. Unencumbered by our forty-pound backpack and our slow pace, I am hoping that he will make good time. Min is in his early twenties, stocky, and about three inches shorter than Trix, but has been a steady, dependable companion on the trip and is very concerned about her condition.

We spend the next hours mostly in silence, Trixie verging on delirium one minute, then ready to lapse into sleep the next. Not knowing if sleep might morph into unconsciousness or coma, I keep talking to her to keep her somewhat alert. Much more quickly than I had expected, Min returns with reinforcements and the disappointing news that it is too late for the helicopter to make a flight in daylight today and that we will have to wait until tomorrow. The reinforcements to my dismay are pitiful. One skinny thirtyish fellow who is dressed like he is out of a 1970s episode of *Coronation Street*. Tweed jacket, V-neck sweater, dress shirt and pants (shoddy). But to give him his due, he does wear a toque and a muffler obscures the lower portion of his face. I am in disbelief, but recriminations in this situation would accomplish nothing. Min introduces me to Dorjee, our alleged saviour.

Speed is of the essence. After helping Trix to the bathroom for one hopefully last bout, I get her bundled up and we load her up piggyback style on to Dorjee. I should also mention that Dorjee is even shorter than Min and wearing winkle picker dress shoes. Without a backward glance Dorjee takes off down the trail, the limp arms of T wrapped around his neck. With dread in my heart I watch them disappear into the gathering gloom as the temperature starts to drop and the trail starts to turn to ice.

Min and I restuff the backpack and wrap ourselves up in all our warmest clothes and follow them down the mountain. I kept expecting to round the next bend, catch up with them or maybe see them in the distance. But there is nary a trace. Going downhill and with Min carrying the rucksack surely we must be making faster ground than the two of them. At this point stress starts to sow the seeds of panic, the mind starts to formulate dire scenarios. "What happens if they have missed the trail? They could freeze out here overnight. He certainly didn't look like a guide."

"What happens if he slips on the ice and goes over the edge? Those shoes are just plain dangerous in these conditions."

And on and on.

We eventually reach Machermo and our guest house, by now in total darkness, and to much relief find that T is already in a room and in bed with a hot water bottle, the audacious Dorjee having burst into the teahouse some forty-five minutes ahead of us. Trix is still obviously very sick, weak, and can barely stay awake. We are still none the wiser as to what had caused this illness. But if it was AMS, the only 100 percent effective treatment is to descend, and we are now 300 metres lower than when she was afflicted. Was that a sufficient drop? I have no idea.

I get Min to show me where the porters' rooms are and ask him to have himself and Dorjee on standby in case things get really bad during the night. If the worst came to the worst we might have to head farther down in the dark, not a comforting thought still being above the snow line.

After feeding Trixie some tea and clear soup, I climb under the pile of sleeping bags and blankets into the bed and watch her through the night as she sleeps. If anything is reassuring it is the fact that her breathing is easier, which may indicate that the breathlessness she had experienced earlier had just been caused by the exertion at altitude.

I don't think I have ever been more happy to see a sunrise. As I go outside to check the weather, Min saunters up in his calm manner to let me know that the chopper has just left KTM and will be here within a couple of hours. I ask to see Dorjee to thank him for all he has done, but, alas, he had already left with his group on their way up to the lakes. "Who was that masked man?"

The six-seater Eurocopter AS 350 touches down for us around 9:00 a.m. Trixie is still unwell and truly "out of it" as we help her into the chopper, where she slumps limply into her seat. It is a subdued farewell to the mountains. Min and I are treated to a flight through spectacular scenery, en route back to Kathmandu. Flying over sections of the trail it somehow doesn't seem possible that we have been walking for seventeen days and yet we would be back in the city in a couple of hours. But there we are greeted by Chewaang, the owner of the trekking agency and his shiny SUV. In no time he has us at the CIWEC hospital. The care at the hospital is very professional and prompt. Samples are taken and it is quickly established that giardia is the cause of the trouble. The giardia parasite is most often found in water contaminated by animals. So in all likelihood it was a combination of pack animals on the trail and drinking tepid tea that hadn't been boiled that were the cause of Trixie's undoing. A course of strong antibiotics are to put her back on the road to a full recovery. The cure's side effects and the after-effects of the infection are so draining that it is enough to put Trixie back in bed—a comfortable, warm bed this time.

Trix would later recount that while she was being carried down the mountain drooped over Dorjee's shoulders, that she had felt the presence of a third "being" . . . a guardian angel? Apparently this is not an uncommon phenomenon, known as the third man factor, and it has been reported by climbers, sailors, and shipwreck survivors subjected to traumatic situations. The unseen presence has been given the prosaic explanation that it is the subconscious mind giving the conscious mind a comforting coping mechanism. But try a non-scientific perspective, picture yourself hopelessly ill riding piggyback on some stranger hurtling down a narrow trail in a frozen, barren moonscape as night falls.

The unseen presence has been also been described as being a spiritual protective force. Either way you take your comfort wherever you can find it.

We are relieved to be back in smoggy, chaotic twenty-five-degree Kathmandu. We contact our kids back in Canada to fill them in on what has happened and get them to submit our insurance claim for reimbursement of the cost of the helicopter flights.

Their relief at our eventual good fortune is palpable, but their assumption that this would end our high-altitude jaunts is misplaced. When I tell them "the trip was fantastic and if you have any chance you should come with us on the next one," it only evokes a stunned silence at the other end of the line.

Fortunately or unfortunately, depending on how you rank your anxieties, we were spared or deprived of the return bus trip due to Trixie's emergency heli evacuation from the Gokyo lakes. It is an immense relief to be comfortably back in civilization, yet at the same time we are rueful that we hadn't exited the mountains under our own power. This perfect state of conflicted emotional contradiction is as good a frame of mind as any to reintroduce ourselves to the caprice of Nepal's cities.

I knew that T had fully recovered when a couple of days later she announced that it was time to go shopping. Amongst the souvenirs we bought a bronze double-ended sceptre, called a Dorjee. A symbolic artifact used in Tibetan Buddhist rituals.

Prophetically enough, the word *dorjee* means "lightning bolt."

Chapter 11

The One Two Three of ABC

I didn't want a shower anyway.

"YOU WILL HAVE TO SPEAK UP I AM WEARING A TOWEL."

—Homer Simpson

"IT'S NOT A REAL ADVENTURE IF YOU HAVE TO PAY FOR IT."

—Edmund Hillary

After a medically required intermission (apparently heart arrhythmia and hiking at high altitude in remote areas are not a good combo) of three years, we return to Nepal in 2016

Seeking to share our love of the mountains and Nepal, we convince our twenty-something kids and one of their partners to join us on Nepal's most well-known and popular trek. We set off for the spectacular scenery of the ABC (Annapurna Base Camp) trek, also known as the apple pie circuit because of its relative sophistication (some tea houses have ensuites). We comprise an eight-person contingent: five Caucasians and our three Nepali musketeers.

Pemba, our guide, who is a dead ringer for a twenty-two-year-old David Niven, cuts a dashing figure—curly black hair, pencil-thin mustache, and pencil-thin legs to match. Appearances as usual are not as they appear. He is an accomplished guide whose next gig will be to take a wealthy American to the summit of Everest. This will be Pemba's third attempt, his two previous plans to summit thwarted by the shutdown of the mountain, firstly because of an avalanche tragedy claiming the lives of sixteen sherpas in 2014, and the April 2015 earthquake.

The porters, Chhirring Tenzing, whom everyone calls CT, and Sonam are perfect travelling companions. Sonam, a laughing, smiling, imp-like bundle of happiness clad in school cap, short pants, and backpack slung low reminiscent of a Himalayan Angus from AC/DC. CT, our Mr. Muscles and the shepherd of the group, making sure that we stay on task and on track while the others deliver tummy rubs, sing, crack jokes, and generally clown around. All three are twenty-two years old. I wonder what happened in 1994.

Natural disasters have a habit of causing spikes in the birth rates. When the power goes out folks get frisky. The birth rate after Hurricane Sandy jumped by 30 percent. The theory didn't seem to fit in Nepal. Natural disasters are not uncommon and the power goes out all the time . . . so maybe, just maybe, the power didn't go out twenty-two years ago and maybe, just maybe, it was an opportunity to try a few "things" with the lights on for a change! If you have any better ideas send them on a postcard to see below[11]

Out in the mountains, creativity is also needed to provide power. Energy sources are more progressive. It is not unusual to find a mule train recharging their batteries under a bank of solar panels at the end of the day or a water wheel on a mountain stream providing power for a tea house and turning a prayer wheel at the same time. The prayer wheels are said to gather goodwill while simultaneously purifying negative energy. Prayer wheels, which originated in Tibet, are found in settlements throughout Nepal. Tibetan customs have lived on more successfully in Nepal than in their homeland, which was invaded by China in 1950. Keep those wheels turning.

We spend the second night of our nine-day hike in Landruk. The river Modi far below slices the valley in two and the twin "city" Gandruk sits on the side of the chasm opposite us. The history of the settlements isn't exactly clear. The local population of Gurung people are reputed to have originated in Mongolia and some sort of Romulus and Remus spat resulted in the split. The men's fearlessness is legendary; in former times, the area was a prime recruiting location for the esteemed Gurkha regiment. The excellent Gurkha museum in Pokhara showcases the regiment's valour in past battles in Afghanistan and Egypt. The villages are, by Nepali standards, pretty affluent and reflect that military ethic: clean, well-built, and well ordered.

Our daughter Scara, having found our pace too pedantic, has branched off with Pemba on another longer loop trail and will reconnect with us two days from now.

Each day we would hike somewhere between eight and twelve kilometres, which doesn't sound like much. But context is everything.

---

11 http://www.fpan.org/

After you cover the first couple of kilometres of an unending path comprised of a twisting switchback of uneven rocks and steps, the goal for the day seems ballsy. The overall round trip of 140 kilometres is beyond comprehension.

I console myself with the fact that I am covering about four times my average Canadian daily quota, most of that done between the fridge, the car, and the couch.

We gradually climb out of the lowland landscape (1,600 metres or so), travelling through trail sides carpeted with tiny white and violet blossoms and cliff sides above us sprouting orchids. Masses of caterpillars squirm their way across the rocks.

All is not a *Sound of Music* production though; all this sophistication brings a lot of hikers, all tricked out with the latest equipment. The trek is fairly strenuous due to the topography: there are thousands of stone slab steps and bottlenecks where congestion can happen.

This can be frustrating (well, maybe only if you are me). A behemoth heaves into my view, leading me by about twenty metres. My imperceptibly faster pace narrows the gap after about fifteen minutes. This chap is severely the wrong side of 250 pounds, and held together with knee braces, elbow pads, mittens, and a foreign legion cap. I pull out to blaze past this Terminator clone, he decides to take a breather at this crucial moment and spread-eagles his arms out like Rio's Christ the Redeemer, trekking poles dangling limply from his wrists, and stops.

Trek rage bubbling barely beneath the surface, I gasp out, "Fine day. Mind if I squeeze by?" while thinking, *Move over, buddy. D'ya think you own the mountain?*

I struggle on past—free, but, no, not to be outdone, he starts off again. I hear the click clack of his poles on the stone steps behind me. No matter how I try, the relentless metallic monotone keeps pace with me. I manifest all the paranoia of Captain Hook being hounded by the crocodile that swallowed the clock in Peter Pan.

"Click clock. . . . Click clock."

Walking for hours among this picturesque landscape gives you plenty of time to reflect—what else are you going to do? Thank Buddha I have no phone. It may be just the selfish interests of the trekkers that we meet, but most of them are just as happy to be as unplugged as we are. This happy arrangement can't last for long. The cell connection is an undoubted boon for the villagers and they are adapting quickly. I spend some time ruminating on the Terminator incident and I come to the conclusion that the problem had nothing to do with him. It was with me, with my own ego, vanity.

"How could an unfit, overweight, semi-invalid possibly be keeping pace with me?"

This all may be self-evident to you, but it was an "Ah, grasshopper" moment for me and one I am sure I wouldn't have had, had I had my smartphone fired up. And had I known how many hads I would have had in that sentence before I had started it, I would have had second thoughts about filling you in on this revelation.

Don't worry. Basking in my new found awareness, we soon arrive in Chhomrong at 2,210 metres, the highest permanent settlement on the trek. It's a charming hamlet complete with a German bakery dishing up delicious pastries and pies. Comfortable accommodation with hot (warmish, actually) water and a fine dinner of *momos* (steamed savoury dumplings, a Tibetan speciality) bring an end to another splendid day.

The menus when trekking are pretty limited, bland, and repetitive, many would say. But I find that an appreciation for what it takes to get the food here, a happy tiredness and gratitude that there is no cooking or dishes involved goes a long way to making these simple meals enjoyable. Sonam and CT certainly lick their chops at the thought of the porter's staple meal (morning, noon, or night) of *dal bhat*, a mix of lentils, rice, and occasionally spices or vegetables. An army marches on its stomach, after all.

Another day up the trail we meet up with Pemba and Scara. Curiously, Scara is carrying the pack and Pemba is limping. He had rolled his ankle and was on the gimp, nothing too serious. Still, it wouldn't look too good to his Everest client if he turned up at base camp using a walking stick. He would have to be back to full fitness by the beginning of May.

Rather than aggravate the injury further, we stow one pack with the tea house owner and redistribute the essential gear amongst the remaining packs in readiness for the last two days of ascent. Trixie gets to work massaging the ankle, doing reiki and soaking his foot in warm water to some effect. By the next day, he is OK to hobble along with us without a pack. Before setting off, Trix ties his shoelaces for him, it looks for all the world like a mom seeing her son off to the first day of school.

After a hot day of hiking, I decide to take advantage of the facilities. It is a pretty upscale tea house, complete with a pay-per-use shower stall with hot water, conveniently located just to the side of the dining patio.

I enter the booth, strip down, and drape my clothes over a piece of string thoughtfully tied to the bars on the window at one end and the propane pipe feeding the hot water heater at the other. I turn to the controls—a bewildering array of choices are available. Some training in how to fire up a nuclear reactor would have come in handy.

The heater itself has three knobs, one each for winter, summer, and firepower?! To multiply your possible permutations there are no fewer than six taps available. To do what I had no idea. All of this paraphernalia was presumably required to coax water out of a handheld shower head tied to the ceiling by a piece of wire and connected to the water supply by five feet of salvaged garden hose.

I gamely start fiddling with the controls, like some mad scientist but without the white lab coat, hoping by random luck to hit on the right combination. "Firepower," I reason, has to be the key to turning on the propane that will heat the water. But, no, I can't even get a dribble of cold water from this Heath Robinson contraption.

The three-degree air temperature is taking its toll. The physiological reactions of the ages take over, goosebumps erupt, my teeth start to chatter and the parts I hold most precious shrivel alarmingly. My feet feel frozen to the icy slate floor, my legs numb from the knees down.

I concede defeat, wrap my towel around my waist, and with a brisk pace like some wannabe Gandhi, weave my way between the dining tables crowded with trekkers, out enjoying a beer and the sunset. I find the owner and explain my predicament. He blithely informs me that "Yes, we are having very many problems with this hot water thing. We keep adding new ones but they all break. We have no hot water for many years, you must just turn the garden tap on in the cabbage patch around the corner."

It's dark by now. I gather my clothes and pass on the prospect of a three-degree shower inside a refrigerator.

After the penultimate day's hike we spend the last night at Machhapuchhare, otherwise known as fish tail, base camp (MBC) lodge. At 3,700 metres, it is freezing cold at night and the digs not nearly as salubrious as the tea houses in the villages down below.

Further sprained ankles are a distinct risk. The toilets are of the Asian squat variety and trying to aim your pee while wrestling with layers of insulating clothing doesn't help with the accuracy. With pee freezing at minus-five degrees Celsius, answering the call of nature could lead to a fate worse than death!

On the final day we depart, early, at 6:30 a.m., to beat the clouds that will roll up the valley later in the day and obscure the mountains that we have worked so hard to reach. The sight is awe-inspiring. The trail enters from the east into an amphitheatre of monstrous summits.

We gaze up, slack jawed, at the massive peaks. Annapurna is actually the name of a fifty-kilometre-long mountain range made up of several peaks. Arranged all around us are Annapurna One, the tenth-highest mountain in the world and first 8,000-metre mountain ever climbed, her sisters Annapurnas Two, Three, yes, and Four, and Annapurna South and numerous other peaks of over 7,000 metres.

Machhapuchhare nicknamed the Matterhorn of the Himalayas is behind. The view from this angle explains the reason for her other moniker, "Fish Tale." The rising sun unveils its dazzling white cleft summit ridge, like some Moby Dick albino whale tale sinking behind the smaller mountains in the foreground.

Going back down the mountain is always easier and we have the time to visit the hot spring pools down on the valley floor next to the icy surging mountain river. We soak our stiff joints and generally relax. Well, at least it is easier for the guys to relax; the ladies tell me that the creepy guy that mans the changing shed isn't up to speed on the "Me Too" movement, if you get my drift.

The last day leaving the mountains is always bittersweet. On one hand, all the creature comforts of the city beckon. On the other, we'll miss the grand vistas and all the small treasures we encountered on our journey. The deafening silences when alone on the trail, the thousands of butterflies that greeted us as we neared the trail head, the camaraderie and small kindnesses exchanged on the way.

An added bonus was being able to share the experience with our kids and to delight in their enjoyment of the mountains. They will be back, but busy lives may mean that it might not be for a while. In the meantime they leave us behind and bugger off down the mountain at breakneck speed. There's only so much bonding anyone can take. They want to get back to Pokhara in time for the Hindu celebration of Holi. It's a no-holds-barred, rough-and-tumble tradition that is part trick or treat, part food fight, part anarchic street battle. Nepal is rich in tradition and culture. It would be a shame to miss it.

Well, there is an idea: tradition and culture. How could we combine that with trekking . . . ?

We needn't have speculated. Nepal has an answer for everything.

Chapter 12

True Grit in Mustang

Fancy meeting you here!

"BE YOURSELF IS ABOUT THE WORST ADVICE YOU CAN GIVE SOME PEOPLE."

—J B Priestley

"YOU'RE OFF TO GREAT PLACES, TODAY IS YOUR DAY, YOUR MOUNTAIN IS WAITING SO GET ON YOUR WAY."

—Dr. Seuss

After our children's departure for Canada, where careers and clients await, not to mention bills to pay, we arrange another trek. This second journey will take us into Mustang (no Western connections here, just a bastardization of the name of one of the main villages, Manang). In any event, Mustang is a small former kingdom within Nepal that sticks like a thumb, some might say a sore thumb, given the politics of the region, into what was the independent country of Tibet until China's 1951 annexation.

We have a two-man crew this time. Entry into the "kingdom" requires that you are accompanied by an accredited guide. And guides, especially ours, don't hump tourist backpacks and so we also have a porter. Our guys are the next generation of trekking assistants—two pretty city boys, guide Deneesh, twenty-two, and porter Prakass, nineteen. Prakass, slim but with a powerful build, has androgynous features, oriental eyes, a cupid's bow mouth, pointed eyebrows like two black miniature Everests on burnished bronze skin. The Buddha carnate with a Fifth Avenue haircut. If I looked like him I could easily wile away an hour or two every day in front of the mirror. Deneesh, resplendent, diamond stud earring, hiking pole, dust cover for his day pack, gloves to protect his hands from the sun, designer clothes, hairstyle, and backpack. A tidy, dandified example of self-importance, uniform in height and circumference of his head, 5'2". His hands on hips semi-swaggering gait is seriously reminiscent of someone very familiar whose name I can't put my finger on. Until, that is, when Deneesh buys himself a cowboy hat. A more useless, ill-suited item of vain millinery you could not imagine. Nevertheless, the hat gives me the final clue as to his hidden identity: John Wayne. For better or worse we have our very own pint-sized version of "The Duke."

I had hoped for a more deferential aide-de-camp, maybe a Carson out of Downton Abbey type of a character. I'd even have been magnanimous enough to let him leave the silver salver at the trailhead.

Delusions of grandeur shattered and facing the facts that a) we'd bought the time-limited trekking permits for US$50 per person per day, b) a guide is mandatory and c) the chances of contacting our trekking agency to arrange a replacement guide were virtually nil, we decide to press on. And to give John his due, he never did seriously let us down. However, as you can imagine, having to interact with a martinet in a ten-gallon hat (still a few gallons too few for the size of his ego) is a good test of our diplomatic, negotiation, and compromise skills.

Anyway, enough of the character assassination and on to the details of the fourteen-day trek. We fly into a small airstrip in a valley at 2,700 metres located by the town of Jomson at the western end of the Annapurna circuit trek, courtesy of a reliable twenty-one-seater Canadian-made Twin Otter. A spectacular way to arrive, flying between 7,000- and 8,000-metre peaks. After disembarking, our major disappointment is hearing that for portions of the hike we will be walking along the road being built between Jomson and the Tibet/China border. Somewhat subdued, we plod off, leaving the aviation age behind. We won't see or hear a plane nor will there be so much as a distant contrail to date the timeless sky until we return two weeks from now. Our misgivings about the trail turn out to be baseless, the "road" being more of a cart track. On our first day, we cross paths with two Jeeps, a motorcycle, and no trekkers. The scenery is desolate, barren, abandoned, spectacular, and beautiful. Indescribable and just to prove it, here is my description. It was as if the creator had taken a Photoshop course and plopped the Alps in the background, the desert mountains of Nevada in the middle and the Grand Canyon at your feet. With little imagination, all manner of gigantic iconic world edifices can be envisioned in the towers and crags of the middle (sandstone?) strata, which have been eroded over the millennia. Petronas Towers, Beehives, the Sphinx, Anne Hathaway's cottage, Ganesh (the Hindu deity with the elephant's head), Gaudi's Casa Batlló, the Playboy Bunny, and Angkor Wat, to name a few (OK, so not Anne Hathaway's cottage, I was just testing how far I could take this thread).

And yet, strangely, amongst all this otherworldly isolation and grandeur, we turn a corner and come across a group of four guys with trowels fixing a culvert, the micro and the macro of it all. This all resides in the world's deepest gorge (depending on whose tourism department's stats you believe in), three miles from Annapurna One's summit to the Kali Gandaki River below.[12]

And so the days pass, steady sunshine low twenty-Celsius temperatures walking along the paths in the "hills" at altitudes mostly between 3,200 and 3,800 metres. The amazing scenery a bonus (the main event for me, actually), considering the trek is billed as a cultural experience. Culture it does have in spades: a glorious mix of religion, superstition, and fables, castles, caves, kingdoms, monasteries, forts, palaces and gompas, kings, monks, bandits, invaders, traders, lamas, and gods. A fluid complex history where you shouldn't expect to hear the same explanation twice. Each day brings its own little treats.

In one canyon about a four-hour walk from the nearest village we come to a stone staircase that leads up to a cave used by retreating (the adjective seems misplaced as they go there to advance their enlightenment) Lamas for some serious navel contemplation. Ascending the stairs I somewhat guiltily reach the entrance to the refuge about 200 metres up in the rock face. I consider heading back down when confronted with a brick wall about seven feet tall barring the entryway. But then I see a small scrap of paper stapled to the door accessing the cave, its message an ambiguously terse "entry fee 100 rupees." Unsure how to proceed I weigh my options– Do I knock first and risk disturbing a meditation? Does this only apply

12 https://en.wikipedia.org/wiki/Kali_Gandaki_Gorge

if I am accompanied by a monk? Are they just happy for any funds they might come by? This isn't a high-traffic zone, after all.

I assume the latter hoping that whoever might be inside might greet me like a "first footer" at New Year's in Scotland. I listen, there is only silence. I peer through the cracks in the door, I see no one. Tentatively I open the door, which creaks loudly and enter with my 100 rupee note leading the way clutched in my hand to demonstrate my honest intentions. I must admit to feeling kind of intrusive and naughty, but what is the worst that can happen? Delivering spankings is off limits for Buddhists I understand. Once inside I feel even more uneasy, like an innocent witness who has stumbled upon a crime scene.

The living area is about 100 square feet of unsquareness, a couple of mats at one end, a dripping pipe which leads to a small stream trickling down the rock wall, a steaming soot-black kettle sitting above the glowing embers of a smouldering fire. Two larger chambers lead deeper into the mountainside—one houses a massive boulder about twenty feet in diameter, of which every square inch has had the Buddhist mantra "*Om Mane Padme Hum*" (hail to the jewel in the lotus) hand-chiselled into it. In the other cavern sits a golden Buddha statue (how did it get here?), about ten feet high surrounded by sputtering brass butter lamps. There is no one around but there is certainly someone around.

After a few minutes taking this all in and still feeling like I am prowling around my neighbour's house uninvited I take my leave, moved that there are places in the world where individuals whose frame of reference is so different from the rest of us are still there and available to us should we ever figure out that we need them.

The farther north we get, the closer we get to the Tibetan plateau, the views of the Himalayan mountains recede. Himalaya in Nepali means mountain but somehow saying the Mountain Mountains sounds more appropriate than redundant. The highlands become more desert, sandy, and dune-like. Scrub like bushes bind the hillsides together against the continuous onslaught of eroding winds and trampling herds of goats that leave a latticework of dust gullies punctuated by moguls of green. Not much else survives, other than the occasional dwarf juniper. I squeeze a juniper berry between my thumbs inhale, God, what I wouldn't do for a G 'n' T. Get me a helicopter, quick!

It's not all solitude, of course, although trudging along the more remote mountain trails you fancy you might be more likely to bump into Marco Polo or Genghis Khan than someone from Canada. The older inhabitants still look as if they are from that era. We walk alongside locals from time to time as they are out going about their daily business. A tiny old lady particularly sticks in my memory. She barely comes up to my chest, her leathery, wrinkled skin attests to the days, months, and years she has spent out in the glare, dust, and wind. She has ventured out to pick up a few things—dung, mostly. She totes a *doko*, a traditional large cone-shaped basket, capacity up to fifty kilos. The basket has no straps. The full weight is taken by a band of cloth (called a *namlo*) attached to the basket and wrapped around her head, and her back, which is bent forward like a half-shut penknife. The white headband makes her look like LeBron James, same skin colour too. The mule dung will make good fuel for her fire. She is a doyenne of dung, a connoisseur of combustibles. She spots a fine specimen and, with her own brand of geriatric athleticism, deposits it in her *doko* with an effortless one-handed reverse slam dunk over her head, barely breaking stride for a routine two-point basket. Just another day at the office.

On we march toward our final destination and turning point, Lo Manthang. Sometimes as we intersect with the road we see signs of more civilization: powerless powerlines, three scrawny wires heading uphill to some dysfunctional power plant. Nepal just can't get it together when it comes to electricity. Yet it has all the sought-after basics: fast-flowing mountain rivers, endless sunshine, and predictable strong winds. I never once had to grit my teeth on this trek as each day promptly at 11 a.m., a combination of sand and a howling wind took care of this for me.

A typical day would see us setting off around 8:30 a.m. Our trek would last between five and seven hours so each evening before supper we would have time to explore that night's village. The winds would often have pummelled the locals into submission and a retreat indoors so by this time the cobbled passageways and alleys would take on a ghost-town feel with ponies and cattle as the only street life. There is invariably a gompa or fort to explore and if you can track down the custodian of the key to the padlock for the building, you can find yourself alone peering at eight-century-old tapestries, frescos, and artifacts under the glow of a single forty-watt light bulb. The only sop to security being that you can't take photographs in case word gets out that there are priceless pieces of art just sitting there for the taking. In case any of you are thinking of getting into some archaeological looting, be warned: there are often temple dogs in attendance. Himalayan mastiffs that haven't taken the first lesson at Buddhist doggie class: "do no harm."

As is often the case in Nepal you don't have to go looking for help, it just finds you. On our way up to one monastery we are intercepted by two soldiers of the Gurkha regiment who quiz us with the Nepali equivalent of name, rank, and serial number—i.e., "What country you from? What is your age? How many children?"

Interrogation completed and curiosity temporarily satisfied, they immediately adopt us as "Mom and Dad" and provide us with a military escort up to the monastery where we pose with each other in cheesy photos. Everyone loves having their picture taken; maybe the solution is to replace the M16s and AK-47s with iPhones—cheese is all you need. Our "sons" take their leave from us to head back to their barracks, their remit is to help build the road to China and incongruously keep the Chinese on their own side of the border. I guess you have to be a bit schizophrenic when you have a neighbour that size next door.

We reach Lo Manthang, the walled city, hub of the region and capital of the lost kingdom. It is still impressive but stuck in the fourteenth century, no more a centre of progressive urbanization. In its glory days it outshone its European contemporaries in sophistication (indoor toilets!). Formerly the trading gateway between China and India through the cleft in the Himalaya created by the Kali Gandaki River separating the Dhaulagiri range to the west and the Annapurna range to the East. Currently the only exchange are the waters of the Kali Gandaki flowing south into the Ganges and the winds funnelling north from the Gangetic plains each afternoon. The new road when it is completed will undoubtedly change all this. For now the only traffic jams occur at dusk each evening as the streets are chock-a-block with goats as the goatherds guide their flocks to their pens within the city walls each night.

The hike south is as spectacular as the way north as we are for the most part taking different trails. For the last leg, rather than leave the restricted zone via our original entry point, we decide to exit via Muktinath, which requires us to ascend to a high pass at 4,300 metres. Nepali bureaucracy being what it is requires that our exit stamp be obtained from the same post that provided the entry stamp. To facilitate this, "The Duke" has to sashay on down the riverbed to the registration post to take care of the paperwork and head us off when we reach the other side of the pass.

The remaining three of us study our map to determine our best route. We seek some local advice from the cook, Druba, at the teahouse we are staying in. The map-reading skills of our porter Prakass are rudimentary at best, he's also a graduate of cooking school. Fingers trace options across the contour lines, these guys are having a rare old time—great guffaws and thigh slapping as Druba's index finger stops at a dead end on a 6,000-metre peak. Turns out that Druba hails from downtown Kathmandu.

Anyway, I try to instill some decorum. "Cut out the comedy, chaps, let's get serious here."

The voice of reason ignored, we set out. What could possibly go wrong when too many cooks are involved?

It is a long slog to the pass but with the promise of stunning views of the Annapurna range from its north side we are determined to get there. Distractions along the way include smashing avocado-sized black rocks known as saligrams. The inside often contains awesome fossilized remains of mollusks. OK, yes, it is just a rock and may not be awesome in the sense of the latest awesome video of a cat playing the piano. But there is a sense of awe in holding in your hand a beastie 450 million years old, which was actually in the ocean back then. It was then abouts that the Indian subcontinent drifted north, crashed into Asia and created the crumple zone that is now the Himalaya. The property values probably took a hammering then too as the nearest waterfront ended up moving 1,700 kilometres to the southeast in the Bay of Bengal.

Five hours and many smashed rocks later, we reach the pass. The afternoon winds are at their fiercest and most concentrated as they stream over the ridge. Wind speeds are at least forty knots and gusting. We weave left and right, like sailors on a heaving deck. But the view. . . . What view? No view . . . . the mountains still loom overhead, dull shrouded in their afternoon cloak of clouds, taunting, "If you want to see us in our glory again you will have to come back."

Unfazed, we make our bouncy two-hour descent into Muktinath, a Lourdes-type pilgrimage site for Hindus and Buddhists. This is our only disappointment. Muktinath is a shambles, a dusty one-street town, like something out of a chapati Western. Decrepit buildings in various stages of repair and construction, mule trains ferrying up and down the main drag, a group of Sadhus playing ludo on the stoop, street vendors, the first garbage we've seen in two weeks, beggars, piles of luggage with Delhi airport tags stacked outside of charm-free concrete block guest houses. Yikes.

After a decent meal of chow mein—the Nepalis have taken to it the way the Brits have taken to butter chicken—we stretch our weary limbs out on the couches in the lobby. Believe me, it isn't as ritzy as it sounds. Deneesh (how can anyone with such a small head have such a big head?) has his head in Prakass's lap. Prakass tenderly braids Deneesh's hair. No one bats an eye. It is common to think of countries like Nepal as being socially backward and yet warmth and caring are much more in evidence than in the West. It's common to see guys hand in hand deep in conversation or walking down the street. They aren't gay, not that it would matter. Nepal is a leader in Asia of legalizing LBGTQ rights. They even have a box for me on their immigration form, male, female or other. I wonder what would happen if I tick two of them. Still, me with my Western liberal enlightened mind (no laughing, please), how would I feel about such intimacy? Of course it is all theoretical. I don't have that much hair.

The next day we visit the shrines on the hill, which have an altogether different vibe, a carnival atmosphere so unlike the intimidating monument-like cathedrals of the West. These are living, social, active places. The devotees are eating, bathing, chatting, laughing. Everyone seems to enjoy a good party, which seems to be the key to a thriving religion. We do our bit, smash a coconut, bathe our feet in holy water, light a butter lamp, get blessed by a minister. He sticks his finger in a grubby candle holder and daubs a sooty black thumbprint *tikka* on my forehead. This guy isn't even a religious minister but the minister of information, one of a group of political ministers touring the area. Could be the Nepali version of kissing babies, I guess. Spiritual batteries recharged, we decide to get out of town rather than spend another night in Dodge.

For our last day/night in the zone we stay in Jharkot, another medieval town where, as luck would have it, they are holding their annual archery tournament. Great fun observing these highest of highland games. The guys all decked out in their finest hats and brocade white silk shirts. Thirsty work, this bow and arrow business. As the afternoon wears on, the flow of rakshi (the local hooch) and chang (the local millet beer) and the beat of the drums increase. As the accuracy of the marksmen alarmingly decreases and their competitiveness increases, we figure we will deke out before the real fireworks began. Boys will be boys.

Tired but severely impressed, we say goodbye to the prayer flag-coloured (red, yellow, green, white, and, yes, even blue) mountains of Mustang as we step onto our airplane/time machine for the flight back to Pokhara. It is a beautiful flight back but doesn't compare to actually walking amongst the snowy peaks, we will return.

"Tis better to have trekked and been taunted than to have never trekked at all."

OK, Shakespeare it ain't, or Tennyson, for that matter.

Chapter 13

The Man in the Moon Brings Me Sunshine

Jimi, the Author, and the Man in the Moon

"IT IS ALWAYS FARTHER THAN IT LOOKS, IT IS ALWAYS TALLER THAN IT LOOKS, IT IS ALWAYS HARDER THAN IT LOOKS. THE THREE RULES OF MOUNTAINEERING."

—Unknown

"Clear, unscalable, ahead
Rise the mountains of instead
From whose cold cascading streams
None may drink except in dreams."

—WH Auden

It had been three years since our last visit to the Himal and Trixie and I were impatient to do some real hiking again. Plans formulated and flights booked the countdown of months tapering into weeks and then days, we finally arrive in Nepal in April 2019.

But before we can get our boots dirty we have to get there. We board a bus that will take us from Kathmandu to the trailhead of our treks at Soti Khola. It's only about 200 kilometres northwest of the capital, but it will take us over nine hours. What would pass for a goat trail most anywhere else in the world qualifies as the highway in Nepal's backcountry. The road, although unpaved and chokingly dusty, is good by Nepali standards. Well, maybe by my standards, i.e., no nail-biting narrow dirt tracks hanging over a cliff edge to oblivion.

Road travel is imperceptibly improving in the country—better infrastructure, some serious highway regulations, bans on passengers riding on the bus roofs (roof surfing). There are even vehicle roadworthiness inspections, even though 90 percent of the vehicles in operation would have been condemned in Canada ten years ago. Our bus's departure is delayed by an hour. A police road check is the cause; the officers had decided that the cargo on the roof of the bus (a shipment of air conditioners) made us dangerously top heavy and susceptible to tipping over. A forest of hands and arms safely unload our cargo onto the roadside.

Finally we are off. Thirty minutes later we are caught up in our first traffic jam. A travelling minstrel takes this opportunity to hop on our bus and serenade us on his *sarangi*, a traditional fiddle-like folk instrument, for the next twenty kilometres or so. He passes his hat around for some donations and gets off at the next snarl-up, crosses the street, and catches another bus back in the direction that he just came from.

Another twenty kilometres down the road, a van overtakes us and shepherds our bus to a stop on the side of the road. After a brief confab between the driver of the bus and the van, the hatch of the van is popped open and large boxes are dragged out. Hmm, these look kind of familiar—ah, yes, these are the same boxes of air conditioners that the police had removed from the roof back at the bus park. Undaunted, the crew gets to work and piles the cargo back onto the roof; they must have upgraded to Amazon Prime shipping.

Our two-man crew for this hike are Krishna, forty-one, and his brother Mahesh, twenty-three. Two less similar siblings you would be hard pressed to find.

Krishna the guide has worked his way up through the ranks—porter, then cook, then assistant guide, and now guide. Stocky, about 5′4″, with a friendly demeanour, and although he is from the Khumbu region, is well acquainted with this trek—it will be his ninth time.

His head is perfectly round, and only two-dimensional, although that might just be an optical illusion as he occasionally wears a cap and it doesn't seem to fall off. His face is a perfect brown version of the man in the moon. His eyes are narrow and slitted, four deep creases radiate from the outer corner of each eye like starbursts. He has chubby cheeks, a marshmallow nose, and a crinkly permanent smile. Sprigs of spiky black hair are scattered around the circumference of his visage.

Throughout our twenty-two-day trek, this inscrutable mask will betray nothing of his changes in mood, if indeed he has any. For the next twenty-two days I will be the earth to his satellite, constantly watching, gathering data, and analyzing changes in my behaviour. Me and my shadow.

Mahesh, the second youngest of the other eight siblings (six more brothers and two sisters), will be our porter. He looks quite different from his brother, who more fits the characteristics of his Mongolian ancestors whom he figures came to Nepal five or six generations ago.

Mahesh is puffier around the eyes, has a broader nose, fuller lips, and a wisp of a moustache, and often sports a bandana. He doesn't just look like Jimi Hendrix, he *is* Jimi Hendrix. A dead ringer, proof positive of reincarnation. Jimi is alive and well and carrying bags in the Nepali Himalaya for twenty dollars a day. Should I tell Jimi about his previous life or will that break the cycle of his path to Nirvana and Kurt Cobain?

The valley our trail passes through is being transformed as a result of the earthquake reconstruction efforts and is augmented by tourism expansion. For our first night we are treated to a three-storey lodge complete with ensuite, a nail or a piece of string to hang your towel on could make the difference between deluxe or a standard room rating.

I continue to get entertainment out of language misunderstandings. Seeing many ducks in the village I try to arrange to have some put some on the menu for tonight. Guide book not to the ready, I try to communicate my wishes with a few barnyard-like sounds and only succeed in horrifying Krishna. He misinterprets my sound effects as a request for dog, my quack quack sounding like Nepali for dog, which is *kukura*. So if it looks like a duck and walks like a duck, be careful—it might sound like a dog. To the relief of the ducks, we get tucked into SpaghettiOs instead. The baffling old-style trekking pricing conventions still prevail—the room is still the cheapest item on the menu. We head off next morning, skirt a couple of ducks having a quackie—it is springtime, after all.

Our journey is really a combination of two treks. After hiking north for four days we will branch east into the Tsum valley for seven days before doubling back and continuing on the Manaslu trek for the remaining twelve days. The whole region is very close to the epicentre of the 2015 earthquake and the damage is still greatly in evidence. Lots of aid has been provided to re-establish the villages and the infrastructure has seen major upgrades. The British Gurkha regiment has built numerous suspension bridges across the deep gorges and canyons that typify the geography in this area. These footbridges save the villagers hours of travel time and make the transportation of goods and materials by mule train a lot more efficient.

Construction of a major road to Tibet is well underway, and what a feat of low-tech engineering that is. The contours on the map are stacked closer together than the whorls of my fingerprints. In places the road is literally carved into the rock. Small men with jackhammers on a sheer cliff face work tirelessly, like termites chewing a notch into the side of the canyon. Hard hats, masks, and all the other typical safety paraphernalia are noticeable by their absence. The first day of our trek traces the path of this would-be road.

The drillers are followed by another group of just as small men. They look younger, like they might be playing hooky from school. These guys are equipped with ten-foot-long steel pry bars, flip flops, and bare hands. Their job is to deal with the rock dislodged by the drillers and blasters. With nothing more than muscle power, day in day out, they manhandle the debris over the precipice and down into the canyon below. Finally bringing up the rear is a sole Caterpillar,[13] which uses its massive bucket like a broom to sweep the boulders, that were too big for the grub crew to deal with, over the edge into the chasm.

Soon enough we leave the dust and hubbub behind and the surroundings become lush, green, and welcoming—so welcoming, in fact, that someone has laid out the red carpet for us. It is the tail end of the rhodo season and the path in long stretches is littered with the fallen petals from the scarlet blooms of these native plants—trees, really. Huge nettles and clumps of wild ganga proliferate the trailsides. According to Vandana Shiva, "In nature's economy the currency is not money, it is life." Nonetheless, they only take cash in these parts

13 https://www.youtube.com/watch?v=DPWXouDsZhc

and as I won't see a bank or an ATM for nearly four weeks, my wallet starts out the thickness of a paperback.

We soon adopt the trekkers' daily routine. The moon brings the start of each new day with a 6:30 a.m. knock at the door. I slowly open the door. The man in the moon's sunbeams infuse the room.

"Gooda sleep?"

"The best, and you?"

"Fine."

This is our standard exchange, as he offers us two steaming mugs of ginger tea from his tray.

"Breakfast ready at seven."

We have placed the order the night before, and he is gone.

Breakfast eaten, kitted out for the day, bags packed and collected from the room by Mahesh, the last chore before setting off is the community toothbrushing ritual. The guests loiter in the courtyard around the water faucet mounted on a concrete wash station foaming at the mouth, wondering where to spit. Not into the wash station—there are usually dishes stacked there—not on the cabbages in the garden—gross. In the toilet only, if you are lucky, there are usually only about one for every ten guests. We usually opt for surreptitiously over a wall or out on the path if no one is looking.

Garbled frothy goodbyes said to acquaintances made the previous evening, the commute is underway by 7:30 a.m. Rush hour finished by 8:00 a.m., and another groundhog day (or is there some sort of daily reincarnation going on?) is in full swing.

The hiking fraternity on this route is eclectic—groups as large as a dozen, individual trekkers, couples that linked up in Kathmandu using social media, young, old, in between, North and South American, Thai, European, Israeli, first-timers and veterans. Consequently, the paces are all different so there is plenty of solitude although the earthquake-sponsored building boom has meant that the mule train traffic is plentiful. It is more common to see mules laden with bags of concrete and rebar than food and propane supplies these days.

On one occasion we are held up at a traffic jam of thirty mule trains of ten mules each, crossing a suspension bridge in convoy. Everything that goes up the trail goes on foot and a new younger breed of trucker herd the mules. Their kit commonly comprises windbreakers, lash, Nike sneakers, cell phones, and funky dyed haircuts. Fewer are the old-school more patient veterans, Nepali toque, T-shirt, flip flops, and pocket full of rocks variety.

After a couple of days we branch off from the construction and the gorge side trail along the Budhi Gandaki River and head into the Tsum valley. It's some valley, the Tsum valley—broad, verdant, and surrounded by 6,000- and 7,000-metre snowy, white-capped peaks—a spectacular setting. And to top it off we are blessed with crisp air and clear, sunny skies.

However, although we are in Nepal, this region is culturally Tibetan and therefore Buddhist, and as we all know, the first truth of Buddhism is that all life is suffering. Naturally I am sick—not with any of the exotic options available here, but a filthy, streaming cold. I wrack my nasal cavities to come up with a metaphor that might do the secretions justice. Warning: some readers may find the description offensive: lemon curd.

I do my best to focus on the blissful surroundings and stretch out on a big flat rock and bask in the sun. The heat of the sun seems to have a heavy tangible physical dimension to it, like the weight of the lead apron you wear at the dentist when getting X-rays. It feels marvelous after the days of this lousy cold.

Krishna and I debate about going much farther today; there is a decent-looking teahouse nearby. Debate may be a stretch—the one shortcoming in Krishna's impressive array of skills and qualities is in his lack of English.

Communication is a challenge—as my inquiries escalate, his responses deescalate. The longer my probes for information, the shorter his responses. Eventually, the power of his moonbeam freezes time and space.

I admit defeat and ask simply, "Here?"

He nods.

We have arrived.

It proves to be a good choice. The owner, Dawa, is a live-wire entrepreneur. The tea house is only a couple of years old, the rooms spacious with views of the mountains and within earshot of roaring waterfalls.

It's spring and there is plenty of activity in the valley. A neighbour is out in his field tilling the land, getting ready to plant his crops. He plods behind an ancient plough pulled by an ox, he sports a pair of Bose headphones. Opportunistic puppies come and visit in search of handouts and companionship. A rider on his way to a wedding up the valley gallops by on his pony bedecked in silk scarves of gold and white. A nun from the *gompa* we visited earlier in the day wanders by the gate and shouts out to us the Tibetan greeting of "*Tashi Delek*." The usual "*Namaste*" hello of Nepali is the lowland language and isn't spoken much up here. Nothing much but a perfect afternoon (lemon curd aside).

In the evening over dinner and a couple of Lhasa beers the owner fills us in a bit about valley life. Three of his kids go to the Dalai Lama Buddhist school in Dharamsala in India and Dawa gets to see them every couple of years. His fourth child goes to boarding school here in the village about a hundred yards away. He is home on the weekends—tonight, in fact.

Dawa still has two feet firmly planted in the seventeenth century: he goes to Tibet for the groceries, which is saying something when his trip to the mall involves him traversing a pass with his yaks and donkeys at nearly 6,000 metres. Europe's highest mountain, Mont Blanc, is around 4,800 metres. It is still a more efficient trip than getting to Kathmandu and, besides, he likes that Lhasa beer. He doesn't need a passport as long as he speaks and looks Tibetan, he is good. The only thing he has to make sure to do is hide his locket with the picture of the Dalai Lama for fear of being arrested as a dissident. In mid-sentence he bolts from the room, hurtles down the stairs, and scatters some neighbour's intruding cattle from his stone-walled yard. Someone had left his gate open.

Tonight he is helping his son with his homework learning English. The boy will speak four languages: Tibetan, Nepali, Hindu, and English. They sing along with the English alphabet nursery rhyme songs courtesy of YouTube. Four opposable digits at home in the twenty-first century.

It is all a curious mix. There isn't running water in the buildings and dishes are washed across the path in a nearby creek. His wife multitasks, while shepherding the cattle out to pasture, she spins raw wool onto a drop thimble, which becomes woolen yarn that she will weave on a hand loom into blankets. Meanwhile, the man of the house offers to make us some butter tea, a concoction composed of yak butter, salt, tea leaves, and water, traditionally mixed in a tall wooden butter churn-like contraption. I ask to see how it works and he proudly pulls out an electric blender?

All buttered up, we retire to our room and drift off to sleep to the sound of waterfalls and the occasional barking dog.

The next morning as the Moon delivers the tea I can see over his shoulder that there has been snow overnight. It has settled low on the surrounding valley walls like a coating of icing sugar. Much of it will melt in the heat of the day and start its 1,300-kilometre journey to the sea, seeping first into the Gandaki river then merging into the Ganges then morphing into the Padma in Bangladesh before emptying into the Bay of Bengal.

Not all tea houses are as idyllic as this one. Many can be crowded or perched on windy hilltops with the roar of waterfalls replaced by the flush of a toilet next door through the quarter-inch plywood walls. This, combined with the slam of the tin bathroom doors and the explosiveness of Nepali cuisine, can be like living the event firsthand in Dolby surround sound. Fortunately, these cacophonies reach their crescendos before 9:00 p.m. Everyone has eaten and headed for bed by this time. Bladders generally more youthful than ours and the terrors associated with a night trip to a tea house latrine are usually enough to minimize any nocturnal activity. But you have been warned, choose your room carefully, especially if there is an inside toilet.

Eating, as you probably have figured, isn't the main draw here. The diet is fine, but being a Buddhist region, eating creatures is out, fruit and dairy produce is so perishable that by the time it gets to higher parts of the trail it just isn't worth the effort. So that leaves starch, every manner of starch—potatoes, rice, noodles, lentils, millet, buckwheat, bread, and pasta.

The menu is the same at every tea house. Two sheets of spiral-bound laminated plastic whose only originality is manifested in the size of the font, the colour of the paper, and the originality of the spelling mistakes. By the end of the trek you will have subconsciously memorized every culinary delicacy on offer to the extent that you can recite the menu by heart. I will probably never forget that the cost of a room for a night was 600 rupees while a beer would cost 650. About $8CDN. A small pot of tea means a two-litre thermos.

When you are off your Wheaties or haven't had your ten to twelve hours of beauty sleep, being presented with these options has all the visual and gastronomic stimulation of an optometrist's eye chart.

Well, enough with the whiney First World bitching. It really is remarkable though how the innkeepers manage to keep such a consistent standard of service considering the difficulties that they face. Virtually everything they need, including fuel, is carried here by man or beast via twisting mountain pathways. Twice we passed donkeys that had paid the ultimate price. The trail is very steep and very narrow in many places and those poor creatures had gone over the edge and fallen to their death. In both cases they still were fully laden with their cargo. Such was the precariousness of their inaccessibility that no one had tried to retrieve the goods, yet. This will not be for long. Nepali ingenuity knows no bounds.

There are more risks on this trail than we are used to. They aren't so much associated with falling but more about being hit from above. It is better to start off early in the morning when rockslides are slightly less likely to happen. In the heat of the day the soil dries out and the wind picks up, which all adds to the likelihood of the rocks and scree becoming less stable. There may also be some karmic retribution happening as the herbivores (blue sheep) up above dislodge rocks on the unsuspecting omnivores beneath them. Someone must have leaked the information that I am a carnivore.

I don't take it personally. We exchange reports with a big Mancunian who has just had a close call down the trail. He has the perfect onomatopoeic accent to recount his near miss, his goggle-eyed pupils a testament to the vividness of his recent brush with death.

"It were a grate rock that landed raight besides muh wee a masseeve thoomp. It were about this size." His hands spread apart, modeling the dimensions of a duffle bag.

Krishna of course is already alive to the potential dangers and has been on the alert the whole morning, steering us to safer spots for our rest and snack breaks. Having a rock or your head end up in your sandwich could ruin your whole day. Krishna's cred just keeps growing. The sandwich equivalent here is half a buckwheat pancake slathered in peanut butter; a dollop of ketchup on it wouldn't be a good look.

Approaching the junction where our valley side trip rejoins the main Manaslu trail, we have to face our own test of courage. A section of the trail about twenty feet long has vanished, the narrow six-inch-wide path we were on petered out in front of us. A landslide, made up of a slurry of gravel, small rocks, and dirt, had buried the path on a near vertical portion of our route. There haven't been any attempts to recreate the track, we are the first on the scene, so the rockfall must have just happened that morning. The conditions are still unstable and a small, steady stream of scree continues to flow hundreds of feet down the face above and below us.

Unfazed, Mahesh and Krishna, after waiting for a lull in the flow, step towards the gap and, using a stick, scratch a narrow groove into the debris to create a crossing for us. When he is finished, he starts stomping on the ground to see if it will hold, like some member of the Irish land mine-clearing operation, except that he doesn't have his eyes closed and his hands over his ears.

It is amazing how brave and/or foolish you can be when there is no choice; there is only one path into the valley so this is the only way out.

After thirty-six years of marriage, I am learning the benefits of talking things through—it has been a slow process. Paradoxically, Trixie has figured out that debate is sometimes futile. I like to think that she learned that from being a mother, but I suspect it came from being a wife.

Be that as it may, we discuss the situation that we are faced with. In silence. Telepathically.

Satisfied with their handiwork, without a word, Mahesh takes the lead. Trixie's left hand in his right, her right hand in Krishna's left, they tiptoe their way across in single file like they are dancing the Dashing White Sergeant on a balance beam.

Safely on the other shore, they beckon me to join them.

I make my squeamish dash across the exposed area. Nearly there, I hear something dislodging from above—a rock, maybe just a pebble, I wasn't looking back. Just then I lose my footing as I scramble to the other side. Ever present Krishna is there to reach out and grab my backpack handle and swing me onto my butt.

It may be a beautiful sunny morning but it is a comfort to know that the Moon's gravity is there for me twenty-four hours a day.

Chapter 14

Peter Pan

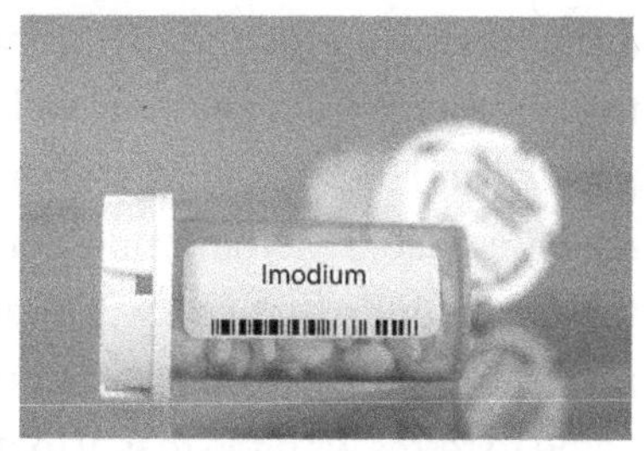

Apple Pie à la Imodium

"THE EUROPEAN TALKS OF PROGRESS BECAUSE BY THE AID OF A FEW SCIENTIFIC DISCOVERIES, HE HAS ESTABLISHED A SOCIETY WHICH HAS MISTAKEN COMFORT FOR CIVILIZATION."

—Benjamin Disraeli

"LIFE IS SHORT AND THERE WILL ALWAYS BE DIRTY DISHES, SO LET'S DANCE."

—James Howe

Leaving the verdant Tsum valley behind us and retracing our steps, we eventually rejoin the main trail heading North again in the direction of the Larkya La, one of the longest mountain passes in Nepal. At 5,100 metres, it will be the high point of our circuit around Mount Manaslu. This monster of a mountain dominates the area at an impressive elevation of 8,156 metres. The days pass pleasantly. As the Himalayan treks get more well known, they are becoming more popular and the amenities are gradually improving. Lunch stops are readily available. Morning, noon, or night as you approach the villages the first sounds that you will hear will be the hiss of steam under pressure. But before your taste buds get carried away, you have to come to terms with the reality that it isn't the sound of cappuccinos being whipped up for you but the sound of the ubiquitous Himalayan kitchen appliance, the pressure cooker, preparing hearty *dahl bat*.

Coffee culture is not yet "a thing," although we did encounter one funky trail-side shack staffed by a young enterprising Kathmandu cook who had set up shop. He had obviously done his market research. A Bob Marley poster on the wall and "Stairway to heaven" on the boombox. Irresistible and probably the best worst cup of java I've ever had.

It isn't plain sailing all the time. By the time we reach Lho, a village three nights away from the high point of the trek, we have to make a decision whether to attempt the 5,100-metre pass or turn around. There isn't much of a debate really. By this time we are pretty much out of everything: time (the permit will expire), energy (two torrential bouts of diarrhea separated by two weeks of hacking feverishness), and out of patience with the fickle weather.

The Himalayas aren't exempt from climate change; the high pass normally open from mid-March has only been intermittently clear and it is now late April. The previous night's thunder and attendant downpour would have brought more snow and again blocked the pass.

By this time our goals have become more modest. Summoning our remaining enthusiasm and energy, we opt to head up to Shyla, the next village, a couple of hours farther up the trail, where the views of the mountains are supposed to be spectacular if the weather is clear. Few folk seem to be making this choice. We meet several groups who are actually heading down. They bring tales of no room at the inn from the two remaining stops before the pass. The snows have caused a log jam of trekkers waiting, hoping for the blockage to clear. Folks are sleeping in the dining rooms and storage areas of the tea houses.

When we arrive in Shyla it is deserted. It is an unremarkable settlement of fifteen or twenty hand-hewn rock two-storey houses, timber framed with blue corrugated metal roofs. We haven't seen the sun or the mountains all day. The warm winds from the South clash with the cold mass of mountain air to create a dense cloudy mist. It adds an eerie ghostly atmosphere to the empty town. The only sound of civilization is the chip chip chink chip, chink of villagers hammering away at rocks to provide materials for the construction of more guest houses to rebuild and replace those devasted in the 2015 earthquake. It is a continuous soundtrack that plays from break of day until sunset. Seeing folks in the gloom squatting on piles of rocks whacking away with small hammers it is hard to not think you are in some kind of parallel universe visiting a gulag or penal colony full of volunteer rock crushers.

Eventually we arrive at our destination. "Welcome to the Shining" our spartan digs seem to promise. At least it will provide us shelter from the howling wind. The hostess is a smiley Tibetan lady who proves to be more Florence Nightingale than Jack Nicholson.

She supplies us with hot tea and soup, which we consume recumbent in our sleeping bags lying on our bunks in our room. There is never any heat in these inns and in this case no electricity in the room, so rather than sit in the extra gloom created by the tinted windows, we eat with the door open. It is six degrees inside the room and six degrees outside.

We can smell the fire that our host has made outside for the batch of rakshi she is brewing up. I have acquired a taste for its faintly sake-like flavour. We can hear the snap of the prayer flags as they thrash in the wind.

Having dragged myself this far I am getting impatient about what the chances are that we might see something tomorrow. Now having had the opportunity to see Krishna's interaction with his brother and various guides and innkeepers along the way, I realise that he is naturally taciturn. I am not hopeful that I will get an unqualified assessment.

So totally unfairly I expect Krishna to add oracle and meteorologist to the list of his job duties. Not surprisingly, he is reluctant to commit. As much as he would say was

"I tink," waves his arm in the general direction of Tibet. I get a rare chance for a glimpse of the dark side of the moon as he turns his head, it is black.

"Mumble mumble mumble . . . tomorrow maybe." Two vigorous nods of the head.

"Mumble mumble mumble . . . so muchy windy." A winning smile and a chuckle.

"Mumble mumble mumble."

His shoulders slump down, another big smile with evident relief that the issue of tomorrow's prospects have been laid to rest. It's a remarkably efficient way of solving problems. You just stop talking about them! The eye creases deepen, the moon beam intensifies, happy to be back in non-controversial territory. We have reached détente.

He proffers the goddam menu. I order a plate of fries and a coke for old times sake. I ask Trixie "Remind me again why I am not standing in the lineup for the buffet on the Holland America?"

Dinner time rolls around right on time at 7:00 p.m. Krishna lets us know that it is ready. Lo and behold, our innkeeper has made a fire in the small pot-bellied stove in the dining room and we are the only guests. Krishna as usual does his impeccable job of discreet but attentive helpfulness. By some small miracle there is apple pie for dessert. Krishna had seen our disappointment at it being dropped from the menu due to a lack of apples and gone door to door to rustle up enough for a pie. He should be a maître d' in a five-star hotel. Where else would you get this sort of service?

The following morning the weather has improved little. After breakfast, we pack, I take another two Imodium and we prepare to retrace our steps down the mountain away from Larkya La and the challenging transit of the pass that we were edgy about. The loop around the mountain is done anti-clockwise, east to west to take advantage of the better views and gentler gradient than the western approach, but for us the west side was destined to be an unknown. We felt worse for Krishna than ourselves as he had undertaken the responsibility for the success of the whole venture as his personal duty.

Just as we are about to shoulder our day packs and start back, Krishna bursts into our room with uncharacteristic boldness and an impatient "come quick . . . come quick." He ushers us upstairs to the rooftop where a lively wind is buffeting the day's laundry. The world is immediately a better place. There in the distance stands Manaslu, one of only seven 8,000-metre peaks in the world. The winds have briefly drawn back the curtain of clouds shrouding the peak and given the four of us grandstand rooftop seats. Relief mixed with joy, we snap away for a good fifteen minutes before the clouds roll back and envelop the spectacle.

After our tantalizing glimpse of what might have been and with no lunar loss of face, our smiling little band sets forth for the lowlands and the many riches it promises.

Maybe we don't get as high as on other treks, but we certainly travel farther in kilometres. With nothing to do but walk and think, strange thoughts start to pop into my head. I ruminate on how transformative the weather is to these high places, the seemingly idyllic life of the monks one day living in the heavens amongst glistening, snow-capped mountains framed by clear blue, blue skies, then the next day as the clouds roll in, it transforms into a socked-in devil's moonscape, a frozen, barren, uninhabitable landscape as desolate as anywhere on the planet.

The gloom gathers again and envelops us as if in a cold embrace and I wonder: *Maybe the mountain doesn't want us here.*

A couple of days later we near our starting point. Our exertions are made easier thanks to the series of amazing suspension bridges constructed by the British, the Nepalese Gurkha army, really, over the decades. Those were yesterday's miracles, which save villagers and their animals days in travel. But now we encounter the construction zone again. When completed, the new highway will cause a seismic shift. It will create its own vacuum, which will suck the life and young people out of the villages dotted along its route. As we clamber over the construction debris, we feel a bit superior with our ability to eschew the technology and the road.

One thing is for sure once the traffic starts whizzing by you: you don't feel quite so noble. The trekkers will move on to more remote areas. Who wants to hike beside a highway?

Within a generation, the road will succeed in doing what the earthquake failed to do—that is, to eliminate a way of life and a culture. The conveniences that the road promises will be irresistible, its use will become addictive and before long contemptibly familiar. New horizons will open up, the lure of further sophistication in the cities of Kathmandu, Lhassa, and beyond will draw the young into their vortex. Soon the remaining communities will become dependent on priced commodities and hard currency. After centuries of self-sufficient existence, modern economic viability will determine the fate of these small societies, it won't take long before they have vanished. All of the skills and knowledge that were developed over generations in order to support an independent self-reliant community will wither. The diverse skills in meteorology, agriculture, medicine, animal husbandry, music, law and order, construction, storytelling, engineering, artistry, spirituality, and astronomy will atrophy.

The next generations as they are subsumed into mainstream humanity will gain vast exposure to button-pushed information, touch-screen knowledge that is ten seconds deep and an internet wide. Something gained, to be sure, but so much to be lost. It is a common story that is now told in even the remotest parts of the world.

It is an irony as the richest of the city dwellers travel to the ends of the earth to experience antiquity and the unspoilt glories of nature. Maybe there will be some sort of equilibrium reached. As the underdeveloped world speeds toward consumerism, the youth of the developed world are perhaps becoming disillusioned with materialism and are heading in the other direction, towards conservation, uniqueness, and a search for deeper meaning. Is all of this progress or just simply change? We will have to wait until we reincarnate to find out.

My nose jars my brain back to more mundane matters. Heading south, you smell the villages before you see them. The acrid smoke from the wood fires is being blown up the valley from the next settlement. It is time to step it out: nature is calling again.

We roll into a tea house, the first to arrive. Our senior's pace going downhill is still faster than the hiker's tempo coming up from below.

We get settled in. It's a fairly new guest house and our room has its own Western-style toilet. I retreat to the ensuite, hit my head on the low door frame, soak trousers in the permanent one-inch-deep puddle of water on the floor, ride the throne-side saddle (you couldn't fit a child in the available space between the lavatory and the door). The floppy lid collapses on me when I sit down. Plumbing isn't one of the skills that the mountain people have mastered . . . yet.

Ablutions completed, it is time to relax. We have the inn to ourselves, and although the trek is coming to its end there are still small treats to savour. We sit anonymously on the second-storey breezeway daydreaming to melodic Hindi music wafting up from below.

The guest house owners' preteen daughter enters the empty courtyard below unself-consciously and begins to dance. Slow, fluid movements, swaying in graceful innocence, beautiful, lost in the rhythms, no sense of time, suspended in the joy of the moment, her spirit and motion blended as one. Fingers and hands flowing through the air in sinewy ballet like so many waves caressing some far-off shore.

The song comes to an end, she exits stage left, reboots the music and returns for another performance. For all the graceful effortlessness of her moves, it's clear that she has put hours of practice into perfecting her choreography.

After dinner to bed, sleep as usual comes quickly for me after a long walk in the mountains. Spookily, I awaken in a cold-sweat panic, having dreamt that I was being eaten butt first by a giant clam—I am scarred for life now.

The next morning, when Diki, our dancer, brings us our chai tea she tells us that the music is called "Yeshu Naam Pukare"[14]_Between stifled sobs she let out that she had been practising for tomorrow's church celebration in the next village. That dream is now dashed.

14 https://www.youtube.com/watch?v=UL_kTNraTU8

Mother had had to play the heavy. She has said that Diki can't go because too many trekkers have arrived and there are dishes and sheets to be washed. We do our best to console her—there are few things as moving as seeing a youngster's dreams crushed. The girl is heartbroken—a real Cinderella tragedy.

After breakfast we set off, a clamour of raised women's voices coming from the kitchen deters us from making our usual goodbyes. Tonight's destination will be Arughat, the last stop on the trail before we catch the bus back to the city. An hour down the trail we are passed by the singing, skipping, beaming figure of Diki. The racket that we had left behind at the tea house has been caused by her auntie giving Diki's mom a blast about depriving her daughter of her time in the sun. Losing one's cool isn't considered cool in Nepal, but I guess some things are just too important for aunties to let go. Diki is one happy dancer.

The last piece of trail looks pretty familiar by now as do some of the mule trains that under their relentless pace have probably lapped us a couple of times. I should be Facebook friends with a couple of the lead donkeys by now. We stop in for lunch at the same new tea house that we visited on the way up. A number of the guest cottages and the outdoor restaurant look like they have been shelled. The poor despondent owner has ploughed all his savings into the venture and now he stands amongst the devastation. Some overzealous construction worker labouring on the new highway perched above the valley has used too much dynamite. The resulting blast has launched car-sized chunks of rock down into the valley below. Miraculously, no one was injured but at least half of the guest cottages were rendered uninhabitable.

Whether the owner will get any compensation is doubtful. Whether it makes sense for him to rebuild is another matter. Now that he knows that the highway is going through, he wonders how long the trekkers will continue to use this trail.

At the end of a long, difficult day clambering over construction debris, I say to Trixie, "I am tottering over these rocks like an old lady," then think to myself *seeing the stamina and agility of the old ladies here, I should be so lucky*.

It's our last night in the mountains. It's still early but dusk by now, the tropical timetable at work. The meals are becoming more ambitious. Krishna brings us our dinners—mounds of chow mein on battered tin plates, each delicately placed two-handed in front of us, paper napkins neatly folded, a greasy ketchup bottle thoughtfully placed just within reach. The moonbeams shine as brightly as at any time in the last twenty-one days.

After dinner our little family of four sit down one last time for our traditional nightcap—two bottles of beer and four glasses—and raise a toast to each other.

My shadow begins to fade, Neverland recedes into the gathering nightfall, I will miss them both. This must be how Peter Pan felt.

Part III

STAYING LOW ON TOP OF THE WORLD

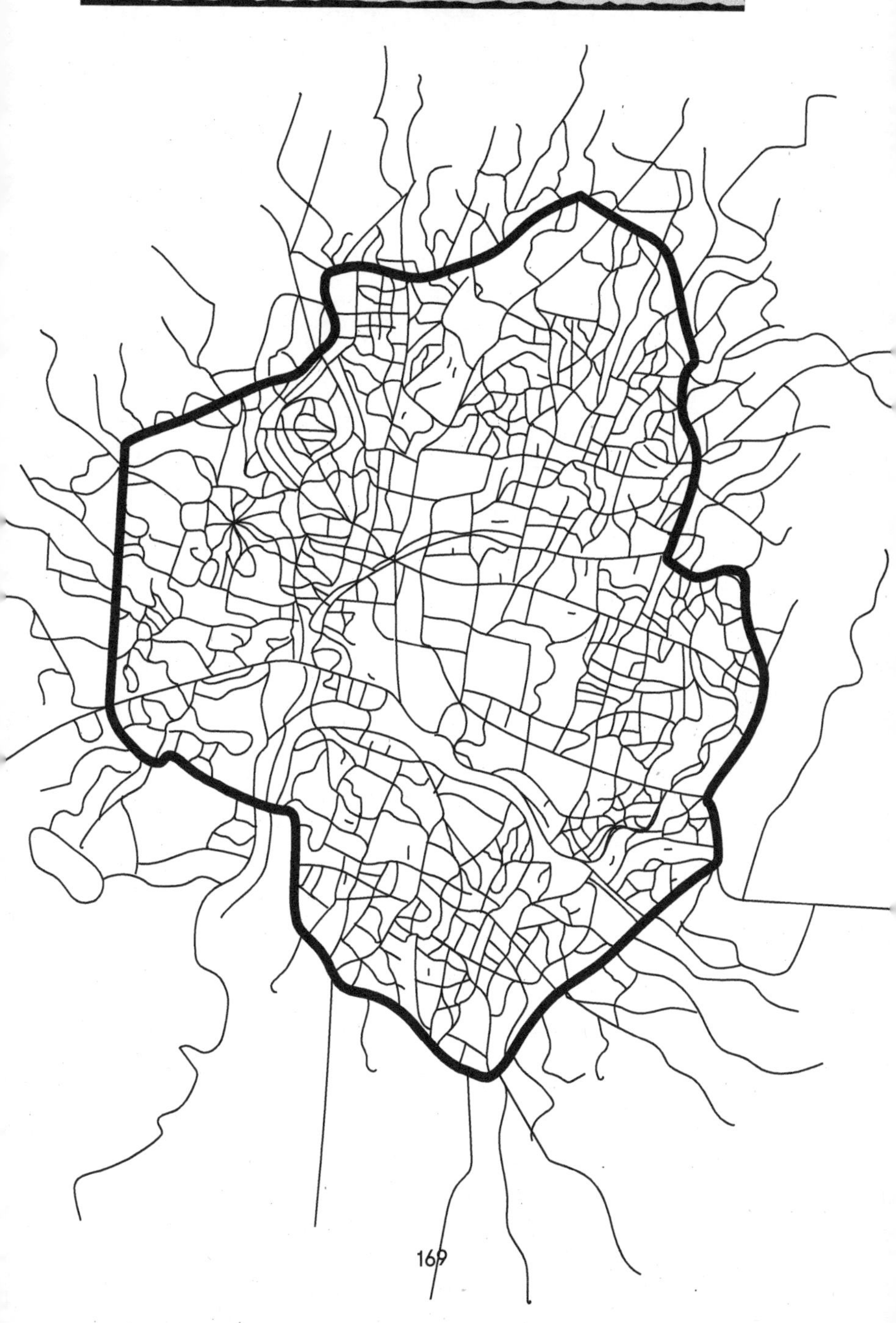

Chapter 15

It Was the Best of Times and It Was the Best of Times

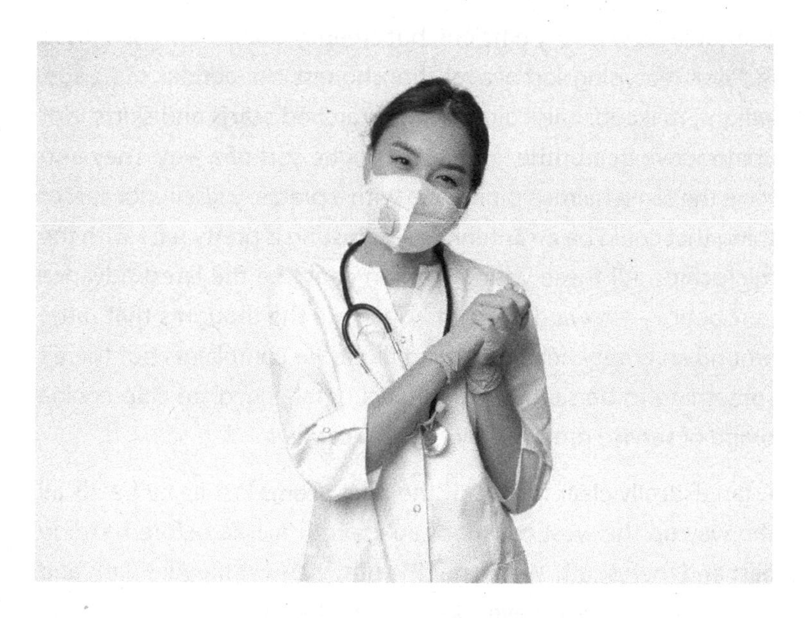

It's the same for every star.

"AIRPLANE TRAVEL IS NATURE'S WAY OF MAKING YOU LOOK LIKE YOUR PASSPORT PHOTOGRAPH."

—Al Gore

"YOU'RE NOT A STAR UNTIL THEY CAN SPELL YOUR NAME IN KARACHI."

—Humphrey Bogart

Nepal's towering treasures are not easily accessed from Western Canada. A tale of two cities will clarify how we got there.

Our preferred route requires that we start the vacation with a numbing eleven-and-a-half-hour flight from Vancouver to Seoul on Korean Airlines.

The cabin crew is very efficient, but creepily clonish. This isn't just a racial stereotyping sort of a reaction, honest. Uni-gender, same age, weight, makeup, hair colour, same starched scarfs and skirts. Not unattractive in a brittle, fragile, meringue sort of a way. They also have the same hairdos pinned up with a pretzelly fascinator sort of thing that could be an antennae—Samsung is pretty nifty with the microchips. All these young women could be the latest advance in robotics—(steward)dessbots. Such are the thoughts that rattle around an empty head on a long flight. No complaints but there's something to be said for the multicultural chocolate chip cookie brand of service provided by Western carriers.

A fantastically clear flight but the pilot seems lost as he heads all the way up the west coast of Canada into Alaska before heading east and then south. We do get the best views of the Aleutians and Kamchatka that we are ever likely to have. He gives some explanation about the jet stream and the curvature of the earth being the reason for the diversion. I'll do my own simulation with a globe and a piece of string when I get home.

We spend three days in Seoul, a fast-paced city with the modern infrastructure you'd expect from a city that hosted the Olympics and World Cup in quick succession. What I wasn't prepared for was the size and scale of the place. We go up to the observation tower in the centre of the city. Looking to the horizon in every direction, we see forests of skyscrapers. Seoul is a city of 10.5 million souls (sounds better than the demonym Seoulite), twenty-five million in the greater metropolitan area, in an area of 2,500 square kilometres.

Mind blowing when you think that every Canadian west of Ontario (an area of over four million square kilometres) could be housed here.

Our experience with the Koreans is mixed, like any place, I guess—brusque and pushy at times, probably world champs at musical chairs if the scramble for the seats on the subway is anything to go by. And yet on other occassions showing oldworld chivalry—numerous times we had seats offered to us by young folks on the subway, I'm sure all to do with our jet-lagged appearance or the fact that we were visitors in their country. Not because we look old—repeat, not because . . . although respect for elders is an important cultural tradition.

English isn't commonly spoken, but if you whip out a map and look lost, which we frequently do, someone will soon stop and help out.

In fact, there are not many Caucasians around at all. In one artsy/trendy shopping district we visited I attain quite the celebrity star status. I have one teenage schoolkid do a tape-recorded interview with me for his school project. Questions include what good and bad habits I have.

Me: "Riding my bike and eating organic food." Riveting stuff—the poor kid'll probably get a D.

If only I'd remembered to mention the refuge for pygmies in the Dzanga Sangha jungles of the Central African Republic that I've been running, he might have stood a chance. Later on, a university student comes up to me and whips out her cell phone and fires off a couple of dozen shots of me for an arts poster of foreigners she's working on. Yeah, right. Is there anything the paparazzi won't say to get an exclusive shot?

Then to top it off a woman follows me into the men's toilet in the underground. Is this what Brad Pitt has to put up with? Anyhow, turns out she is the cleaning lady. I guess the white coat should have given it away. Still, it is the last thing I expect. It seems a very conservative country to have coed washroom cleaners. Oh well, the stardom is fleeting but it doesn't do any harm to be an exhibit for a change. I will have to remember that when I'm tempted to be snap-happy in Nepal.

We decide to take in a few slices of Seoul life:

- Baseball game with 30,000 enthusiastic fans, cheerleaders, live fan wedding proposals on the jumbotron between innings, combined with an eclectic music soundtrack, surfin' USA followed by Andrea Bocelli.
- Visit fancy malls with the latest exclusive designer labels, the youthful city folk eager to splurge on the clothes that will give them instant status in the global pecking order.
- Eat at night market stalls. Interesting approach to food hygiene. Cook takes grubby cash from customers, washes hands in fish tank containing live octopus, then separates frozen chicken kebabs before tossing them on the BBQ. I gather David Attenborough is planning to do a special on the symbiotic relationship between the restaurateur who replenishes the octopus's camouflage supply with the ink from the grubby bank notes—isn't nature amazing?[15]

High-tech wizardry extends to the toilet. The control panel provides cryptic hints at the various functions—mystical hieroglyphics such as a happy face, is that a whale spout or a mushroom cloud? A selection of fifteen buttons, built-in heater, the deluxe version comes in Corinthian leather with optional heads up display and ejector seat.

Tells your weight maybe before and after, too much information but it will probably end up being another app on your next shitbit, oh er sorry, Fitbit. Maybe a nuclear attack alert would be more useful

15 https://www.scientificamerican.com/article/the-mind-of-an-octopus/

as Seoul is just fifty kilometres south of the DMZ with North Korea. It might just give you enough time to kiss your $%# goodbye.

Talking of exits, we leave for Kathmandu, a five-and-a-half-hour flight and at least a century away.

After an uneventful flight, the *Lonely Planet* took a beating, and on a viewless night arrival we make our way to immigration. The paper form handed out to us on the plane gave me the chance to select M, F, or Other. I have the opportunity to put it on the record that I identify as trans-species. The paperwork turns out to be superfluous, the process has gone high-tech. Now confronted with a bank of six or so mismatched computer terminals and a plane load of 450 jet-lagged fellow passengers as bewildered as me, I go for the least controversial and hopefully most expeditious option and select M.

The first machine is out of service—this you have to find out by pressing all the buttons. A sign would save us all a lot of time. The second one won't read my passport. Manually enter details. Name of street we are staying at? Ya gotta be kidding. I enter "Smith." It seems to pass muster.

A whirr and a clank as the air conditioner (note: not air conditioning) shuts down and the arrivals hall is plunged into darkness. A nostalgic welcome back to Nepal, a power outage. General murmuring and shuffling of feet ensues. An interminable thirty seconds later the lights come back up, the air conditioner picks up speed with a chop-chop-chopping sound like a vintage helicopter being fired up. The masters of our destiny awake from their slumber, fans begin to whir, cursors flash perkily, and screens glow with intimidating supremacy.

I start again with entering the data. Four screens into my life history, the screen freezes and the dreaded "Have you saved your work?" pops up. Buggered if I know. I press yes.

The screen goes blank, the "contact your network help desk" alert glares back at me and the machine smugly refuses to cooperate (that's a laugh) further. I move to the line queueing up for machine number three; fifteen minutes later, I am ready for my next duel with technology. In the land of Karma I do my best to think positively, speak, OK, beg the machine in soothing tones, caress its housing, let my fingers fall like dewdrops on the keyboard. I am blessed and reach the final step—the photo finish. I lean forward intimately to get a better look at the instructions, glasses on the end of my nose as *thunk flash,* the picture is taken. Buddha, damn it.

The Prince of Darkness spits out its spawn. The photo isn't too bad, my bald spot doesn't quite make it into the picture, but I do seem to have a second head popping out of my left shoulder. Oh, crap, the guy behind me in the line was leaning in over me trying to get a sneak preview of the process. I'm not going through this torture again and decide to take my chances with the immigration officer at the desk.

I figure if he has a problem with the photo I will ask him if I can change the M on my form to Other and explain that I am a Siamese twin. Ingenuity not required: he doesn't even bat an eye and stamps my chit, but asks to see my boarding pass instead. Give me a little Hitler bureaucrat over a machine any day.

I am able to retrieve said pass from the bowels of my daypack. His majesty now satisfied that I have indeed arrived by commercial airliner rather than by UFO from planet Zircon, the clot grants me admission to the Republic of Nepal.

Now to find our luggage. But before that we must pass through security and the one X-ray machine available for all comers. Thankfully, the bedlam in the immigration area has the effect of stringing out the arrivals so the flow-through the checkpoint isn't too bad. We then traverse an open zone festooned with "This is a no metal zone,"

"No Metals" signs, and a skull and crossbones or two. But what to do with our assortment of belt buckles, coins, water bottles, cameras, umbrellas, and stuff? You have probably figured this out, the answer is obvious: ignore the signs.

The bags are there. Phew. We are met by our driver Giri from the hotel. A couple of *Jom Joms* (Nepali for let's get going) later, and we are off. The vitality, chaos, and energy are a rush; it is great to be here. The contrast in the way of life is stark. We enjoyed Seoul, but this is analogue not digital, chaos as opposed to order, vitality versus sterility—it feels good. Kathmandu, a city of one million, stops, starts, wheezes, pops, fizzes, bobs, weaves, stalls, swerves, clatters, and belches a petri dish, no, a swamp pond, of evolutionary soup. A city planner's worst nightmare with a street map that looks like a web spun by a spider on crack. Seoul, a city sprawl of twenty-five million in the rearview mirror, appears as a unified organism where traffic flows, pedestrians stream, and sophisticated transport systems pump a plasma of humanity through interconnecting veins.

Seoul too big to fail, Kathmandu too chaotic to succeed. Wonder which has a more negative impact on the environment? *Bistari bistari* (take it easy) there, boy. What the heck? We have bigger fish to fry. We are going hiking.

Chapter 16

Headless in Kathmandu

I spent all day getting dinner ready and now you tell me the Joneses are vegan?!

"LET THEM EAT CAKE."

—*Marie Antionette*

"ANIMALS ARE SUCH AGREEABLE FRIENDS. THEY ASK NO QUESTIONS, THEY PASS NO CRITICISM."

—*George Eliot*

Kathmandu is a name that conjures up all sorts of images, and it doesn't disappoint. Chaotic, polluted, vibrant, colourful. And we arrive on garbage day. As a bonus, the major festival, Dasain is on while we are there. It is celebrated all over the country by Hindu and Buddhist alike. Durbar (palace) Square is the place to be.

It is one of three UNESCO sites in the vicinity. It's by no means a cordoned-off look-don't-touch monument. You have free reign to roam around the palaces, clamber up and down the temple and stupas' steps, watch the traffic and crush of sightseers swirl around the antiquity. In the '70s, the hippies pretty much camped out here, their only remaining legacies being Freak Street and the occasional hash seller. Now it's very much a gathering place for locals as well as tourists.

During the festival the kids fly their kites as a reminder to the god Indra that it is time for him to stop the rain. Families bring their animals there for live sacrifice. This sacrifice will supposedly appease the bloodthirsty demon god Kali. We witness a preemptive strike, so to speak, when a pigeon gets tangled in the string of a kite in flight and garrots itself, dripping blood on the street below. A strange collision of events that results in the bizarre good luck of killing two birds (simultaneously making contact with both Kali and Indra) with one bird, so to speak. Or maybe contacting three gods, seeing as Ganesha, the god of luck, was clearly involved. There are more characters to this franchise than Marvel and DC comics combined.[16]

We head down to the square to watch the action—it's still garbage day. I'm curious to witness one of the sacrifices. There's a crowd of about fifty folks gathered outside one of the temples, at their centre is a post that a goat is tethered to. Three guys, presumably the goat owner and two family members, stand close by. This general loitering goes on for about a half hour. Maybe the goat's lawyer is

16 https://www.dummies.com/religion/hinduism/core-beliefs-of-hindus/

attempting a last-minute plea for clemency from the state governor. I don't know because nothing is being said. The goat is a picture of contentment, munching on a pile of hay. If he had known that he was on death row he may have opted for the more traditional steak dinner followed by cheesecake as his last meal.

Without preamble, the three move to their tasks. One snugs up the rope tethering the goat's head, one takes the goat's hind legs and gently manoeuvres the goat back as far as it can comfortably stand. The third takes his kukri knife from its scabbard. The goat stands nonchalantly oblivious, smiling its goofy goat smile. The owner raises the blade high, glinting mesmerizingly in the sun.

Swoosh.

It's over faster than you can say, "Let them eat cake."

The head, severed from the torso, drops to the ground. The torso topples on its side. It's a clinical exercise carried out dispassionately, like slicing the top off a soft-boiled egg. The crowd is similarly tranquil, no frenzy or bloodlust, almost reverential, like a Sunday afternoon crowd gathered round to watch a street-corner game of chess.

The owner drags the carcass off for his family feast, the crowd disperses, all that remains is the trail of the goat's blood.

I can't say that the event is cruel or indulgent, but it isn't a spectacle I'd look forward to experiencing again. You might make the argument that it is time to go all twenty-teen and say that Kali should become a kale and carrot smoothie-thirsty demon and we could just slice the top off some winter greens, but I don't think we are there yet.

As long as I never have to visit a First World slaughterhouse I can continue to delude myself that my meat grows in shrink-wrapped styrofoam trays and happily go about my business.

We spend the evening wandering around Thamel, the tourist district. Fabulous little shops with all kinds of unusual knick knacks and souvenirs and antiques made last week. Trixie's ready to start our souvenir shopping. Before we left Canada I had already reached peak consumerism, and am now rolling down the other side and gradually gathering speed. Nowadays I get more satisfaction from getting rid of stuff than I do from acquiring more. Give me a trip to the dump over a trip to the shops anyday.

So it's no hardship for me as the self-appointed chancellor of the treasury (party pooper) to issue dire warnings about our own personal debt clock and lessons to be learned from the Greek experience. It's a tough job but someone has to do it. My arguments prove to be superfluous when the realization sets in that we would have to lug the stuff around for six weeks. Purchases have only been deferred, only quantitative easing can save us now.

They sure know how to celebrate in this part of the world. They should, as they get lots of practice. As luck would have it when we return to the capital after our treks, another festival, the festival of Diwali, will be on and the creatures this time will be getting the royal treatment. Dogs, who are the guardians of the gates to the afterlife, would be necklaced with garlands of marigolds and have colourful bindis painted on their foreheads. Every dog will have its day.

But for now this is the last night in Kathmandu before going trekking. Jet lag is now over and we have adjusted to the pace of Nepal's city, which is frenetic. Despite the frenzy there seems to be an underlying friendliness to the chaos. The driving habits are mental (is there any other million-plus city in the world without any traffic lights, stop signs, or road markings of any kind?), but I don't get a sense of any road rage. The blasting of the horns seems to say, "Watch out, pal, I'm coming through."

I witness a fender bender between two motorcycles. The mirror comes flying off. A couple of momentary scowls, then some banter back and forth between the riders, turning to smiles and real laughter, they pick up the pieces and drive off. Pretty remarkable when the motorcycles were probably the most expensive possession they had. Yet we get the willies every time the stock market has "a bad day." It seems the outlook here is not so much "life is cheap" but more "life is too short."

I have one last errand to complete before hitting the slopes: I have to meet up with Ali to retrieve our backpacks. He is an embroiderer of considerable artistry and he has been stitching the names of our Nepali hiking teams on our bags for me in Devanagari script, the traditional alphabet still in common use here. The writing is intricate, beautiful in its own right, but totally indecipherable to me.

Over the years we have become friends with Ali. He is Muslim, one of a small minority group that represents only 4 percent of the country's population. In his humble way he is a shining example of humanity to us. His faith is near palindromic. "DOG is my GOD," as he would say. His devotion to the canine comes at some social cost. Many of his Muslim alumni take a dim view. Dogs rank somewhere at the bottom of the popularity stakes, along with pigs. But his compassion knows no boundaries and isn't limited to four-legged creatures but all God's (or maybe in his faith, Dogs') creations, including humans.

On this occasion we meet him just back from an overnight mission on his motorcycle to the monsoon-flooded, ravaged Terai district to deliver food and medical supplies that he has scrounged up from local businessmen. After Kathmandu's earthquake in 2015, he housed homeless earthquake victims for weeks. He regularly ministers to the sick and homeless at Chatrapati Chowk.

We gather our bags and walk with him on his rounds as he feeds his pack of homeless gods. All is not always a slam dunk—even gods can get a bit territorial, Ali has the scars to prove it. He knows feeding the animals isn't a permanent solution. He collects funds for a neutering program he organizes. Well, organizes isn't the right word—he just acts and when he has enough funds he books a vet for the day, kidnaps the dogs, again at peril of more physical injury, and, on his motorcycle, delivers them for their surgery . . . no biggie.

There will be NO NOBEL FOR THIS NOBLE MAN, nor would it occur to him to expect one, he is just doing what any one of us would do. Right.

Dog si taerg halla rabka.

We prepare to head out of town. It is garbage day again.

Chapter 17

Voyage of the Crammed

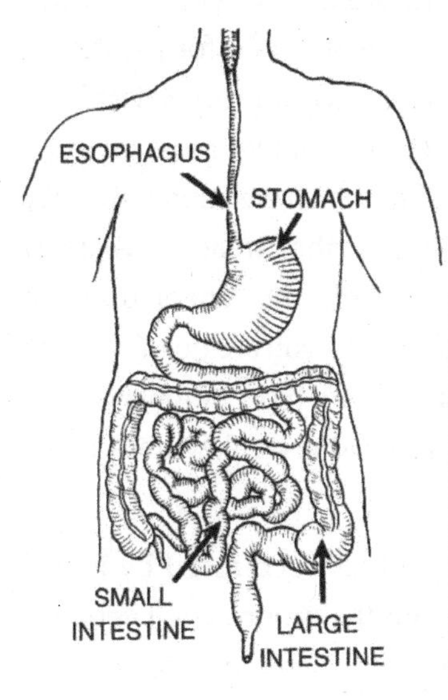

No guts no glory.

"THEY WERE SETTING OFF ON AN ADVENTURE AND HORNBLOWER WAS ONLY TOO CONSCIOUS THAT IT WAS HIS OWN FAULT."

—C S Forester

I DON'T MIND DYING. I JUST DON'T WANT TO BE THERE WHEN IT HAPPENS."

—Spike Milligan

Nepal is a jewel that sits on the crown of the world atop the Himalayas. Over a third of the world's population surrounds its borders. Melts from its glaciers and the heavy monsoon rains make it a key source for many of the region's major rivers. It has huge potential as a supplier of hydroelectric power. India and China are thirsty neighbours and hungry for power in all its forms. There is no need for plantation owners, miners, gunboats, or militia, as corporations, bankers, economists, and globalists have contrived a stealthier, more sanitized form of colonialism: economic colonialism, which we euphemistically call globalization. The mountains don't share their treasures willingly though. Whether you are planning a hydroelectric dam or just want to go for a walk surrounded by natural beauty, you are going to need to come to terms with travelling on Nepal's high highways. And when I say highways, I mean rock-strewn, dirt donkey track roads teetering on the edge of oblivion.

Undaunted by the horror stories gleefully recounted by fellow hikers we are determined to get up into the mountains. Every bus trip up to the high altitude villages degenerates into cliffhangers of the four wheeled variety. Spring and fall are reputed to provide the best conditions, we have tried both. Read on and judge for yourself.

Another early morning departure, this time we will travel from Kathmandu (KTM) to Surabesi, the trailhead for the Langtang trek in the north of the country. The main trekking seasons in Nepal are in the spring, late March to early May, before the hot monsoon rains sweep the country. The second season is in autumn and runs from September through to early November, before the bitterly cold winter settles in. We are travelling in early September to avoid all the unpleasant weather, aren't we clever?

The bus ride is a trip not to be savoured at the best of times, my dose of the Kathmandu quickstep just an added horror. Our destination is only 117 kilometres away, but the bus ride is scheduled to take nine hours. A glance at the map gives a pretty good indication why.

It looks like someone has miniaturized a photo of an intestine and Photoshopped it onto the map as a section of road!

On this occasion we are riding on a public bus. The pickup is in the middle of a chaotic commercial street in downtown Kathmandu. Folks are getting ready for the day, sweeping garbage out to the road's edge and setting fire to it. We hold our feet to the fire and tiptoe through piles of smouldering rubbish to get to the bus. Gahljan, our guide/porter, has snagged us seats a couple of rows back from the driver's cab, and we settle ourselves in.

A queen has come to see us off—raven black hair, a scarlet sari trimmed in gold, she seems to glide like a ghost over the trash, taking her son in school uniform to class. We set off with not a berth to spare. The trip becomes alarming as we get higher, the road becomes a muddy track clinging to the side of the mountains.

Our crew, however, is amazing, the skipper (driver) massive steering wheel in his lap is all business, thank goodness. The few times that I do look through the front window I see him spinning the wheel from lock to lock like Captain Hornblower in a gale, one minute staring out into eternity the next down the barrel of a slippery mud track. The sensation is like being piggybacked on a skier about to launch themselves down a double black diamond slope. No sense of control or balance. A clench everything, nerve-jangling experience, like watching your own open-heart surgery.

The mate (driver's helper), a kid who looks less than twenty, permanently hangs out the passenger door and, through a system of whistles and bangs on the side of the bus, while moving, of course, communicates with the skipper as to whether we're about to go over the edge or not. The system seems to work—it better work, it has to work. If you go over the edge, which happens all too frequently, it's over, unless you are lucky enough to have your momentum halted by rolling on top of some unsuspecting farmer's shack perched on the side of the mountain.

The third member of the crew, purser, collects the fares. He has a wad of notes in his hand the size of a brick of butter (probably about fifty bucks' worth). How he keeps track of who pays for what I've no idea.

More people and their belongings pile on all the time. TVs, carpet underlay, backpacks, cooktops, Google "everything" for a more comprehensive list. The tanks of propane next to me smell like they're leaking, though not to worry half of the bus windows don't have any panes in them. At least they're wedged in with sacks of rice so they can't roll around.

By this time there's probably as many people on the roof as there are inside the bus. The mate is sent aloft to collect the dues, while the bus is still moving of course. The purser stands watch at the door, he's a money man though, and takes the importance of this job way too casually for my liking.

Just to add to the fun it starts to drizzle, the windshield wipers smear the mud across the glass. The monsoon rains have lingered longer than usual this year so the roads are slick and treacherous. The roof surfers clamber down the metal ladder and swing themselves in through the passenger door, while we are still. . . . By now we're probably well over a hundred strong in a bus fitted with sixty seats. Quite comforting in some ways, we're sitting on the "upside" of the bus so the crush of humanity obscures the downside windows and the view of the precipice. We are happy to stare at the rock wall, waterfalls, and rockslides out of our window.

It is a means to an end, there is no other way to get up to the mountain trailheads. If Trixie has anything to do with it, it is never to be repeated. A couple of helicopter rides later we learn to be careful what you wish for!

For the remainder of the ride we do our best to induce a trance-like state, eyes open but unseeing, body relaxed, swaying to the motion of the bus, muscles soft and pliant, all the better to shock-absorb the jarring clatter of the wheels in the potholes and mind in sleep mode.

As a coping mechanism it is better than setting your hair on fire, but still has a ways to go in turning the experience into a barrel of laughs. Maybe a bit of practice is all that is needed to achieve zen calmness. After all, the Dalai Lama spends about seven hours a day in prayer, mindfulness and meditation.

Is this all really happening? Yes. And as if to prove the point, the experience is reincarnated two years later when we are back in Nepal to sample another trek, this time in the Ganesh Himal range. Perhaps you would have thought that we'd have learned our lesson after the torment of our last charabanc experience, but as I've hinted, the options that would reliably deliver you to your trailheads untraumatized are, well, they don't exist. After our last cunning plan flopped and still being naïve enough to think that there must be a way to avoid the worst of the road conditions, we have decided to hike early in the spring season this time. I am a veteran of the mountains now, so I've got this all figured out.

I have also made many refinements to my hiking wardrobe. Gone are the garments that passed the "looks good swanning around the yuppie trekking shop" test but failed the "how does it feel after wearing it without being washed for two weeks?" test.

Gone is the quarter-zip polyester popover that ended up smelling like a dead animal had been trapped inside. Gone are the cotton T-shirts that never dry. Rest stops became torturous events. At each stop you would shed your pack to cool off. A good idea, but your T-shirt cooled off a lot faster than your body. When it's time to get going and reshoulder your backpack it feels like you have a sheet of ice sandwiched between your load and your still steaming back rather than a T-shirt. The heavy Frankenstein hiking boots have been shunned in favour of lightweight, non-waterproof trail runners. My hiking shorts, replete with more pockets than a mob of wallabies, are staying home.

I now sport lightweight shorts with only two slash pockets, which I keep empty except for my hands and a hanky. Up top I wear a multipurpose paisley-patterned short-sleeved silk shirt, which looks like it was bought at some random Indian bazaar on a whim and has spent its life at the back of a sock drawer. Which it has.

The whole ensemble is topped off with a bright green full-zip fleece cardigan. The overall fashion vibe isn't so much Ed Viesturs getting prepped for an assault on K2 as Mr. Rogers getting ready to paint his garden shed.

I feel very much on brand. It's called style and some of us just have it. Others are destined to be mere followers of fashion.

Any trekking or climbing equipment can easily be bought or rented from any number of shops in KTM. I know better than to skimp on the sleeping bag so I have rented a top-of-the-line model for a dollar per day. It proudly sports both the Patagonia and North Face logos. They were probably sewn on in the back of the premises by the owner's wife when she was on her tea break.

On this occasion we opt for the "leisurely" twenty-four-day excursion with views into the Everest region (you may remember it from Part II). It's a route that starts with two bus rides of about six hours each that take us to the lower trailhead at Bhandar (2,100 metres) that all the old mountaineering expeditions used to take. Even although it's a much longer hike to the mountains it's a cunning plan whereby we avoid having to use the new route through Lukla airport (which you can find on YouTube under "the most dangerous airport in the world".[17]

17 https://www.youtube.com/watch?v=ICmx-WGfHCE

It will give us a much more gradual opportunity to acclimatize, get fit and avoid the crowds that fly into Lukla.

The first stage of our bus journey takes us from Kathmandu to Jiri. Riding the buses in Nepal is an exhilarating experience. The views are spectacular enough to make you drive right off the road.

We again have the typical three-man crew: driver, conductor, and communications officer (CO). Our communications officer's multimedia array consists of whistling, shouting, and banging on the side of the bus. He's a whippet-thin guy, about twenty years old, a human dynamo, and as skittish as a squirrel after five cups of coffee.

His primary duties are rustling up passengers. It appears that whenever there is a throng of folks strung along the side of the road, that it constitutes a bus stop. The driver slows to a crawl as he approaches the lineup, the CO jumps off the moving bus and runs through the crowd shouting out, *Jiri, Jiri, Jiri.* Meanwhile the bus is gaining speed as it nears the end of the line. The driver either slams on the brakes if he hears the CO's whistle, presumably meaning he's found a customer or accelerates to escape velocity just as the CO leaps back on the bus. If they were trapeze artists their timing couldn't be better. He's quite the showman.

The driver is no slouch himself. He is fluent in horn language and seems to be able to carry on conversations with his fellow drivers with a kind of Morse code made up of beeps of the horn. An exchange might be:

Bus A *beep beep:* "It's OK to pass."

Bus B *beep beep* "OK, I am coming," then overtakes.

Bus B *beep:* "Great, thanks."

Bus A *beep:* "No worries."

One hopes that this is the case, but given that Nepal is documented as having 123 languages spoken as a mother tongue, a nationally understood beep language of the road isn't guaranteed. And seeing how people drive, that would be my guess. One can see the potential for confusion. What may have actually being beeped was:

Bus A *beep beep:* "There is a cow in the middle of the road."

Bus B *beep beep:* "OK, I am coming through."

Bus B *beeeep:* "Why didn't you warn me?!"

Bus A *BEEEEEEP:* "Your mother wears army boots!" Or words to that effect.

Hindi music blares out over the Marconi sound system. It seems peculiarly Celtic. The flutist could easily be James Galway, the piper Paddy Moloney. Only the nasal vocals, Kate Bush kicked up an octave, and the over-and-under rhythms of the tabla give it the Nepali flavour. In any event it's the perfect rhythm for driving on these roads. We're only overtaken three times in the six-hour journey. Two hundred kilometres in six hours and it feels like you are flying. The trip passes remarkably quickly: the near misses, ever-changing complement of passengers, and glimpses of everyday life provide free must-watch entertainment. Whether it's an old man sitting on an empty food carton proudly emblazoned with " MSG Free" warming his hands over a pile of burning plastic; a human chain—women, wouldn't you know it—passing freshly made cement blocks hand to hand from the cement yard to a truck parked on the shoulder of the main road 100 metres away; or a herd of goats passing us in the opposite direction on the top of a bus, the show never ends.

The next leg on the bus from Jiri to Bhandar is only forty kilometres and, over four hours, proves to be less enjoyable. Although we are in the dry season, the early spring snowmelt from the mountains means that the dirt road is in intimidating shape. So much for my master plan to avoid the end of the rainy season's challenges. A couple of times the wheels are spinning so freely it feels like we will be stuck. You can only marvel at the determination and nerve of the driver embarking on this trip every day, quite a different skillset from the flash and dash of the city boys.

What could have possessed us to endure another white-knuckle odyssey? The only reasoning I can come up with is that it is something akin to giving birth to a child. You go through all that pain and suffering for that moment of elation. The brain then compartmentalizes and separates the two extremes and leaves room for a fresh starting point. So it was for the last bus ride, we have been able to suppress the horrors of the last trip and stash them in some mental "do not open" storage bin.

I share this realization with Trixie, mother of our two children. It isn't as well received as I expected.

After a stunned, expressionless few seconds, her features settle into a lingering gaze somewhere in between hostility and disbelief. Finally moved to speak, she utters, "Sometimes I think that the average donkey we meet has more brains than a man." End of discussion.

Conditions worsen as the bus climbs ever upwards to the high pass that will take us over into the next valley and eventually to our trailhead destination. Let me remind you, the joke about travel in Nepal is that it is "a little bit up and a little bit down." The driver tries to gain some momentum in order to make it up the steep incline just on the far side of the approaching hairpin bend. Halfway round the corner the bus slews to the right then slithers toward the cliff edge on the left as the bald tires try to gain traction in the mud. No dice. Undeterred, the driver backs down the hill to get a longer run up. He must try this four or five times, with no discernible difference in the results. Other than maybe for the passengers getting more panicky by the moment. Well, maybe just the white passengers are getting whiter, and we are the only white passengers. It doesn't inspire much confidence when the conductor and CO abandon ship then too.

By this time it becomes apparent that a change in tactics is required, the passengers in the front half of the bus are told to get out and push, leaving the rest of us to provide weight at the back over the driving wheels. A Nepali merchant who is sitting across the aisle from us helpfully interprets the mayhem as it unfolds. He does this over sacks of corn seed that are stacked in the passageway; he is en route to his shop in the village. The bus is packed. Our porter/guide Min had bribed—such an ugly word, maybe incentivised would be better—the two original occupants of our seats to surrender them to us back at the terminus, and he is currently riding on the crowded roof of the bus with the two displaced but now richer Nepalis.

Well by now, true unadulterated fear has set in, and decisive action is required. It's a combo I admit I'm not renowned for, but it is amazing what adrenaline can do. I grab Trixie's hand and exclaim "we're getting the hell off this bus" and bolted.

"Where are we going?" says Trixie as we clamber over the clobber, making for the exit.

"Anywhere . . . anywhere but here!"

The sight that greets us certainly justifies the action we have taken: the bus is in the mud up to its rear axle and fish tails dramatically from side to side as the driver gently feathers the gas pedal. Some of these swings will take the wheels within two feet of a virtually sheer drop of hundreds of feet. I can't help thinking with some embarrassment, the number of times I heard or used the metaphor "this isn't a hill to die on" when I worked in the civil service. We really do devalue our language with overuse.

Nepali improvisation and doggedness are not easily denied. Having freed the bus from the ruts and reversed it back down the hill yet again the rag tag band of would be sappers set about filling up the ruts with boulders and "paved" over the top of them with branches and vegetation. It was early for Palm Sunday but with this added little bit of traction combined with the muscle power of twenty or so of Sherpa pedigree our prayers were answered and we escaped our treacly trap and continued round the bend, up the slope and on our way again.

The rest of the journey passes relatively uneventfully, other than on one occasion—it is dark by this time and the driver must have been either distracted or dozed off and would have driven off a cliff had the passengers in the front not all shrieked at the same time. Rather than there be any recriminations, howls of laughter ensue from the front of the bus. Maybe it is just gallows humour.

But I can't help thinking to myself: *Next time, let's try and get on a bus where the driver is a Hindu or Muslim instead of a Buddhist. Someone who isn't quite so confident about his reincarnation.*

Chapter 18

I Am Bat

If I might reply to the honourable member.

"DON'T JUST DO SOMETHING, SIT THERE."

—*Sylvia Boorstein*

"NEVER BE AFRAID TO LAUGH AT YOURSELF, AFTER ALL YOU MIGHT BE MISSING OUT ON THE JOKE OF THE CENTURY."

—*Dame Edna Everage*

That's the thing about Nepal, its trekking is in a class of its own but in its own quiet way it is packed with so many other treasures that the traveler could miss out on. With that in mind, we return to Pokhara, the adventure capital of Nepal. Its affluence and good dining are evidenced by the locals' waistlines approaching Western circumferences. Tourism is only slowly coming back to normal after the seismic jolt given to Nepal's economy as delivered by the 2015 earthquake. In the meantime, bored shopkeepers wait for the upturn, reading newspapers, thumbing their iPhones, playing solitaire, scanning the empty streets like dustbowl farmers eyeing the sky for signs of rain. These guys know it is all about hits/eyeballs.

If you can call it good news, the proliferation of worldwide calamities and the resulting blanket media coverage tends to numb our reactions and fog our memory. Memories are short and the "rains" will soon resume.

The friendly relaxed vibe of the town has you wondering how far we really have come in our progressive liberalized society. It is common to think of countries like Nepal as being culturally backward throwbacks to Victorian morality where nudity and public displays of affection with the opposite sex are offensive. Yet warmth and caring between people here is much more in evidence than in the West.

The selfie culture is alive and well, the Nepalese just as infatuated with their electronic mirrors as we are. Only a couple of decades ago the Japanese were the brunt of western scorn for their snap happy ways, turns out maybe we were jealous, technophobes, or just too cheap.

Now that we've been physically put through the wringer on the trek, we (and I use that word loosely) decide to exercise the spiritual being by enrolling in a four-day yoga session at a retreat just outside of Pokhara. It's the quietest place we've been to so far in Nepal. It's in a rural area on a hillside overlooking a lake, as is the fashion for these sorts of places. The centre is a striking lime green and pink building sitting 600 metres above Phewa Lake and 700 metres below the summit of Mount Sarangkot. Sarangkot is the hub of Nepal's paragliding activity and also the birthplace of parahawking[18]—(read it and be amazed).

We soon discover the place is a blend of scout camp (there are jobs to be done, Karma yoga) and boot camp (up and at 'em at 6 a.m., and a set timetable of events throughout the day). We start the day with pre-meditation—premeditated torture if you ask me. I am required to twist my body into positions I couldn't even manage when I was a fetus. While in one of those contortions, the yoga master asks us to relax and make ourselves comfortable. I look around for a couch—nothing doing. While sitting cross-legged on the floor we're supposed to chant, "So hum, so hum," which means—well, I don't really know what it means. The master tries to translate for us but he speaks very softly and has a whispery accent. The best that I can figure from his explanation is that it means "I am bat" or possibly "I am bad" maybe but even less likely "I am dead." I'll go with the bat thing. After all, they have a monkey god Hanuman and an elephant god Ganesh, so the odds are pretty fair.

Anyway, the chanting is supposed to quiet the mind for the hour or so that we are going to be under. Fat chance—my knees are screaming at me after ten minutes. From now on I'm going to be early for class and snag some prime real estate at the back of the class where I can rest my back against the wall.

The meditation concludes with a chant of "Om," a moving spiritual moment except for an irritating discordant undertone. More of an "Owum," like some poor zombie might have stubbed their toe. I sneak open one eye, have a shifty dekko, but can't spot the culprit. There must be a cockney somewhere amongst the assembled.

---

18 www.parahawking.com

Other events include nasal cleansing. We each have our own "neti pot," a utensil a bit like an oversized meerschaum pipe. The bowl is filled with salt water. As you bend down from the waist and tilt your head to the side, you then insert the spout into your nostril. Alternating sides, you pour the solution in one side and it magically flows out the other—nasal flossing, I guess. For the grand finale, you straighten up and then stick your thumbs under your armpits, flap your arms like a chicken, and violently exhale through your nose to expel the last droplets. When you have twenty people doing this in unison it sounds like all the riders on the Tour de France pumping up their bike tires at the same time. Fortunately, no one takes any of this seriously so it's lots of laughs.

Next, an hour of yoga—more pretzel-like contortions. Stick the left big toe in the right ear "anne mek de nih toss de floss" (touch your knee to the floor). Given the vagaries of Nepal bathrooms I can see the potential benefits to all this flexibility, other than that I'm just about flexible enough to sit on the fence.

After all this it feels like I've put in a full day already (you're probably thinking the same thing), but no, it's now only breakfast! After breakfast, a choice: either a steam bath in a contraption that looks like a cross between a fish smoker and the casket a magician uses to saw his assistant in half or a mud bath. I usually opt for the latter. On the rooftop of the centre a group of us swimwear-clad whities gather.

Recipe for Nepali gingerbread men

- Take a half a dozen Caucasian men and women.
- Slather in mud.
- Place flat on a rooftop in Pokhara.
- Bake for ten minutes under the Nepali sun at twenty-seven degrees or until crispy and wrinkled.

- Obtain fresh supplies of Caucasians and repeat every three to four days.

After we've baked, we get up, stand around chatting like we're at some cocktail party for Aboriginals. Here's mud in your eye.

"Yes, I much prefer a good Pinot to a Shiraz, don't you?"

All the while thirty or more colourful paragliders spiral above our heads in an azure sky. I feel like I'm living in a Salvador Dali painting. It's a strange old world. Time to head for the showers before my watch melts.

Activities in the afternoon follow a similar pattern, with the added threat, er, treat (how similar those words are) of an hour of chanting. I am really lapping it up—back straight, neck elongated, eyes closed, chin wagging from side to side, channelling Stevie Wonder.

Ending the day's official program on a lighter note I find myself the beneficiary of a twenty-minute endorphin rush delivered courtesy of Hasya yoga, or laughing yoga, to the uninitiated. Interestingly, Kafka of *The Metamorphosis* fame also published a collection of short prose on meditation. So, in a nexus of art imitating spirituality imitating life, our acharya has us lie on our backs like stranded beetles. Knees up to our chests, fingers pointing skywards perhaps wriggling around a little to get over our inhibitions. He then instructs us to focus on nothing at all, set our minds in neutral and then commence to laugh for absolutely no reason. It is a fake-it-till-you-make-it sort of exercise that actually works. I think that it was the only class that I got a passing grade on.

It should be mandatory for all the national governments of the world, that before they start a session of debate, they perform twenty minutes of Hasya yoga on live TV before they are allowed to speak. It could replace those phony scripted photo ops of bitter politicians shaking hands and smiling through gritted teeth. It could catch on.

I could picture some being more willing than others, Obama a big daddy longlegs, Merkel probably game for anything, Mandela, for sure. A few imposters of course would join in. Our guy Trudeau will do anything for a Facebook moment—boxing matches, donning traditional Indian dress, taking a knee. Some of course would self-select out Putin, Xi Xiang, Erdogan. Donald, can you imagine? The only thing bigger than his vanity is his insecurity.

Bush a maybe if it wasn't for Cheney, the devil on his shoulder. Others should be forced to perform. Can you picture anything more delicious than Pelosi and McConnell?

It also just might reintroduce some sense of dignity to the proceedings. I'd have a lot more hope for progress if I were to see the Ayatollah and Netanyahu kick off a meeting with them on their backs, feet in the air, giggling their heads off. It's time to try a little more humility and a little less machismo. Time for our leaders to take the issues of the day seriously instead of themselves.

All in all, a fun week. We meet some cool, idealistic, accomplished young folk (I am the senior citizen), but as they say, all good things . . .

I did find out what "So Hum" means: "I am that". . . . "which is conscious." "Ho hum," "Ho kum," I'll stick with "I am bat,"—it's what worked for me. But just maybe I'm not as blind as when I started the week.

Given an honourable discharge from the program, Trixie and I plan to press on to Chitwan, Nepal's premier wildlife national park. The combination of an embargo by India on delivering fuel, the recent plane crash just outside of Pokhara killing twenty-three tourists, and the failed monsoon have stalled the economic recovery in the region. Nepal needs our support so it's a great time to be there. No lineups, the best guides and hotels are available, the trekking is quieter than usual and the service is great.

Rather than drive to the park we book a two-night river rafting trip from just outside of Pokhara down the Seti Khola to just outside the park. Being the tail end of the dry season the rapids are a gentle cruise with a couple of class two and three rapids thrown in to keep you on your toes.

At night we retire to our rubber room. The raft has been hauled out of the river, inverted and propped up on one side by the canoe paddles, the effect is much like sleeping under an open car hood. The weather in these lowlands bordering India is warm and humid with few insects. Perfect in fact, for sleeping outside under the stars.

We reach Sauraha, the main village, with access to the park. We are now in the far south of Nepal in the jungle of the tropical lowlands. The big attractions here (unless you are a birder) are wild elephants, rhinos, and tigers. The wildlife is at its most active at dusk and dawn so we arrange for an early safari the following morning.

Bleary eyed, we are poled across the Rapti river in a dugout canoe. The river forms the park boundary. We are met by our guide on the far bank and introductions complete, we clamber aboard our open jeep in the dim 6:00 a.m. light.

Our first order of business is the pursuit of the elusive tiger and we actually come across some evidence of them. Namely, the field where a mother and daughter were out collecting various roots and vegetation to put in their curry and then were eaten by a tiger; the lake where an environmental cleanup crew were extracting invasive water hyacinth and were eaten by a tiger; and a tiger's footprint. Although I have a sneaking suspicion that they send out a man with a giant rubber stamp making footprints in the sand before the safari groups set out for the day.

The other fauna are less elusive, elephants, deer, an assortment of exotic bird species, monkeys, crocs, sloth bear, butterflies, jackals and many, many rhinos all in severe need of liposuction. Collateral evidence of the rhinos' presence is hard to miss too, given that the equivalent of 1 percent of their body weight, which is up to 1,600 kilos, goes in the front end every day. So it's a frequent occurrence to stumble across a thirty-pound mound of what comes out the back end too. I don't know how much they drink—suffice to say if you have ever seen a firehose in use . . . .

Along the way we learn new direction-finding skills – if you are ever lucky enough not to know which side of the equator you are on and don't have a sink handy to watch which way the water swirls down the plug hole, just check out which way the strangler vines wind round the trees. Clockwise in the north—at least then when you are about to die you will know which hemisphere you are in! See, hiring a guide is always worth it.

Using all navigational aids at our disposal we return to town for the evening. We buy a few bananas on main street and feed them to the elephants coming home from a day's work carrying tourists around the "bufferzone" on the edge of the park. The pachyderm commute snarls the traffic for a while, but who is going to argue?

This Terai region of Nepal is mostly inhabited by an ethnic group known as the Tharu. That evening we decide to take in one of their cultural shows. It is a Nureyev meets Bruce Lee kind of a spectacle as men whack at each other with Kendo-like sticks while performing ballet-like spins and leaps. Impressive and quite some fun. When we leave it is pitch dark, the streets unlit and ill defined. Not to worry, all we have to do is make use of another useful navigation aid—the trail of elephant turds down the middle of the street leads to our hotel. It is way easier than trying to follow a trail of breadcrumbs.

Day two we hang out for a while and creature watch—the neighbouring property has a three-elephant garage. The mahouts lovingly scrub their . . . their what? Beasts, isn't it, nor animals. Pets is closer to the mark and so is partners—how's that? Next, a facial, a rinse, and then they apply the makeup—colourful chalk-like markings. To show our appreciation we pass our breakfast bananas over the fence to them. Whether all the working animals in this area are treated this well is very doubtful.

There is a business convention for Nepali insurance salesmen at the hotel (must be the big demand for life insurance given all the people being eaten by tigers). A truly universal experience: slightly corpulent men in dress shirts and slacks, cellphones pressed to ears, talking in loud, self-important tones while absentmindedly adjusting belt buckles and fly buttons.

For their entertainment a cultural event is staged by the Tharu on the grounds of the hotel. Predictably, something unpredictable happens, in this case a stampede of the performers and the audience when a couple of rhinos (the collective noun being appropriately a "crash") crash the party (or, more accurately, the fence) and the performance and meander up to the riverbank that separates the town from the park. The pachyderms' indifference to the humans calms and reassures the panicked crowd, who soon decide the animal show is the main attraction. The performers, knowing when they have been upstaged, join the onlookers.

Grateful for having the good fortune to witness the impromptu rodeo, we retire to our rooms, for we return to the capital on the morrow. There we will have a delicious last Indian meal at the Third Eye restaurant. We will get the royal treatment from the maître d', who we have dubbed the "Suaver," the epitome of discreet attentive service. His dulcet tones being his signature identifier, the light being so low in the dining room that you can barely see the cutlery. That only visible thanks to the Suaver lighting a candle for us, the only clue to his whereabouts being provided when the flare of the match illuminates the white of his dress shirt which contrasts with the black of his bow tie, dinner jacket, and face . . . the invisible man.

But I am getting ahead of myself. My apologies. I had hoped to reach Kathmandu in the usual logical sequential manner, but my hallucinations of mutton Rogan Josh have proven to be irresistible.

Chapter 19

What to Do about A 'Do in Kathmandu

Just a little off the top, if you don't mind.

"I ALWAYS WANTED TO BE A HAIRDRESSER."

—David Beckham

"WE DON'T NEED TO WORRY ABOUT THE CORPORATE GIANTS BEING TOO BIG TO FAIL, WE SHOULD WORRY ABOUT THEM BEING TOO BIG TO TRUST."

—Otis T Hackenbush

What is Ben Gunn doing in my bathroom?

This isn't what I expected to find returning to our Kathmandu hotel room after nearly three weeks away in the mountains. On closer inspection, it would appear that I have more in common with the marooned mariner from Robert Louis Stevenson's novel *Treasure Island* than just a hankering for cheese.

The skin is wrinkly and weather beaten, hair longish, unkempt, a tufted grey mop, a slight stoop in posture, and the face covered in the grizzled white beard you'd expect after twenty days of trekking in the Himal. Oh, oopsy, it's my own reflection in the mirror. Changed and not for the better, that's for sure. On the trail the tea houses' amenities don't usually stretch to mirrors—vanity isn't much of a thing.

Now reacquainted with myself, I take the time to anticipate the sumptuousness of my surroundings. I can feel my primitiveness of the weeks melt away. Even my thoughts become more sophisticated. *Wow, that bathtub really resonates with my inner being. I am truly blessed to have survived my growth experience*. Yes, I am back in civilization.

Finally my gaze fixes on the temple, the altar of all that is great in this world, the holy grail that receives instead of gives. A magnificent gleaming white goddess, that thing of unparalleled beauty—the toilet. This is clearly porcelain you can have a relationship with. My imagination soars. I give myself permission to have some alone time—it's my body, it's my choice. The possibilities for luxuriating are endless: perhaps linger over a crossword, read a chapter of *The Snow Leopard*, take the time to learn to knit.

But visions of my Ben Gunn alter ego plague my psyche. My mirror image has a repulsing effect, somewhat like Narcissus in reverse. I need to escape the ugliness, and fast. Knit one, purl one will have to wait. Time for a shave and a haircut.

I make my way to Thamel, a region of the city that has been a long-time favourite of visiting foreigners. One of the terminuses of the famous hippie trail of the 1960s was Freak Street in Thamel. These intrepid trailblazers travelled an overland route through Turkey, Iran, Afghanistan, Pakistan, and Kashmir to get there. It would be considered borderline suicidal to undertake that journey nowadays. What went wrong?[19]

I step into the hairdresser's salon—a hole-in-the wall operation roughly six feet wide by seven feet deep and a little over six feet high. Four stations, two stylists on duty and an extra chair for the manager. A cozy set-up. I am the only customer.

After "Namastes" all around, I sit down and we get down to business. We negotiate a price—300 rupees, about three dollars, the outrageous tourist rate, but what the heck, I've a lot of whiskers to get through and I am sure he will put the three dollars to a much better use than I would.

He gets to work, lathers me up, and takes out a new blade for his razor. I am all spiffed up in no time. He wipes the last of the shaving foam off my lips with his finger then proceeds to give me a facial, drowning me in all manner of unlabelled unguents massaged into my face, presumably with the intent of exfoliating my dewlaps. The grand finale comes when he takes out what looks like dental floss, wraps a twelve-inch length around his index fingers, then scrapes it down my face like he is using a cheese wire.

But maybe we are not done. I must have unintentionally signed up for the "Spa Utopia Touched by an Angel Indulgence Package," for my transformation is not yet complete. His pointed scissors disappear so far up my nostrils it looks like he is taking a COVID sample instead of

19 https://www.thevintagenews.com/2017/09/06/the-hippie-trail-once-a-symbol-of-freedom-and-enlightenment-today-is-synonymous-with-danger-and-war/

snipping off a couple of rogue nose hairs. All cranial thatch attended to, he proceeds to do a head massage. To be more accurate, he grips my neck in a Hulk Hogan-style headlock and gives my skull a couple of swift twists that elicit two loud cracks like pistol shots. I hold my hands up in surrender. There's only so much pampering a guy can take.

A couple of Nepali guys come in for a trim—business is picking up. It is getting a bit like a Guinness Book of Records event: how many tonsorially challenged people can you fit in a Mini? Just as we are nearing the record, Goliath turns up in the form of a hippie time traveller: an American, about 6'6", waist-length hair and beard. I get the sense that he must have been "travelling overland" for the last fifty years.

He is decked out in Jesus sandals, harem pants, tie-dye shirt and, unsurprisingly, is labouring under a massive backpack with a sleeping bag tied on top. He pretty much succeeds in getting inside our crate, but then makes the fatal mistake of turning around. Because of course the guitar (how could I forget to mention the mandatory twelve-string guitar dangling from the back of his pack?) wipes out most of the meagre supply of lotions and equipment from the counters. He may just have awakened, Rip Van Winkle style, from a hash-induced sixty-year-long snooze somewhere on Freak St.

After a short period of convalescence from my wellness treatment I settle up and lurch back onto the unlit streets. The Kathmandu cityscape at dusk is a scene from a post-apocalyptic movie: potholes, jumbled wires, rebar protruding from buildings at weird angles, mounds of smouldering garbage, piles of bricks, slabs of concrete strewn around. Water trucks loom up out of the gloom and lumber around the debris, dustmasked bandits on their two-wheeled steeds racing for home. A saffron-robed Buddhist monk whizzes by on his motorcycle, a Nazi helmet on his head.

The thickness of the murk and dust exacerbated by the dry season is a soup of pollution that you could scoop up with a spoon. A dog surveys the scene from his vantage point on the top of a rubbish heap. It beats LA.

As I near our guest house my pace quickens in anticipation of my assignation with the splendour of our bathroom. The simple joys are, in the final analysis, the biggest luxuries: a hot bath, a substantial palak paneer dinner, and a comfortable bed welcome me back to a life of ease.

Back in the city now with only one day left until departure it is time to shop and scram.

After three weeks away from any form of mechanized transport it takes some time to readjust to KTM's chaotic roads. It is always a good idea to look out for old ladies trying to cross the street. Not out of any sense of chivalry, it is pure survival-of-the-fittest Darwinism at work. I figure that if they have lived this long they must know something. They usually gather as a phalanx of up to ten in a roughly triangular bowling pin-like formation. I feel least vulnerable being downstream from the group and the direction of the traffic: ten feet separated and positioned about mid-pack, always taking care to be out of range of the "head pin" lest anything goes awry. It's a winning strategy.

Trixie and I have safely arrived in the commercial zone in time to practise some more low-impact tourism, in the twenty-first century building good Karma has gone digital. Every dollar that you spend and every mouse click that you make is a vote for the future you will inherit. To get off on the right foot I have my sandals shoeshined—the shoe shiner's idea, not mine. Oxblood Tevas could be the next hot thing. I have my Raccoon Sixty logo embroidered on hats, backpacks, clothes, etc. My embroiderer, Ali, who has become a friend over the years, tolerates my gimmicky corporate artwork as a side line as he has the opportunity to give free reign to his creative talents when beautifying Trixie's sweatshirts with glorious herons, mandalas, and bodhi trees. We pick up a few nostalgia-evoking souvenirs and I get another shave before we hire a cycle rickshaw for the ride back to our hotel.

In the afternoon we take a cab to the south side of town to a small carpet factory co-op. The building still shows the damage from the 2015 earthquake. The posts supporting the structure look like some concrete-loving beavers have chewed the cement bottoms of the columns down to some pencils of bare rebar.

I find myself haggling with a carpet seller over one of the spectacular multi-coloured patterned wool Tibetan tribal rugs, each one an original piece of art in its own right—it is a stalemate. We have narrowed the gap. He wants $150 and I am willing to part with $130. It's kind of personal, but it shouldn't be—he isn't going to pull the wool over my eyes (ha ha).

Oh, sure, carpet-making is a dying skill. Many of the Tibetan refugees who fled the Chinese occupation of their land in the 1960s are either now too old to work or have transited on to other countries. A few of their children still carry on the tradition, hand-weaving on wooden looms, but the majority of their offspring are now more likely to be abroad, working in factories, maybe even churning out thousands of identical monochrome 3.5-ounce merino undershirts on some production line.

Without a second thought I will happily buy one of those for $140 or more. I might even wear it for a few hours a year for a couple of years. But by way of some twisted biased logic, I have the mindset that these carpet salesmen are not to be trusted, that they are part of some nefarious Madoffian scheme to separate me from my wallet, that there is no tradition of institutionalized integrity in business like we have at home, so buyer beware.

What a lot of yak shit, if the recent behaviour of many of our captains of industry is anything to go by. Facebook, VW, Lehman Bros., Pentax, BP are just a few bad apples. Oh, and then there are Enron, Firestone, Apple, and and and. It feels like the world economy is just some sort of scam, a huge Ponzi scheme where we, by some lucky chance, happen to be at the top of the pyramid.

Thinking these sorts of thoughts rather coloured things, as you can imagine. I figure that if I am serious about wanting to support the continuation of this craft, I should be paying more than he is asking!

Conscience sufficiently twinged, I shut up and pay up, making a grand keep-the-change gesture as I hand over $160 to the stunned merchant.

As the sun sets on the last few hours of our visit, we pack away the Tibetan prayer flags that we have bought—they will flutter outside our kitchen window back home in Canada. In a couple of years, the sun, wind, and rain will reduce them to a faint replica of their former vividness, enough of a reminder for us that we must return. Not that we need one. Trust me, this is an interesting place and the draws are many, but the world is big and the rest of Asia has many rich and unique experiences on offer.

As if to choreograph a grand finale, who should materialize out of nowhere but our friend Krishna, his timing and intuitiveness as impeccable as ever. On the morning of our departure he has come to see us off and has brought Khatas to present to us. These traditional Tibetan white scarves bestow good karma and respect for the wearer.

It is a bittersweet moment as we say our goodbyes to Krishna and the friendly hotel staff as we eagerly anticipate our stopover in the land of the rising sun on the way back to Canada.

Chapter 20

The Power of the Little Green Man

Keep your fig leaf dry.

"THE CITY IS NOT A CONCRETE JUNGLE, IT IS A HUMAN ZOO."

—*Desmond Morris*

"SO AS LONG AS YOU HAVE FOOD IN YOUR MOUTH YOU HAVE SOLVED ALL QUESTIONS FOR THE TIME BEING."

—*Franz Kafka*

A short two-hour flight from the connecting hub of Seoul airport brings us to Nippon to spend a few inscrutable days visiting its frenetic capital, Tokyo, and Kyoto, its cultural centre and historical heart. Banzai! (That's hurray to us anglophiles.)

Our first day walking the concrete canyons of Tokyo confirm many of our preconceptions. No dogs, no police, no garbage, no graffiti, yeah! Speed with order. No joggers, yet everyone stays trim. They get plenty of exercise with the usual pace of life running for tubes, trains, buses. But no one is carrying cameras. Bizarre.

The towering buildings reveal none of the history that fostered their existence. The origins are ghastly. Towards the end of WWII, Japan was subject to a bombing campaign the likes of which had never been seen. Tokyo's wood and paper buildings were kindling to the incendiary bombs that were dropped by the USAF in March 1945. The city was virtually obliterated. In two nights, a million were made homeless and over 100,000 died, more than four times the mortality of the infamous bombing of Dresden in Germany. The fires burned so fiercely that several of the bombers in the second attack wave were destroyed when the pilots lost control of their aircraft due to the super-heated updraft turbulence from the firestorm below. It was the most destructive bombing in human history, even surpassing Hiroshima.

At war's end, this island nation emerged battered but uninvaded. The devastated cities provided a clean slate for the introduction of the latest technological innovations and efficiencies in modern manufacturing techniques and equipment. These circumstances gave the country a huge competitive advantage and led to the" economic miracle," which soon resulted in the country having the third-largest economy in the world. Traditional Japanese values prevailed after the war —regard for family, hard work, attention to detail—and are still apparent to the visitor. The have/have-not divide is less in evidence, high income and inheritance taxes and an aversion to ostentation have helped to maintain stability, even as the economic boom times have passed.

The 1950s and '60s saw an unprecedented reconstruction initiative, but bureaucracy was slow to adapt; it wasn't until the mid 1960s that the ten-storey height restrictions were lifted. When those revisions were made, the skyscraper building boom literally took off and Tokyo truly rose from the ashes.

How better to take in their daunting glory than at night, from street level on the busiest crosswalk in the world? The iconic Shibuya intersection is a five-barred Abbey road album cover for the masses where a Beatle would be swallowed up.

The green man means go, nothing unusual in that, but in twenty seconds a legion of up to 3,000 sushi-savouring souls will stride, saunter, swerve and sidestep their way to the safety of the other shore. By day's end, the little green men will have ushered a total of 2.4 million humans across the divide, seven times the population of greater Victoria will make the peregrination every day. A hundred and forty million kilos of Homo sapiens stampede across an area about the size of a soccer pitch. A human equivalent that lampoons the paltry migration of the two million wildebeest spread across the roomy Serengeti. It's a true wonder of the world, one that you should be an active participant in. Where else can you immerse yourself in your own herd and share a non-contact pilgrimage bathed in one of the biggest neon light arrays in the country?

Our fellow dogies are a dapper species. The many male office workers known as salarymen are dressed in smart dark suits and ties, heading for the train and home or just as likely to the bar to meet up with their work colleagues. The ladies' attire is as imaginative as the men's is conservative. They are dolled up in intricate creations, like Sarah Brightman with buttons, bows, lollipop earrings, and tutu miniskirts.

Strangely, youth abounds. Well, it seems that way in the cities but in reality Japan has the oldest average age, at forty-six years, and the highest life expectancy, at eighty-four, of any country. Nepal, our last port of call, has one of the younger average ages, at twenty-two years, and a life expectancy of sixty-nine. One imagines that the countryside must be like one giant old folks' home full of old, wizening citizens.

The workforce is shrinking faster than the population, which begs the question: how will the society continue to thrive? Sophisticated, undisputedly, yes, cosmopolitan, not so much, immigrants only constitute about 2 percent of the populace and this number isn't significantly increasing either. It is undeniably a monoculture and for all the oddity of our four round eyes, the anti-pollution-masked visages of the Eddokoers reveal not a flicker of interest.

Fame, I guess, is fleeting, and the stardom of my days in India and Seoul only a fading memory. Time to lick my wounds and head back to the hotel, but first we must buy our train tickets, for tomorrow. It is sayonara to the current Shihon, Tokyo, and on to the old capital.

Our groundwork turns out to be a prudent move. The train station is massive, and labyrinthine, a torrent of harried travellers who know where they are going and how to get there. And then there are us two babes in the wood, clueless and without language. Spoken English isn't as commonplace as you might expect. We eventually locate the ticket counter and with a combination of pointing at maps, clocks, and calendars, we finally succeed in making our wishes known. A more pleasant ticket-buying experience I have never had. Our imperturbable ultra-polite wicket operator has the zen-like patience of Ah, Grasshopper. Then as a final flourish rather than sliding the tickets over the counter to these two trying gaigins, he solemnly stands, bows his head, and proffers the tickets two handed, like he is offering the cure for the economy to Shinzo Abe.

Reconnaissance complete, we take the subway to our hotel, noting the ongoing traditional gender roles in the workforce: train cleaners—women, platform attendants—men.

We find ourselves in everyone's worst nightmare. No, not the dreaded "making a speech in front of a crowd" one. The trapped alone in a railway carriage with a bunch of drunks one. A group of six or so young salarymen have been loosening up after work. It's a popular custom to leave the circumspect conservatism at the office tower.

These lads have clearly been partaking of a few Birus, probably a whisky or two and by the look of things, wrapping up with a couple of rounds of Kamikazes, before heading home. The most blootered of the group worryingly flops himself down on the seat opposite us. He exhibits all the symptoms of over-enthusiastic participation.

Sagging to one side with his head supported by one elbow on his briefcase. His eyes slowly close. His pose begins to teeter before the whole arrangement collapses in slow motion. His head slides down his forearm before bouncing off the armrest. This renders him fully awake, but in no way fully conscious.

The first thing that his goggle-eyed stare locks onto is us. Now in his crosshairs predictably he makes the drunkest bee line a bee can make for us. His goal is to engage us in dialogue, if you can call it that. He commences making grand arm-waving gestures, slurring heavily in Japanese. Us deaf to the language nodding agreeingly, smiling, making thumbs-up signs, and saying, "Kirin good!"

The rest of the revellers are drawn to join the conversation. They are the politest bevy of boozers I have yet to meet and are obviously trying to make apologies for their friend and rein him in a bit. Much smiling and bowing follows. Shaking hands isn't much of a thing in Japan, which is probably just as well. Executing the manoeuvre in a lurching, speeding subway carriage with a bunch of foutered businessmen would have been like trying to dock the International

Space Station in a hurricane, doubtless resulting in the need for more apologies.

We arrive at our station in due course. Had our language been in any way intelligible we would have been on first-name terms by now. Instead, our departure is a friendly few bows and a liberal sprinkling of *sumimasens* and we are away. Back in the hotel slumber comes next with 330 kph dreams of the Shinkansen bullet train speeding us past the snowy cone of Mount Fuji, like Fuji film not quite as extinct as you might think. Kyoto here we come.

A dream come true, we arrive in the beautiful city of Kyoto. Spared the bombings of the Second World War, it is home to museums, geisha, culture, markets, green space, and more temples and shrines than you can shake a samurai at. Not to mention food . . . glorious food.

Trixie and I splash out on a stay at a ryokan, a classic Japanese-style inn. Each room is a sliding paper-doored sanctuary with all the latest low-tech attractions: bamboo and paper walls, tatami mats, futon on the floor, and traditional slippers and robes for the guests.

This one has the additional extravagance of having its own onsen,[20] a communal plunge bath filled with water from underground hot springs. Each gender has its own pool and access and there isn't a pair of budgie smugglers to be seen. Adam and Eve suits only. The bashful can either hide the forbidden bits in the steam or with a small handkerchief-sized towel that's provided—totally inadequate for me, ha ha. You balance the folded towel on your head once you are in the water. You then look at the other goofs in the pond and try and keep a serene expression on your face. It's how the samurai learned to discipline their bodies with their minds. In case you are into body art you should note that those with tattoos are not welcome, as until recently they were only used as symbols of gang membership.

20 www.themanual.com/travel/onsen-etiquette-japan/

After our purification we head out for dinner. We fancy some Japanese, tonight, which is in no way as obvious as it might sound. Eating out is a treat. You don't just go out for Japanese food. Each restaurant caters to a specific type. You would be hard pressed to find a Japanese restaurant similar to those in North America, where everything from soup to nuts is typically available. Here, tradition, quality, regionalization, and, above all, specialization is the name of the game—forget about a little bit of everything.

You will find diners catering to one but only one of a slew of culinary styles: yakitori, sushi, ramen, tempura, shabu shabu, suki yaki, udom, etc. Tonight soba is our treat. Buckwheat noodles in a hot beef broth, with refills and eaten with chopsticks. It's a nondescript hole-in-the-wall operation but the simple food is excellent and totally authentic—except for the off-key soundtrack: "The girl from Ipanema"?

It's a lengthy experience for me with my own plodding delivery of slithering bootlaces from bowl to mouth. Local customers come and go. Neighbours firing it down with the clack clack clack of a grandma knitting, high on crystal meth.

I half expect those chopsticks to burst into flames. Others more languorously enjoy every mouthful, slurping candidly, the ultimate compliment, music to any Japanese cook's ears.

As I eat and eat I can feel my waistline and belt start to form sumo-like contours, so enough is enough. We find eating out, pricewise, to be quite comparable to home. It is nice to find that what you see is what you pay for—no tipping, no taxes, a bargain.

Day-to-day commerce is not as current as you might expect—a lot of cash is used and manual signatures still prevail over swipes and taps. Time to pay up and walk back to the hotel. It's a treat to walk the streets of a big city in the dark of night without a care in the world. It's a law-abiding, honest country. The murder rate is the lowest in the world—lose your wallet in Tokyo and 80 percent of the time someone will hand it in to the police. People are so honest they even put nice coat hangers in the hotel closets.

The deer, however, are another story. The next day we take a trip to the World Heritage site of Nara, about a forty-five-minute train ride from Kyoto. Its Buddhist temple is the largest in Japan and also the largest wooden building in the world. We were prepared to be impressed but not to be pickpocketed by deer—1,200 of these loveable protected herbivores have gone rogue. Bands of these brazen bandits (I bet they have tattoos under that fur) roam the grounds and prey on unsuspecting tourists. I am not spared when one of these creatures has the audacity to sneak up behind me, stick its nose in my trouser pocket, and rip out the map I am carrying.

I get off luckier than some. The deer have had their horns removed by park staff to prevent any serious violence—the odd pilgrim being gored wasn't good for business.

Back in the city for our penultimate evening, we continue to indulge in the gastronomic choices available.

For a change we make for a trendy glass and steel joint with wine bottles arranged by the battalion. Nothing stays the same forever. Menus record the evolution of globalization. We give the moussaka and tapas a miss. The fashions of the youth also mark the same trend towards statements of personal style and individuality, the current cosmopolitan conformity of the "me" mindset. It is a shift from the more traditional conservative conformity of the "we"-focused older generation, which came with its own pitfalls.

Cultural norms shape innovations in technology too. The national preoccupation with physical and spiritual cleanliness has, so to speak, found an outlet in plumbing. All manner of gadgetry is available. I find myself being caught up in the fascination myself.

This eatery being a new establishment, it must have the latest in super bowls. Not even needing to go, I go. The anticipation is unbearable. Being a budding aficionado I don't let unfamiliar signage be an impediment. Icons are commonplace: blue for boys is a giveaway and the Japanese Kanji symbol with a little imagination looks like a man running. What could be more apt?

I enter and as I approach my chosen cubicle, a high-tech door slides silently open, and the stainless steel and chrome chamber invites me in like a welcoming air lock on some faraway space station. The lights rise in brightness as the toilet lid eerily opens as the first few bars from *Space Odyssey* rend the silence.

Dun . . . dun . . . DUN . . . DUN!

As the timpans crescendo, I gird my loins for the first movement.

****

We awake the following morning to find that the cherry blossoms have finally started to pop just in time for our departure from the "city of flowers," although for me I would be more inclined to name it the city of food. We have our last breakfast at the ryokan, an eight-course extravaganza plus rice plus soup plus tofu. I am no bean curd convert, but this tofu is a delicious creamy treat, kept warm over your own small burner, a crème brûlée-like delicacy. Kyoto is to tofu what champagne is to Champagne. Who knew?

The dining room is the setting for an east-meets-west admixture—not because we are the only white people present, but more that the Japanese guests are engaged in a sort of cultural mashup. One lady is wearing a kimono/yukata and Nikes, another a zori (Japanese indoor thong-type sandal) and trench coat, probably Armani. The music is all Japanese—piped-in serene kabuki instrumentals. But the compositions are weirdly occidental Ave Maria and then "When you wish upon a star." It's like they are saying, "We are interested in adopting some of the Western ways, but only as a complement to our own style." A sort of a national cognitive dissonance.

Unable to top that for gluttony, we go down-market for our last meal, a little quirky too. We follow handwritten signs down a back street through a courtyard and finally up a stairwell. Arriving is like stepping into your Japanese auntie's apartment and sitting down at her kitchen counter. Yer auntie will make you dinner. Mamasan invites us in and plies us with mounds of steaming noodles.

Fingers too exhausted to eat anymore, I put down the chopsticks. Four other elderly guys are there reading their newspapers and having a smoke. We watch the sports highlights on the small, non-flat-screen TV above the fridge. Some baseball, then the big boys wearing diapers—the sumo wrestlers—fill the screen. I watch the highlights, all fifteen seconds of it. After the same clip is replayed five times in a row it finally dawns on me that I am witnessing the whole match—blink and you'd miss it.

After settling up we make to leave. The hostess intercepts us, bows, nods, and shows us to the door. She opens it and stands there waving as we make our way down the stairs. "Bye, auntie. See ya next time."

Home beckons, time to try my hand at haiku, all that chopsticks work has given me carpal tunnel syndrome—it will be short.

Butterfly feet in the east
Seasons soften
Slowly slowly the memory

Part IV

OCCIDENTALLY DISORIENTED

Chapter 21

Welcome to the Hotel Lilliputia

Life has improved, comrades. Life has become more joyous.

"TWO MIRACLES OF MASCARA, HER EYES LOOKED LIKE THE CORPSES OF TWO SMALL CROWS THAT HAD CRASHED INTO A CHALK CLIFF."

—*Clive James*

"PEOPLE ARE ALMOST ALWAYS BETTER THAN THEIR NEIGHBOURS THINK THEY ARE."

—*GEORGE ELIOT*

Our jaunts to Nepal brought us to the realization that we have as much fun hanging out with our Nepali friends and acquaintances as we did on our actual hikes. So in an effort to bring a less decadent flavour to one of our trips, we decide to try a little volunteering. I contact AFID (Accounting for International Development), an agency that matches professionals with charity organizations for pro bono consulting. It is a bit like Tinder for accountants.

"Sweet, sincere gentleman. Retired sixty-ish accountant seeks needy Asian NGO for mutually satisfying relationship. For a committed short-term assignation.

"Open to trying new things, or just long walks through your ledgers. I am experienced and sensitive. I know that you are out there. Who knows where it may lead.

"Recent picture of your balance sheet appreciated. No cranks, please."

A suitable match having been found, we leave Victoria on a chilly February day and so begins our trip to Cambodia.

It is night when we arrive and, as usual, have our breath taken away as we are swallowed up by the sticky, hot fog of air ever present in southeast Asia. Our hotel is on the northwest outskirts of the capital, Phnom Penh (PP). It will be our home while I am working with the Beacon of Light (BoL), a local NGO headquartered in the city, for the next two months.

The hotel has been recently built. Only two years ago here thrived a rice paddy field. But the proportions are of a strange mix, as if it was something designed by Jonathan Swift. Our first room has enough room for a bed and luggage if you piled it on top of each other. Getting onto the bed would require you to launch yourself from the doorway. One night of that was plenty. We upgraded to a larger suite.

The new room is certainly more spacious and the bubble-gum-sized bars of soap and children's-sized furniture helped create the illusion of size. The common hotel areas are of a different scale altogether: massive, highly polished mahogany appointments. Tables a solid eight inches of thick slabs of gleaming oiled tropical hardwood, stools fifteen inches in diameter so heavy you can only slide them across the tiled floors. Recliners and chairs built of similar lumber of a scale that three people could easily fit on each. Apparently, the culture amongst the rich here is that it is important to demonstrate one's wealth and this is one way to do it. Cambodia's forests are taking a pounding as a result. The Chinese and Vietnam markets being on the doorstep are helping to accelerate deforestation.

I hate to say it but whoever had the interior design contract could have used a little advice on the décor too—a little more Martha Stewart and little less 1950s Moscow stodginess. In the lobby there are a half a dozen pictures of the owner/manager in a variety of Dame Edna Everage frocks, frozen perm, pancake makeup, and pearls. An Asian version of Maggie Thatcher gone goth. She glowers down at you from the walls like she's the chairman of the politburo. This lady of the house has the eyebrows of Stalin and apparently the management style to match. Her obsession with her own image would put an Instagram influencer to shame.

After a few days we start settling in, get to know the staff—it is hard to fake any formality when some of them sleep in the lobby in their PJs. I try a few words of Khmer (Cambodian). By the time I master "good day"—*"johm rib sua"*—it's nightfall. My pronunciation being what it is I could have been describing anything from chickens to candle-making. Anyway, my feeble attempts garner a few laughs from them, so we earn some brownie points for entertainment value. The setting is informal so we soon get to know the other guests, few though they may be. A more eclectic cast of characters you'd be hard pressed to find. I get the impression that Cambodia is the sort of place where an expat can invent whatever past or present they fancy. Trying to create a future is a whole different matter.

As an example, we have Kevin, variously a banker specializing in micro-financing, an executive for Boeing, and an entertainer. He's all trilby, skinny trousers and skin moisturizer, as well as hot air. Fifty-two masquerading as thirty-nine (it pays to be friends with the front desk staff. They have all the scoop that a passport can provide and more).

All we know for sure is that Kev has his country's instincts for money and sharp practices. He has also taken a fancy to the young night watchman, Vibol. We are initially outraged at the shameless seduction of the young man. Gifts are showered, promises of stateside trips are made, it is all a bit offensive. Then in our reflective moments we relent. "Well, they are two consenting adults, so no big deal, right?" Then, "Hold on a second. This is pure deception. Kevin has no intention of sponsoring Vibol to go to the US. Shouldn't we do something?" Fortunately, before we have to figure out what we really think and, more to the point, what do we plan to do about it, Kevin mysteriously bolts from the country.

Then there is the taciturn Takeshi, a nineteen-year-old kid from Japan whose parents sent him to Cambodia to learn English, having failed to do so after living with a Sikh family in Vancouver for a month. I know. . . . I'm not making this stuff up. Takeshi is an enigmatic character who seems to just drift around all day, scuttling away on his keyboard or occasionally running errands or doing dishes. We never do figure out whether he is a guest or some kind of part-time staff. I try to get a bit more of his story, but our conversation kind of peters out when I enquire of him, "Which city are you from?" His reply is a bit of a conversation-stopper in itself. "Hiroshima."

Then there is the staff: Pooneray the cook with his watermelon-sized smile and sideways baseball cap. The three housekeeping girls, shyly charming and relentlessly busy. Their work schedule is regularly fourteen hours a day and seven days a week. All for US$180 per month—about four times the national average. And yet they are grateful. With room and board included, they are able to send a significant amount back to their poor families in the rural areas. Trixie will put her hotel training to good use here, coaching these girls on their English and bringing them up to snuff on Western expectations in the hospitality industry.

Most disturbing of all though is Darwin, a Christian missionary from the American Midwest who is having a nervous breakdown. When he actually snapped he was still living in the parsonage provided by his church. One evening he turned belligerent. His wife phoned the police and he ended up in jail for a couple of nights. Now drugged to the eyeballs, he is billeted in the hotel for an indeterminate period. Poor bugger is in his mid-thirties, has been in Cambodia for nearly twenty years, and has lost virtually all contact with anyone stateside. His wife (Japanese) and young son, whom he lives with here in PP, wants to separate from him. His mission can't have him going off the deep end with the congregation so here he sits in a futureless suspended animation and talks and talks and talks and talks . . . .

He is in a manic phase, and whenever anyone comes near or within view, the monologue commences. It's like his tongue is connected to a motion detector. Any creature, be it a gecko, a fly, or a human—that comes within range of his sensors automatically provides stimuli to verbal synapses and the outpouring begins. His voice has become the endless soundtrack of our stay like some sort of inescapable elevator music provided by CNN. Predictably, this can't last and inevitably he plumbs the depths of the depressive phase. Folks from his church come and stay overnight (stand watch, more like) with him. We try to offer some comfort, but what can you say to a guy whose few anchors in life have melted away? Disconnected from his past, his present a temporary unsustainable solution. Estranged from his family there and in the States, he finds himself face to face with an empty future. It's no wonder he's in such a desperate condition.

The hotel, though well-tended and reasonably priced isn't that busy. It's a twenty-minute tuk tuk ride from the city centre but it won't be long before it is engulfed by the relentless sprawl of Phnom Penh.

An unexpected windfall in the form of thirty doctors from the Midwest US Bible belt arrives one day. They have been redirected to Cambodia to provide some health services to the rural areas. Another flare-up of religious violence in Bangladesh has put their project there on hold. Caution is their byword and they drink only filtered then boiled water, avoiding the local bottled water in PP because there are no standards. The Lord will protect us, but there is no point in taking any chances.

Chinese New Year is a big deal in Cambodia and the hotel owners go for it in a big way. We are invited to the feast. Madam Edna,[21] her husband, and three adolescent children prove to be generous hosts. Thanks to the translation skills of their children, we have some interesting discussions. Of course they aren't the basket of deplorables that we were thinking they would be.

It is always annoying when your prejudices don't conveniently work out as conceived.

21 https://www.youtube.com/watch?v=Ac0CJn0-6tE

Chapter 22

White Man Walking (the Streets of Phnom Penh)

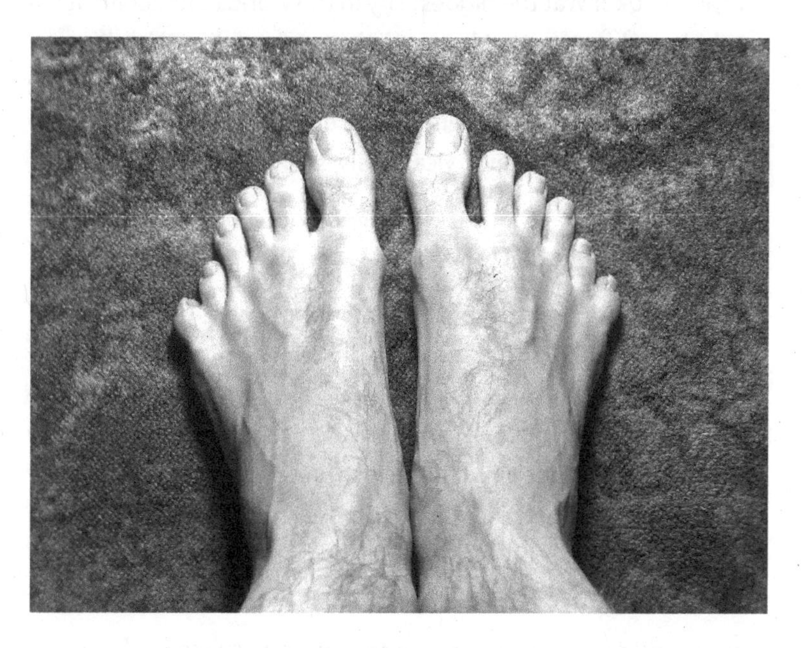

Cambodian abacus

"YOU TALKIN' TO ME?"

—Robert De Niro

"SOMETIMES ALL IT TAKES TO STOP TRAFFIC IS THAT RIGHT PAIR OF RED PUMPS."

—Tommy Ton

So as we fly toward Cambodia, I try to picture what our visit will be like. No helpful imaginings come to mind. Everyone knows about the troubles in the past, and the big temple too. But what troubles! Somewhere between 1.5 and 3 million deaths during the genocide in the late 1970s—roughly a quarter of the population. And what a temple! Angkor Wat the biggest city in the world at its zenith. It is a morbid combination that brings in the tourist dollars. No different, I guess, than anywhere else on earth where the biggest draws are often the churches and battlefields. The emotional pull to experience hope and despair, however vicariously, seems universal.

More of that later—there is entertainment to be had in the hum drum of the day-to-day too.

It is a typical atypical sort of a day in Phnom Penh. The sun rises at its usual time: 6:45 a.m. We are at a latitude of twelve degrees north, so the time of sunrise varies only by an hour or so over the whole year. The orangey glow valiantly tries to pierce the smoggy, hazy layer enshrouding the city. It is the forty-seventh consecutive day of our trip without a drop of rain. The temperature will rise to around thirty-four degrees, not far from its historical high of thirty-seven and not far from its historical low of thirty-one, for that matter.

I am an oddity on my fifteen-minute morning walk to work. No one but mad dogs and white people walk in the morning sun. No one in PP actually walks—anywhere at any time. Sidewalks are scarce and treacherous. Toddlers learn to steer as soon as they can reach their mother's handlebars, kids have their own motorbikes—the 100cc Honda Hero seems to be the model of choice. There is no minimum driving age requirement. As long as your feet can reach the pedals, you are good to go. The schoolyards are packed with motorized bikes and scooters. The parents in this city don't believe in driving their kids to school—they give them a motorcycle instead.

If you do happen to see a bicycle it is invariably being ridden by a white person.

As is common, a friendly motorcyclist will cruise by me, wave, yell hello, slow to a crawl, and offer me a ride. I know by now that the friendliness is real, but also that so is the entrepreneurial spirit. These freelance guys offer "moto" service—i.e., they negotiate a fare with pedestrians at random and deliver them where they want to go. Phnom Penh: home of Uber but without GPS.

I arrive at the office. Things are in full swing. The guitars are out and the staff are singing their devotions. Office attire is bare feet, so I slip out of my shoes—it's an added bonus for an accountant to have both fingers and toes available for those big calculations. It is a pleasant way to start the day. The fact that there is another power outage today further complements the tranquility. The organization is faith-based, but despite the religious overtones and unquestioned faith that the Lord will provide, the pervasiveness of business speak has reached even here. The universality of key performance indicators, strategic plans, capacity building, customer engagement, etc., etc., abound.[22] The executive staff arrive and show me up by all wearing socks.

Later in the day, Piset, the night desk clerk from our hotel, rescues me from another migraine-inducing discussion about "capturing customer-centric data." As arranged, he has come to take me to the dentist. I have shattered a tooth chomping down on a nut. He arrives fully prepared with a kids' plastic crash helmet for me. You don't get this sort of service at the Four Seasons. We make a few guesses about the location of the doctor's office and then we are off.

Piset's English is pretty good but when he dons his full-face crash helmet communications become Ladtke auditions for Darth Vader. We are on our way—well, almost. The gas tank is empty so we stop for a fill-up. It's more of a snack stand than a gas station, the fuel

22 https://www.youtube.com/watch?v=o7_vGIWqgdg

being dispensed from plastic two-litre pop bottles. The cost comes to $2.70. I pay with a US$5 bill, and, this being Cambodia, which has two currencies in interchangeable simultaneous use, I get $1 and 5,000 riel in change, eight notes in all. It gives the old grey matter a workout until you get used to it.

When I say snack stand maybe I should say snake stand. The fast food on offer includes crispy battered gecko, crickets, and snake on a stick. I decline the less-than-tempting amuse-bouche. I camouflage my squeamishness by delivering an Oscar-worthy performance miming the agonies of toothache. I should have auditioned for *Marathon Man*. Opt instead for an Ankor—yes, so it is beer, but it has kind of pain-killing properties, right?

Refuelled, we launch back into the traffic only to stop 100 metres down the road—his cell phone needs topping up now. By now it is well and truly rush hour. The streets are jammed and traffic is painfully slow. PP's disparity in wealth is clearly evident as the Range Rovers and what seems to be PP's equivalent of the Honda Civic, the ubiquitous Lexus RX 300, jostle for position with every other possible example of motorized and unmotorized transport. The creativity of how these vehicles are laden with goods and people is only limited by the unlimited imagination of the drivers. Exactly how many tables is it possible to load onto a tuk tuk? Every journey reveals a new first. My all-time favourite is the motorcyclist who whips past us hooked up to an IV feed, his girlfriend on the back seat riding side saddle holding his tripod stand with saline bag attached aloft like Brittania and her trident.

Traffic lanes do not exist; it is basically organized chaos. I get a little history lesson in the process: a number of PP landmarks still bear the names of former troublemakers—the Russian market, Charles de Gaulle Blvd., Mao Tse Tung Blvd., curiously magnanimous of the city managers given the current worldwide trend to rename anything with a hint of colonialism. I am not expecting to hear about a George Bush freeway in Baghdad any time soon.

The traffic is a living organism with a consciousness of its own, like swirling starlings at sunset, we are but one tiny element in the ebb and flow. The distance between vehicles is maybe six inches on all sides. Our motorcycle is small/narrow even by Cambodian standards. My knees protrude a good six inches out from the width of the handlebars. The hairs on my knees act like antennae as I feel the closeness of our neighbours through them. On some occasions, things are so claustrophobic that I have to squeeze my knees tight to keep from having them brushed by passing vehicles. I keep this to a minimum in case Piset thinks I'm getting overly familiar. He's a married man, after all.

Piset is a good driver and has all the skills necessary for navigating these streets. He is decisive, creative, not easily influenced by traffic signs or regulations and loves to open up the throttle when those few glorious opportunities arise. I look over his shoulder to see exactly how fast we are going. The speedometer reads a disappointingly uninformative zero. We are probably doing about forty KPH. I soon realize that driving in a car here would be madness. Riding on the back of a scooter you are king of the road. It is a thrill a minute and certainly a risky proposition but immensely satisfying as you surge past hulking SUVs stuck mute and anonymous like boulders in a river. The entertainment is nonstop as you jink and slalom past the obstacles, a thousand moving conversations begin and end with an ever-changing cast of characters.

Eventually we arrive at the dentist, close to 4 p.m., but just in time for the last appointment of the day. The office is a gleaming sci-fi set. Everything is tiled and white. The receptionists are cute in their starched pink scrubs, the dentist is in a fetching shade of lavender. We could be on the bridge of the Starship Enterprise. The patients are required to leave their shoes in the lobby and don white Crocs.

My dentist is a taciturn Cambodian fellow who looks about twenty-five. His surgery doesn't have any reassuring certificates from the US or Europe, dang. Well, what the heck, it is either this or run the risk of my tooth breaking again in Nepal, where the dentists' main line of work is usually repairing bicycles.

Thinks to self: *Let's do this*. Two hours later I'm done and reasonably happy with the results so far. All went well except for Piset worried that I had somehow left already without him and phoned me on my cell phone predictably at the crucial moment. The dentist, unperturbed, fished my phone out of my trouser pocket, and answered the call while he still had his left hand in my mouth, pressing the impression mould into the offending cavity. This younger generation, I tell you.

All patched up I rejoin Dark Helmet and we set off on our homeward journey under the rapidly darkening skies. Night drops like a guillotine at these latitudes. Piset shows off his many manoeuvres—up packed one-way streets the wrong way, through red lights, shortcuts through the gas station forecourts, U turns in the middle of the highway, up the railway tracks for a few hundred yards, if there is a semi flat sidewalk try that, weaving his way through the traffic to the front of a jam is fair game too. These are the rules of the road and fully accepted and expected. Any deviation will only cause confusion.

The major intersections of course are where the greatest congestion occurs. Things slow to a crawl as the vehicles skillfully merge. These are also ideal ambush spots. A Cambodian girl, a passenger in a tuk tuk in front of us, has her necklace stolen, ripped from her neck as she sits waiting for the traffic to move. The whole event is over in seconds as the robber springs from the shadows and just as swiftly sprints to safety down an adjacent dark alley.

We pass numerous KTV lounges. This particular strip is all lit up like Vegas. It is still early in the evening so there isn't much action. Young women—girls, many of them—dolled up in heels, short skirts, and makeup, sit in the doorways on plush couches engrossed in their smartphones. This doesn't help to speed up the commute. Later in the evening wealthy Khmer men and foreign tourists will arrive, pick whomever takes their fancy, and head for one of the private karaoke rooms. The girls will ply their callers with overpriced drinks, make small talk, and serenade them with a song or two. They are literally singing for their supper. The entertainment usually does not end there. Money talks and the clients get to decide what else they would like on the menu.

The lounge owners take the cash and pay the girls a salary. The lure of better pay and the pressure to send money home to their families back in the countryside create an irresistible dynamic. And now they work night after night, too ashamed to admit to their families how they earn their money and too responsible for putting food on their families' tables to be able to stop.

Most of the girls are from rural areas and came to the city to work in the garment factories. Over 600,000 workers toil in these sweatshops, most of them on the grueling 996 shift.

That is from 9 a.m. to 9 p.m., six days a week, in buildings where the temperatures regularly exceed thirty-five Celsius, all for US$200 a month. Cambodia has cheaper labour costs than China, so Chinese-owned manufacturing companies have opened scores of factories here in recent years. These intermediary companies in turn sell their products custom made to their buyers' brand specifications.

Most of the buyers are big-name household brands like Nike, Adidas, and The Gap. Its a win, win, win proposition. The corrupt government gets to cream a few bucks off the top granting manufacturing licences, no questions asked. The big-name brands are happy to wash their hands of the unpleasantness associated with the making of their product. They are also pretty happy to pocket the profits made on the backs of someone else's enslaved workers.

But, wait, there is another win: those corporations are then in a position to "give back." They can do this by signing sponsorship deals with sporting superstars. Those multi-millionaires lend street cred to their brands. Nike reputedly signed a sponsorship deal with LeBron James worth $32 million a year. We the masses now have the pleasure of being able to listen to these humanitarians spout off about human rights abuses and watch them run around in Black Lives Matter T-shirts.

Globalization: it ain't the great leveler it was cracked up to be.

Chapter 23

Put A Sock in It

Then the man hides his tummy banana in the lady's twinkle cave.

"IF I THINK MORE ABOUT DEATH THAN SOME OTHER PEOPLE IT'S PROBABLY BECAUSE I LOVE LIFE MORE THAN THEY DO."

—*Angelina Jolie*

"COMMON MEN TALK BAGFULLS OF RELIGION BUT DO NOT PRACTISE EVEN A GRAIN OF IT. THE WISE MAN SPEAKS LITTLE EVEN THOUGH HIS WHOLE LIFE IS RELIGION EXPRESSED IN ACTION."

—*Ramakrishna*

Trying to break out of the bean counter mould, I arrange for Trixie and me to accompany Oudom, one of the HQ supervisors of BoL, on his upcoming visit to a field office in Takeo province, some 150 kilometres from PP. I am not religious and have a bit of a built-in skepticism about faith-based organizations doing humanitarian work. Is it about providing help or is it about gaining converts? I want to see for myself.

The work that the Beacon of Light does is, for the most part, funded by a church in Iowa, and it employs only Khmer staff. The organization's board is a mix of representatives from the USA, a nurse from the Netherlands, and local Khmer businessmen. The nurse is now repatriated to Holland together with five of the six children she adopted while working in Cambodia for twenty-five years. Hers is a story worth hearing, but you will have to make do with this instead.

The board meets a couple of times a year and the expats visit to check on the progress of the agency in addressing their key objectives: street-proofing kids, healthy hygiene practices, sustainable agriculture, and community-building.

On arrival in the village we are met by BoL's regional facilitator and the village elders. The first session that we sit in on is held under the shade of a bamboo thatch shelter. Parents and youths are being briefed on the dangers of illegal immigration. Men, mostly young, are often dazzled by human traffickers with tales of the bright lights and good paying work in Vietnam and Thailand, the ugly truth being that they will find themselves illegally in a foreign country in virtual slavery. Often illiterate, unable to speak the local language, and unable to approach the authorities for fear of imprisonment, they are totally at the mercy of their handlers.

Some parents relate tragic personal experiences of children gone in search of fortune, never to be heard from again.

The attendees have come from the local village and surrounding settlements and have at best a Grade 3 education. Only a few are literate, so the presenters have to use every trick in the book to get their message across. I feel illiterate myself—Cambodian script doesn't give me so much as a clue as to what was going on. There is no point for me in even attempting to try and decipher the flip charts. They all look like someone has randomly emptied a bucket of worms on a sheet of 24X36 paper and then run a steamroller over them.

Khmer script
កញ្ជ្រោងពណ៌ត្នោតរហ័សលោតពីលើឆ្កែខ្ជិល

Cambodian
kanhchrong pnrtnaot rhsa lot pi leu chhke khchel
khe t dauchchea tokkata dab bl

English
The quick brown fox jumps over the lazy dog.

Cambodian: a tricky language to pick up in eight weeks.

All kinds of media, cartoons, role playing, PowerPoint, posters, but mostly dialogue are used. The local language, Khmer, is just as mystifying as the script. Luckily our guide Lon sits behind me and gives me the live blow-by-blow translation. I feel like I am sitting at the UN. Come to think of it, they might be more in touch with what needs to be done if they were to do their work on site. The background soundtrack of the quacking ducks, barking dogs, mooing cows, and the chomp chomp of the goats would be sure to add a certain *je ne sais quoi* to the proceedings.

The next session is a lot more fun but undeniably an even more fundamental topic, if that makes any sense. A group of youngsters are being schooled in the benefits of good hygiene, especially as it relates to food. The message is delivered this time using sock puppets, and, judging from the expression on the kids' faces, the script must have been written by Stephen King. The bug-eyed kids are paralyzed with fear watching as the dastardly Mr. Diarrhea, a brown sock, is stalked and ultimately vanquished by the two white socks, Mr. and Mrs. Soap. A spine-tingling horror production David Cronenberg would have been proud of. With a happy ending and good triumphing over evil, the kids relax. We finish off the segment with the ever-popular "preventing the diarrhea" song, complete with sound effects. It is a transformative experience. I will never own a pair of brown socks again. There is ample scope here for some focus group to improve the racial stereotyping undertones still prevalent in the messaging the old "white good-brown bad" trope still rearing its insidious head.

By now it is time for a short tea break, and some hospitality from our hosts. Oudom obviously isn't confident that our host has seen the brown sock tutorial and promptly thrusts a water bottle into my hand. It helps avoid one of those uncomfortable moments when you have to choose between rejecting someone's genuine generosity or running the risk of exposure to some nasty bugs, of which there are plenty.[23]

Interlude over with, we attend the discussion about STDs. It seems to be a popular topic. There is plenty of chatter and animated participation (no socks this time). I guess when you work and live with animals all day you don't have many illusions or reservations about what is anatomically possible, however improbable. As the conversation becomes more graphic, Lon, our city boy translator, becomes more and more uncomfortable as he struggles to find the right words.

I am still not sure what colour an olive-skinned person blushes, but I am pretty sure, given the beads of sweat on his forehead and heat emanating from him, that that is what Lon is doing. When Oudum turns up on the scene and mercifully ends his torture by telling us that it is time for lunch, Lon looks like a hostage that had just been set free.

---

23 https://www.theguardian.com/environment/2017/jun/28/a-million-a-minute-worlds-plastic-bottle-binge-as-dangerous-as-climate-change

For lunch we have some fried noodles at a roadside kitchen/restaurant. Finished with eating, the BoL team stretches out side by side in the five parallel hammocks in the forecourt, whip out their cell phones, and get caught up on Facebook. Trixie and I decide to go for a walk down to the Mekong River to watch the cattle herders bring their cows down into the water and then give them a thorough scrub, making sure not to miss any of the nooks and crannies. It is a pity Lon isn't there to give us an uncensored description of the proceedings. Nah, that would have been cruel. Bovine scrub-up finished, the men see to their own ablutions. Man and beast emerge from the waters dripping and glistening in the bright sunlight and amble back to the fields.

After lunch we attend the next session, which is about community and, more specifically, land ownership. The graphics need little translation: "Hang onto your land" is the gist of the message. Easy to say, but hard to do when you are a subsistence farmer. Fortunately, the banks are there to help with micro-financing in years of drought, which are becoming more frequent since 70 percent of the forests have been logged since 1979. Micro-finance interest rates are a reasonable 3 percent—well, actually, that is 3 percent a MONTH. Not to worry—those helpful banks will take that pesky land off your hands if you can't come up with the interest.

It has been an impressive day. We say our goodbyes to the villagers and the BoL team, who have all been so patient and gracious with us. I do get the feeling they have seen it all before though, the retinue of curious Westerners checking out what they are up to.

Despite the lack of "Hallelujahs" and "praise the lords," I am now a believer.

These people are making a difference.

Johm rip sua today, gone tomorrow.

Chapter 24

The Do Ron, Ron, Ron, The Do Ron, Ron

DON KING - KING KONG . . . Why the confusion?

"THE ONE WHO KNOWS THAT HE IS CONFUSED IS NOT THAT CONFUSED."

—Zhuangzi

"HE PICKED ME UP AT SEVEN AND HE LOOKED SO FINE

DA DO RON RON RON THE DO RON RON."

– The Crystals

Being retired, planning a vacation is never far from my thoughts. So after a month working in hot, dusty, polluted PP, we figure that it is time for a holiday from the trip and a temporary change of country if not scenery. Our destination is Laos. Our visit will last a week and our jumping-off point is Kratie, a dusty (aren't they all?) town on the Mekong River. Its only real claim to fame is that it is home to the rare Irrawaddy dolphin, an endangered freshwater dolphin whose anatomy more resembles Alfred Hitchcock than Flipper. We are fortunate enough to see a handful of them on our sightseeing boat trip. I can't help but be surprised that they are surviving at all given that the Irrawaddy River is about 1,000 kilometres to the west, two countries over in Burma; maybe they came here to escape the military dictatorship. These dolphins are smart, have brains 20 percent bigger than humans, don't you know.

We are up early as usual for the first leg of our 133-kilometre journey to our destination at the "Four Thousand Islands," situated on the Mekong just across the border with Laos. "How many legs can there be for a 133-kilometre trip?" you ask. Well, four, according to our booking agent, Ricky. "Little bus, big bus, big bus, some kind of boat."

"Where is our ticket? Will the buses have numbers?" I ask.

"No need ticket. My cousin do this lots, no problem, you trust me, I give you my business card and phone number."

Do we have a choice? Anyway, what could possibly go wrong?

The first leg starts inauspiciously. The little bus, which apparently means a minivan, rolls up at 8:00 a.m., instead of 7:00 a.m., due to mechanical issues with the wheel, and needs to be fixed before we get to the bumpy road. It's a small bus with a big heart. By the time we leave town we are sixteen cramped, sweating, ornery individuals trying to act happy and positive. Backpacks on laps, bags of rice underfoot, and the aforementioned defective wheel wedged in between passengers make for fetus-like coziness. If ever I needed an out-of-body experience it is then.

Fortunately on the ride to our first transfer point we have a few stops. Folks stir themselves from their self-induced catatonia, those in the back shimmy out windows to stretch numb limbs as there is no way for them to make it to the door, and thankfully, we unload a few items.

We finally arrive at the promised land at 11:00 a.m., sighs of relief, cold drinks, food, and then laughter. To kill the time before the "big bus" comes at 1:00 p.m., people strike up conversations with strangers. It's a bit like speed dating as folk try to establish each other's travel cred before buying into the latest hot travel tip.

The couple we end up chatting to is a bit out of our league. An Austrian park ranger and her Russian partner, a ranger and part-time tour guide.[24] Not your tour bus type guide, but "you are dropped off in the Siberian wilderness, lose your food-laden canoe over the waterfall, down to your last three bullets, hike out on your own to arrange a rescue party" type of a guide. I let him know that I saw a really big spider at the hotel.

One o'clock passes. "Oh, bus will be here at 2:00 p.m." Variations on this refrain continue until 4:15 p.m. We fill the time predictably arguing with the "big bus number 1" representative about why we have no ticket—thank goodness for cell phones—Ricky, don't lose that number.

The bus lurches into view at 4:20 p.m. Good humour restored, we and about forty others clamber aboard and fill the bus. About five minutes into the trip, the pitch begins. The conductor warns us that we will be late arriving at the border. Fees in addition to the visa fee will be needed. I had already researched what the border

24 https://www.fiftydegreesnorth.com/article/kamchatka-bears-and-volcanoes-tour

visa fee would be. It has some sort of sliding scale where different nationalities pay different amounts—based on what I have no idea.

The Chinese pay twenty dollars while they are busy syphoning off the Mekong River into their hydro projects before it reaches Laos, the French pay thirty dollars despite seventy years of exploitive colonial rule, the Americans pay thirty-five dollars after they dropped a plane load of bombs on Laos every eight minutes for nine years during the Vietnam war. And Canadians? Well, forty-two dollars!

Huh? What! Céline Dion? Stephen Harper?? Justin Bieber??? I dunno. Because we invented the paint roller?

The bottom line is the conductor wants an additional ten dollars no matter what your country—the implied threat is that if you don't pay and try to do your own paperwork, "Big Bus Two" on the other side of the border won't wait for you. Much heated debate ensues, our new travelmates among the most involved, the "Russian Bear" stoically restraining his Austrian partner, who has gone nuclear.

We are into the tenth hour of our 133-kilometre trip, so far so good. Of our complement, about 60 percent, including ourselves, reluctantly opt to use the services of our conductor; the remainder choose to go it alone. We arrive at the border about 6:15 p.m., as the sun is setting, and ours is the only vehicle in sight. The crossing boasts a cold beer and rice shack with two staff and a few flea-bitten dogs. Not another house or soul in sight—except, that is, for a massive new but derelict and unmanned customs/security/immigration checkpoint that wouldn't be out of place in Dover.

Fifty-two dollars later (forty-two plus five dollars for a Sunday plus two dollars for a Cambodian exit stamp, plus a two-dollar processing fee, plus a dollar for an entry stamp), we kiss goodbye to our passports as our conductor plods off into the gloom, a fistful of dollars in one hand and a stack of multinational passports in the other. *Just trust me*, he says.

An hour later he returns, paperwork all taken care of, dumps the pile of passports on a wall, and invites us to rummage around to find one that suits. Reunited with our identity, we trudge across the no man's land in the dark, our goal the dim distant lights of "Big Bus Two." It is a surreal scene as the group of bedraggled travellers lug/drag backpacks and suitcases along the dusty road. It's all *For a Few Dollars More* meets *Bridge of Spies*. We pass the group of self-servers clustered under flickering mosquito-swarmed fluorescent lights outside the Laotian immigration kiosk and wonder where they will sleep tonight.

Safely aboard "Big Bus Two," we head for "some kind of boat." At about the twelve-hour mark of our journey, we arrive at the dock. Oh, joy! Here we are in a new country and, like the rest of the group, we have no local currency and, surprise, the two ATMs are broken. But the boat operator and budding Wall Street banker just happens to have enough kip to exchange for the thirty or so passengers' USD, at a very good rate— "just trust me."

Unfortunately what he doesn't have is a boat going to the Don Kong Island, where we have booked our hotel. In fact, the boat service he is providing goes only to one of the fabled 4,000 islands, like it or lump it—i.e., sleep at the dock until tomorrow. Much wrangling, shouting, calls for the constabulary, etc., ensues to no avail. The Russian Bear sagely murmurs an aside to me: "Zees crowes border treeps nayver are vorkink."

But, wait, a ray of hope! During a lull in the bedlam, Trixie is able to find out that the island he is sailing to, Don Det, is actually connected by a small bridge to Don Kon. Woo hoo! Problem solved.

An enchanting moonlit boat ride punctuated by fireflies and exotic fragrances (hour fourteen) across the Mekong further revive our spirits. On reaching Don Det, we stumble up the sandy beach into the happening party scene that it is famous for. Folks, however, seem to be having too much fun to be bothered providing transportation from this end of the island to our destination five kilometres away. Carrying our backpacks along a rutted dirt road in the pitch black is not an option.

Trixie is, as ever, undaunted. She sets off on her mission. The fact that she has no clue where she is or where she is going has never been a deterrent to her getting there. Resourceful as ever she returns to the group a few minutes later, having tracked down a willing owner of a small flatbed affair, a trailer pulled by a 100cc motorcycle. A couple of hundred thousand kip later, our group, now a Russian/German/ French/ Austrian/Canadian coalition of eight, board the wagon behind our twelve-year-old driver and head off into the dark. We successfully navigate the paddy fields, villages, and the bridge to our destination. The first hotel we come to bears the name we were looking for: the "Pan Arena," but as was our luck all day, it wasn't the one we had reserved but a shabbier version, the owner having built a second, swisher version while retaining the old one.

Still, no worries, we're nearly there. Next, we drop off the other three couples in quick succession. We set off with our driver in search of our hotel, the new "Pan Arena." No luck. We try the side roads, a few dives, nothing more. I decide to take matters into my own hands. These folks' standard of education is pretty poor and, as far as map-reading skills are concerned, I doubt if they could make it to the end of the street. So, with much invaluable prompting and guidance from me, we vainly roar up and down Main Street several times, passing our perplexed travelling companions who have by now checked into their hotels and are having their dinner at an outdoor restaurant. Again we end up in a cul-de-sac with only a decrepit guest house as an option. Not one we are willing to accept; however, the owner is very helpful and offers to phone the hotel and get directions. After a few minutes of chatter, he smiles more broadly. This is finally starting to look pretty promising. He hangs up.

At this point I think you might find the next bit more entertaining (no promises) if you hum the melody from the Crystals' song, "Da Doo Ron Ron Da Doo Ron Ron."

Turns out we are on the "The wrong Don Kon, Kon, the wrong Don Kon." !@#$%

We should have been on "The Don Kong Kong, the Damn Don Kong."

I don't want to know if you noticed the minute difference in spelling, but with 4,000 islands you'd think they'd make the names a little more different and just to pad my excuse a bit, both islands have a "Pan Arena" hotel. And there is another island called Don Khone.

So we head back to the hotels on the main drag, wave to our baffled friends who are still eating dinner, our driver beaming and exchanging jokes with his mates en route (I'm sure he was laughing with us). Eventually, we find a nice little hotel (hour sixteen) at eleven o'clock at night, its restaurant long since closed and, with zero conviction, start negotiations.

"Yes, sure, 300,000 kip sounds fine, whatever that is, and, yes, you can have my eye teeth and, yes, my left kidney, if it is a match for your sister. Just find us a bed!"

This he dutifully does. A cute little thatch and bamboo duplex reminiscent of one of the abodes in the three little piggies' fable. We throw our backpacks on the floor, have a quick wash, and collapse on the bed. Exhaustion overwhelms us. I reach over and turn out the light. The stars twinkle romantically as we slip towards sleep.

What the hell! Those aren't stars, those pinpricks of light are from our neighbours' light in the next unit, glinting through the chinks in the one-ply bamboo wall that divides our suite from theirs and, oh, great, we can hear him snoring.

On with our light again, what to do? We look at each other in silent resignation and seek solace in our meagre provisions. We ravenously delve into a sumptuous feast: one Ritz cracker with a dollop of peanut butter each, a handful of trail mix, and a half a Cliff Bar each for dessert. I reach for a beer from the minibar; it's empty. No worries—it wasn't even plugged in.

Off with the light again.

Lean back, kick off the shoes, hum a few bars of "We're on the Mekong Kong Kong the Mekong Kong Kong." Instantly fade to black. . . .

Chapter 25

Everywhere among the Hmong

Free dinner bell provided by the USAF.

"AMERICA HAS NO PERMANENT FRIENDS OR ENEMIES ONLY INTERESTS."

—*Henry Kissinger*

"THE HARDEST THING OF ALL IS TO FIND A BLACK CAT IN A DARK ROOM, ESPECIALLY IF THERE IS NO CAT."

—*Confucius*

Temperatures by the Mekong are in the comfortable mid-twenties, a pleasant respite from the oppressive heat we've been trying to get accustomed to. Entertainment opportunities are plentiful: cycling around town, visiting local silk weaver operations, haggling over ten dollars on a blanket that it takes the weaver ten months to make—but after a couple of days swimming and eating and generally chilling out, we decide that it is time for a trek.

We plump for a two-day, one-night guided hike in the highland countryside farther north. The foray starts off with a one-hour truck ride to the trailhead accompanied by our ubiquitous guide Ya Li and fellow hikers, two Gallic gals, one a potter who lives in Egypt, the other an itinerant NGO worker. They are old hands at this sort of thing. The four of us constitute a visible minority group, i.e., the only white, non Hmong or Khmu tribespeople in the vicinity for the next two days.

We are dropped off at a dusty roadside village and Ya Li takes us down a jungly trail towards a valley. He thoughtfully whacks down a bamboo pole for me to use as a staff—I feel like Charlton Heston in *The Ten Commandments*. At the bottom of the valley we come to a river and after I fail to part the seas, Ya Li summons us a canoe to make the crossing. Today's hike will take about five hours and take us through brush, jungle and, after about two hours, across farmland.

And on that farm they had some ducks, goats, pigs, chickens, and cattle of mixed gender. I don't know if the Lao are all lactose intolerant, but they don't do dairy; all the cattle farming is aimed at meat production. Suffice to say there is plenty of testosterone on display. We take care not to turn this into a Pamplona event by getting in between the bull and the object of his affection. She's a real bombshell, and by this I mean she has a real bombshell around her neck. It's either an old artillery shell or an old bomblet casing that the farmer has converted into a bell by dangling a piece of cow horn in the centre of it.

The folks in this area have found all kinds of uses for the remnants of the hostilities carried out here in the 1970s. A reputed two million tons of ordinance, 270 million bombs dropped by the US, made Laos the most heavily bombed nation per capita in history. Pretty good going considering that no one had actually claimed to be at war with them.[25] The whole scenario becomes more confusing when you consider that the CIA had several operatives in the area to enlist and train the local Hmong tribe to fight against the NVA (North Vietnamese Army). One of these operatives was Tony Poe, on whom the *Apocalypse Now* character Colonel Kurtz is supposedly based. In any event, the Hmong were willing combatants whose enthusiasm had less to do with any political reservations about communism but more to do with the NVA traipsing uninvited through their land on their way to fight in South Vietnam. As the old proverb goes, "when elephants fight, the grass suffers."

Welcome to the Heart of Darkness.

The Hmong are still a feisty, independent bunch. On our drive up to Luang Prabang I had noticed that every ten kilometres or so there would be a couple of Lao regular army infantrymen armed with AK-47s dozing by the side of the road. This, as it turns out, was in response to an attack on a car carrying five Chinese officials who had died in an ambush the previous fall and a strafing of a city bus in January of this year, fifty-seven bullet holes but no fatalities. Theories as to who the perpetrators are range from bandits, to Hmong unhappy about encroachment on their territory, to Vietnamese who covet the area and don't want to see the Chinese beating them to the punch. Google is a great thing if you know the right questions to ask before you set off, which we didn't. And by the way, while we are at it, forget your Lonely Planet. It is so passé now we seen nary a mention of it anywhere. It is all Agoda certificates of excellence or

25 http://legaciesofwar.org/about-laos/secret-war-laos/

Tripadvisor gold stars, etc. This development probably isn't news to you, but we don't get out much.

Anyway, where was I? Ah, yes, about to leave Old MacDonald's farm. We walk on for about another hour and stop for lunch at a shady spot in a dried-out riverbed. I ask Ya Li if we should be worried about where we sit: "Poisonous snakes? Spiders?"

"No, all spiders and snakes have been taken for eating. You must sit everywhere," comes the reply.

A local couple join us for a few minutes. They have been collecting supplies from the village back at the road. The woman of course has the honour of carrying all the provisions while the husband totes a rifle. It's an ancient single-shot antique that Davy Crockett would have turned his nose up at, but apparently in the right hands it can still bring a bird on the wing down at fifty metres. After a few minutes the man has caught his breath and off they go.

Lunch finished, we carry on ourselves, now padding through bone-dry paddy fields that, three months from now when the monsoon is in full swing, will be brilliant emerald green, vibrant with sprouting rice. We hear a loud crack, a rifle shot from just beyond a scrub hedge. Thinks to self: *It must be "The King of the Wild Frontier."* As we round the corner we see the hunter, he stands cradling "ol' Betsy" in his arms looking down at his kill. As we get closer, it becomes apparent that the kill isn't dead and, for that matter isn't even a bird but a snake. The head and about two inches of torso (what else would you call it?) have been cleanly severed from the rest of the body by the bullet. The body is about four feet long and still writhing. The hunter pokes at the mouth of the serpent's detached head with the rifle; the snake reflexively clamps its jaws around the muzzle. That about ends it.

"So, Ya Li," I ask "What is it about the snake?"

"Oh, it is very poisonous, will kill you. The man will take it home for dinner, very good."

The rifleman is pretty blasé about the whole thing. He picks up the edible end of the snake and, after a few photos is on his way.

Soon we reach the first settlement, a Khmu village distinguishable from a Hmong village because its houses are on stilts and have windows and because the folks are darker and have more Caucasian features. Thanks to Ya Li I am rapidly becoming an expert. The definition of an expert I have heard is "a very ordinary person far from home."

Ya Li advises that we should "take pictures everywhere," which of course we are dying to do. The problem is it kind of feels like treating these folks like exhibits in a zoo, so I end up taking shots of distant shapes standing beside nondescript structures, real Pulitzer material. I think about not bothering at all in the future.

As we take our leave of the village, I ask Ya Li about where to go to the bathroom. He responds in his usual expansive manner: "We have natural toilets, you must pee everywhere." I do my best to meet my urinatory obligations but given the finite capacity of my bladder I decide to target my contribution to just one bush. Scanning around as one does in these reflective moments, I notice the nearby embankment is pitted with holes and festooned with funnel shaped spiders webs. I quiz Ya Li again about poisonous spiders, he responds again with the "no more spiders" spiel. He won't give it to me in writing so I steer well clear.

At dusk we arrive at our overnight destination, a Hmong village. Being Hmong, Ya Li is well connected with the movers and shakers in town. Our digs will be on the grounds of the village chief. In case of any confusion I should mention that the tribespeople don't wander around in loincloths carrying spears. T-shirts, long pants, and flip flops are pretty standard issue. The kids wear spotless white dress shirts, ties, and blue pants or skirts to school.

After freshening up at the household outdoor water pump, we have a wander around the village. The folks are certainly poor, the average Lao having an annual income of about US$1,200. In this village there is precious little that is bought, but because they are self-sufficient in so many aspects there isn't the squalor and desperation that you associate with poverty in India or Latin America. It isn't an easy life by any stretch, but folks seem happy and healthy.

As evening falls we ready ourselves for dinner, watch our chicken being transported into the kitchen on a one-way ticket, share a few informal beers with the chief and Ya Li (we can sit everywhere), discuss world affairs and marvel at the fact that Canada can thrive without being able to grow bamboo. An hour or so later, our free-range organic chicken feast emerges from the chief's house, deelish. Watered and fed, we four whities head for our bamboo beds in the detached bamboo guest room ready for a restful slumber among the Hmong, far from the clamour of civilization.

However, the dogs in the neighbourhood haven't been briefed on our plan and have *eine kleine nacht music* in mind. By way of an overture we are treated to the bark, bark, bark of the local stray dogs for hours on end. Sleep finally comes until the second movement begins at some ungodly hour. The piece evolving adagio as the distant sounds of a clapped-out motorcycle draws nearer and nearer until it finally roars up, parks in front of our house. Its' headlight illuminates the inside of our room, the beams of light casting shadows of the bamboo on the walls like prison cell bars. The second movement follows in short order with the pig, agitato, and dogs again, playing a lively to-and-fro animato piece. An hour or so before dawn, the poultry section launches into the third movement, the roosters in particular delivering their notes *altissimo*. Then silence, the roosters deservedly ignored for their global inability to deliver their *reveille* for the correct time zone.

Just when you think the symphony is over, a soloist takes the stage for the coda. Brrrr . . . brrr -brrr . . . brr- brrrr . . . brr-BRRRRUARRRR . . . BRRRUARRRRR, *maggiore-fortissimo-staccato-troppo*, a chainsaw roar shatters the brief silence.

It will soon be 6:00 a.m.

In this town you can't make an omelette without breaking the silence. It's no small task if you want to have breakfast ready for your visitors at dawn: cut wood, set a fire, and find an egg.

All good things must come to an end and work is calling so we must return to the capital, and the Hotel Lilliputia and its responsibilities.

Ah, the quiet rural life. You can't beat it.

Chapter 26

A Pol Potted History of Cambodia

Pol Pot's reward for being leader of the Khmer Rouge
an unmarked grave. 3 million dead Cambodians

James Quincey, CEO, reward for managing Coca-Cola $16.7 million.
700 million people suffering from obesity,
110 billion plastic bottles a year

"CRUEL LEADERS ARE REPLACED ONLY TO HAVE NEW LEADERS TURN CRUEL."
—*Che Guevara*

"THE PAST WAS ERASED, THE ERASURE WAS FORGOTTEN, THE LIE BECAME THE TRUTH."
—*George Orwell*

For all Cambodia's golden era of culture and civilization, its current incarnation owes much to its more recent history. When independence from France came in 1953, relative peace reigned, but not without new challenges. The region formerly known as French Indochina had only recently dissolved into the three separate countries of Laos, Cambodia, and Vietnam, and they were far from stable. There was a fledgling trend toward urbanization and commerce that created the base for these new independent nations. Vietnam, a long-time regional rival of Cambodia, was at war with itself from 1955 onward. The American ground war involvement would not start for another ten years or so.

Globally, communism was being considered by many disillusioned workers and academics as a viable option. At this time, an unremarkable Cambodian student by the name of Saloth Sar was studying in France.

He had been born the eighth of nine children to prosperous farm-owning Cambodian parents. Although not a gifted student, he was able to secure scholarships to continue his learning in France. Whilst there, he became interested in politics—in particular, communism. Finding the writings of Marx too challenging, he focused his studies on the doctrines of Mao and Stalin.

This banal series of events would have a devastating impact. He would later rename himself Pol Pot and, in due course, take his place with his heroes as one of the biggest perpetrators of mass murder in history.

In the early 1970s, he refined his crude ideology and set out to create a nation independent of foreign interference, based on a non-mechanized agrarian economy that would have no money, and be free of the corrupting influence of intellectuals. He staffed his inner circle with other Cambodians who shared his idealistic revolutionary vision. Many had also had their opinions shaped by the leftist sentiment prevalent in Paris in the 1960s in Paris, a time when it was trendy to extol the benefits of Mao's revolution in China.

Brother Number One (as Pol Pot also was named) would realize his dream by building an army staffed with recruits from Eastern Cambodia. The militia was comprised of adolescent youths and uneducated and impoverished peasants. Many of them were initially inspired to join the military as a reaction to their respected monarch, Prince Sihanouk, being deposed and replaced by a military government. It says something of the lack of sophistication of these troops that their twisted allegiances saw them fighting for a Marxist revolution at the same time as a prince. Such was their desperation that the irony of the situation never tempered their resolve. What they were against was never in doubt, the urban proletariat, but what they were fighting for was much more ambiguous. Hatred trumped logic. The peasants were revolting.

Pol Pot's army, the Khmer Rouge (Khmer an ethnic group making up over 90 percent of Cambodians and rouge because of the "red" communist ideology) would conquer the capital, Phenom Penh, in 1975, and mark the start of the new era by dubbing it "Year Zero."

And then the real insanity began. Towns and cities were emptied virtually overnight. Citizens were forced to relocate to the countryside, often with no shelter or food available. Pol Pot's cadres set about purging the intelligentsia and bourgeoisie; these arbitrary descriptions were applied randomly and included shopkeepers, teachers, people wearing eyeglasses, anyone with the ability to speak a foreign language. An estimated 20 percent of the population died, some three million people.

The country is still recovering from the horrific genocide inflicted on its people by the Pol Pot regime. Even now you will seldom meet anyone who hasn't experienced some personal or family suffering from those times. The monuments to those killing fields are scattered across the country and in larger centres, like the one we visited just outside of PP, are major tourist attractions. The memorials are pretty primitive and undeveloped, which is exactly the way they were when the killings took place. Auschwitz without the technology.

The ordinariness of it all makes it harder to comprehend what actually happened. The stories told by survivors can be listened to on rented handheld recorders and bring it all too shockingly to life. For all its banality, this is the sort of place that you won't forget.

The centrepiece of the memorial is a transparent monolith containing the skulls of a few thousand of the slaughtered. The wounds in the crania are coded with coloured sticky dots: red for hammer, blue for hoe, yellow for club, black for bullet, etc. There are precious few black dots; this backward country had few weapons and ammunition was treasured. Farm implements became tools of execution. If the Khmer Rouge had had the organizational abilities or the technology of the Nazis, the massacre would have been even more catastrophic.

As you stand there before the glass obelisk where only inches from your face thousands of empty eye sockets stare back at you, it is hard not to feel voyeuristic, but there is something compelling about it all. Wrapping it up in our sophisticated language, genocide, liquidation, ethnic cleansing, seems to diminish what actually happened here. There was nothing clean about it—a slaughter, extermination, brutal hands-on mass murder.

The monument reaches skyward like some sort of malfunctioning spiritual tractor beam with its cargo of souls trapped in limbo. The skulls seem to be silently pleading, "God, take me from this hell on earth." Was that what these poor souls were thinking as their mortality closed in on them?

Did the killers know before this all started what they were capable of? One wonders if the victims were that much different than their executioners. Do any of us really know what we might do in the right/wrong circumstances?

In 1977, as all this horror was playing out, a twenty-four-year-old Khmer Rouge battalion commander was defecting to the Vietnamese. His name was Hun Sen and he would return with the invading Vietnamese army in 1979 and topple the Pol Pot regime. Brother Number One and the remnants of the Khmer Rouge army fled to the western hills bordering Thailand.

International politics being what they are, China and some Western countries, including the USA, continued to recognize Pol Pot's regime as the legitimate government of Cambodia and enabled the regime to have a seat at the UN council of nations until 1982. Presumably the self-serving thinking was: "it is better to have a wacko genocidal maniac as a representative of a country than the Russian-backed Vietnamese installing a puppet government in Phnom Penh." The old "if one more domino falls to communist ideology, democracy is doomed" trope. The fact that the USA had its nose bloodied by this same military in the Vietnam war probably still stung a bit.

During this time the Chinese continued to supply arms to the Khmer Rouge and, mysteriously, weaponry identified as being of US and Swedish origin also surfaced in KR hands. A Don Corleone-inspired mentality of "if your enemy is also my enemy, we must be friends" seemed to govern Western policy.

Hun Sen, having further ingratiated himself with the occupying Vietnamese, steadily rose through the ranks and became prime minister in 1985 at age thirty-two. Another truly ironic state of affairs. Hun Sen, a crafty but poorly educated peasant who joined the army as a seventeen-year-old, would become a ruthless, dictatorial, billionaire prime minister for life while his predecessor, Pol Pot, a Marxist revolutionary from a comfortable background, would end up dying of a heart attack at seventy-two. His funeral was an unceremonious affair. He was cremated on a pile of old tires in the jungle close to the border with Thailand with only a few aging comrades looking on.

Cambodia has emerged from these years of turmoil, genocide, civil war, and occupation by foreign nations little better off, still governed—most would say ruled—by Hun Sen. There is no doubt that he is a juggler with many balls in the air, skilled at parlaying the guilt, paranoia, and aspirations of the superpowers (Russia, USA, and China) into massive aid funding. He was also quick to spot the opportunities that foreign business interests would bring. In the process, he has amassed a personal fortune from a poverty-stricken country.

From the buzz of activity in PP you could be forgiven for thinking that the country is flourishing. Money is certainly in evidence, there is no shortage of flashy cars, expensive shops, and restaurants. Buildings materialize virtually before your eyes; all the essentials—condos, casinos, luxury hotels—abound. The nice-to-haves—hospitals, sewerage systems, garbage disposal, clean water, electricity and streetlights—will presumably follow if needed.

Empty, newly built gated communities incongruously sit like deserted islands of affluence as a sea of windswept plastic garbage laps at their protective walls. The workers that build these palaces cook their dinners over open fires in the tin-roofed shanty town just down the street. It is their home for now, but also soon to be consumed in the frenzy for development.

But where does all this money come from? Illegal activities such as drug trafficking, predatory logging practices, human trafficking, money laundering, and misappropriated foreign aid all provide the haves with more haves. But graft flourishes at all levels.

Private schooling is profitable, so available. Public education is rudimentary and sporadic. Teachers can't rely on a paycheque coming regularly so ask for "contributions" from parents and extra cash for things like setting and marking exams. Good marks cost a bit more.

However, it is at the government level that the corruption is at its most rampant. Take the central lake in Phnom Penh, Boeung Kak, for an example. It was expropriated by the government who then forcibly evicted the 18,000 residents. A ninety-nine-year lease of the property was then granted to the wife of one of Hun Sen's cabinet ministers. In short order, the ninety hectares of fresh water lake were filled in with sand, a lot of it dredged from the banks of the nearby Mekong River, destabilizing it in the process too. Chunks of this valuable real estate were then sold to Chinese developers. If you are interested in learning more about this shocking travesty, watch the award-winning documentary *Every Bird Needs A Nest.*[26]

The business ties with Vietnam are still strong, but the dominant player is now China. And with Hun Sen still at the helm, the saying goes that "Cambodia is for sale." It may in fact be more accurate to say that, with Hun Sen in charge, Cambodia has been sold. Forty-five percent of the land and twenty percent of the coastline have been leased to foreign investors. Corporate colonialism's occupation is complete. A hundred and fifty thousand landowners have been displaced as Cambodia assumes the status of a wholly owned subsidiary of China.

Factory work has replaced farming for many Cambodians. Dozens of foreign-owned garment factories employ women working for sixty-seven cents an hour for sixty-hour work weeks. When out for our post-dinner evening strolls we would see truck loads of women being emptied out onto the unlit streets near our hotel. This would be at seven o'clock at night. We would never see them in the morning. They would be at work before we had even gotten up. We have entered some strange twilight zone, some weird inversion where corporations have the same rights as individuals, but clearly an individual hasn't got the same rights as a corporation.

26 https://www.youtube.com/watch?v=dH5gjirUKA8

Government has mandated a 10 percent increase in the hourly wage rate. This is no Robin Hood scenario. The increases would come into effect just before the 2018 general election. The garment workers of course now have no land and often live in shanty-town housing complexes provided for the workers by their employers or wealthy government business owners. When salaries increase, the rent soon follows suit. The lord (Hun Sen) giveth and the lord taketh away. What happens when all of that disillusionment boils up?

With newspapers summarily shut down, political parties banned, dissidents arrested or assassinated, and media and TV outlets managed by Hun Sen's family-owned companies, it is clear that the dynasty is being built to endure. The question is: how long will the people tolerate this abuse of power?

As the SUVs get bigger, the authorities get more arrogant, and the walls get higher, you have to think that this is not going to end well.

History never says "goodbye," only "see you later."

Chapter 27

Pinocchio Meets Lara Croft

Pinocchio Land will grow up to
be a real country one day.

"I WOULD LIKE TO BE A ONE-MAN INTERNATIONAL FASHION PHENOMENON."

—Karl Lagerfeld

"THREE THINGS CANNOT BE LONG HIDDEN-THE SUN, THE MOON, AND THE TRUTH."

—Buddha

Expecting that either: a) I might run out of work at the NGO or b) they might be glad to see the back of me for a while, I had scheduled a second week's vacation toward the end of my two-month assignment. Now was our opportunity to add to our knowledge of the country and pay a return trip to its funkier neighbour Laos.

And so just like that we find ourselves on a bus heading to the coast to the low-key resort town of Kep, on the eastern shores of the Gulf of Thailand, for some R&R. It had a slow-paced lazy town feel to it, relaxed and informal. Its seafood is famous country wide, especially its crab. We eat our meals wandering the waterfront munching on barbecued squidcicles, slurping dragon fruit smoothies, licking the crumbs of deep-fried coconut bread from our fingers, all bought from the myriad seaside stalls. Or we splurge and visit a restaurant, sit on sun-bleached red plastic furniture, and tuck into a famous Kep crab platter. Have a couple of Angkor beers and slowly sink below the horizon with the sun.

Our hotel is on an unspoilt hillside overlooking the town. There are obviously big changes already in the works—a five-kilometre highway into the downtown area that is connected to nowhere at the other end has already been built. The CPP (the ruling party for the last thirty-five years) posters are everywhere, so we know who is behind it. Their motto seems to be: "build first, stifle questions later." You can't stop progress, as they say.

Our bellies full of crab and our eyes and memory cards full of oceanside sunsets, we head back inland to Laos, which if it does have a claim to fame it is that it must be the oddest-shaped country in the world. It is landlocked and looks as much like a profile of Pinocchio as anything else. His hat in the north is squished down by China and Burma, the back of his head and long neck are bordered by Vietnam to the east, his nose protrudes deep into Thailand in the west. The Mekong River flows out of his nostril, over his lips round his chin to his throat where the capital Vientiane sits, then down the long border of his neck, which settles on the shoulders of Cambodia in the south. It is centrally located on the Indo-China continent in the middle of nowhere, so to speak. It has an area about the third the size of France but with a border nearly twice as long, about 5,000 kilometres. It seemed a bit like the various neighbours and colonialists had just reached the limits of their endurance and said, "OK, that's far enough, we'll draw the borders here."

The sample of the six million population we have met are nice, friendly, and laid back, the joke around these parts being "the Vietnamese plant the rice, the Cambodians watch it grow, and the Laotians listen to it grow." I kinda like it. We spend a few days relaxing back on the 4,000 islands close to the Cambodian border, eating fresh fish and fruit, taking boat rides, and touring the island on rented bikes (the bikes are expensive—an outrageous 10,000 kip for the day, about CAD$1.25). We go view the waterfalls—rapids, we would call them. It was about here that the French gave up their exploring—this clearly wasn't going to be their St. Lawrence of the East. It works for us as an idyllic spot to go for a cooling dip.

After our mini break we were scheduled to head north supposedly by big bus but at the last moment we are reassigned to a mini bus. Uh-oh, here we go again. But no, our travel agent's buddy needed his van dropped off in Luang Prabang, our destination. We have the virtually new Hyundai to ourselves—luxury. The scenery is different too as we leave the flat, dusty lowlands behind. We leave the worst of the winter or dry season behind too. No snowploughs but water trucks patrol some of the main streets dousing the dust down. Residents off Main Street stand hose in hand sprinkling their driveways in their ongoing battle with the elements. It beats shovelling it, but just barely.

It's an enjoyable ride and, if you are easily amused, there is plenty to keep you entertained. A herd of cows stops in at a muffler shop—they have a sale on, its pure Far Side. Folks wear the traditional pointy bamboo hats, great for keeping their cell phones dry. It's Saturday afternoon. The boys are having a game of soccer in a dried-out paddy field, the backdrop is stunning mist shrouded, steep tree covered, camel humped karst mountains seemingly rising vertically from the valley floor like a scene from some travel poster for the Yangtze River.

Luang Prabang is Laos's tourism hub. It is a former capital of the country situated in the northwest at the confluence of the Mekong and Nam Kahn rivers, lush dense forest and jungle on all sides. It is definitely touristy, but like a few other smallish destinations dwarfed by natural beauty, it manages to get away with it. For some strange reason it reminds me of Banff with its long main street lined with shops and restaurants. Yet it is a fusion of old Buddhist tradition, palaces, *wats* (monasteries), temples and monks, and its French colonial past, stately villas, street-side cafes, and limitless dining opportunities. Its main drag hosts an evening market where local craftspeople and artisans sell their own wares. There are even stretches of unbroken sidewalk. Still, it is no place for the unwary as the local dogs are quite liberal in mining these freeways with their autographs—how much more Parisienne can you get?

Luang Praban strives to retain its culture and traditions. It has many *wats*, ten in the historic quarter alone. Maybe an average of thirty Buddhist monks occupy each of these temples. Each morning they get up early to watch the tourists and locals that kneel at the sides of the two main streets. They take a good look at them all as they stride single file in a procession three or four hundred strong, dressed in their saffron-coloured robes. As the monks make their circuit, the devotees, tourists and locals alike offer up candy, rice and money to them in a sort of reverse Halloween ritual, a tacit "please take my treat and give me a blessing" expression on their faces.

If the monks are motivated/moved/in the mood/hungry/directed/ programmed/ divinely inspired (nah, they don't believe in a god)/ cosmically predestined, or whatever it is that stirs a Buddhist monk to act, they may extend their alms bowls to the assembled so that they may fill them with their offerings. Their bowls fill up quickly; at some bottlenecks, the debris resembles the aftermath of a water station at a marathon race, so they have to be discerning in how much they load.

Gastronomically contented and climatically refreshed, we take our leave of LP and, for the next phase of our peripatetic interlude, hop on a flight to Siem Reap in Cambodia, which is the jumping-off point for Angkor Wat, the largest city temple complex in the world. Tourists flock here. It is now well and truly a Mecca-like Mecca whose pilgrims are from all over the world, except maybe I am not too sure if there are many Thai visitors seeing as how Siem Reap translates to "Siamese Defeated."

We approach the *wat* from the south, first travelling through the forest outskirts of what in the twelfth century would have been the suburbs of a city of some 400 square miles, nearly the size of LA. In due course, we come to a river, but it is no river—actually a 660-foot-wide moat. An 1,150-foot causeway connects the temple complex to the shore (London Bridge is 880 feet long). And to help you globetrotters out there get a sense of perspective, just the temple covers 820,000 square feet (Versailles is 720,000), rises to a height of 699 feet (Trump Tower is a plebeian 663 feet), and is constructed from about five million tons of rock (the Great Pyramid of Giza is about six million tons).

Two and a half million visitors a year come to marvel at the sights. Today from our distant vantage point it is easy to fancy that all the visitors are ants swarming toward a giant birthday cake. Once through the crazy, crowded bottleneck of the causeway, things are a lot more roomy. At its zenith, Angkor, the capital of the Khmer empire,[27] was

27 https://www.ancient.eu/Khmer_Empire/

a city of over one million, and was, at the time, the largest, most sophisticated settlement on the planet.

It is one of those places where you wonder how many times you can say "wow" and "incredible" in one day so we end up staying three days. No matter what you think, it is possible to get tired of taking photos of intricate stone carvings and colossal feats of architecture, so you start to scan around to find something a bit outlandish, quirky, or comic. During one of these pensive moments out of the corner of my eye I sense rather than spot something. Then I focus in: What's that Chinese guy up to with his fancy camera and telephoto lens? Hold on a minute, the cheeky bugger is taking pictures of me!

So there I am not exactly Saville Row suave, at the end of a two-week jaunt through steamy Southeast Asia, dressed in the remaining clean clothes I have ferreted out from the bottom of my backpack. These are the wrinkled rejects that will only do "in a pinch."

Blue checkered shorts, beige safari shirt, green socks topped off with a jaunty bucket hat, although I have had repeated warnings about the bucket hat—apparently nothing says "old cooter" like a bucket hat does. How outlandish, quirky, or comic could it be?

The whole thing is an outrage, an invasion of privacy totally lacking in sensitivity. But what to do? There's not much I could do, ha, other than return fire. My point and shoot is no match for his Canon. Guerrilla warfare is my only option. I duck behind a stone wall, hide out of sight, and hold my breath until he walks past me. Then, with silent cunning I step out behind him and let him have it. Torpedoes away! I loose off three or four shots before he knows what hit him. Lara Croft Tomb Raider in a bucket hat. It is a big day for me.

He turns, stunned and open mouthed. He lowers his barrel in defeat. I smile to let him know that I'm not interested in unconditional surrender. He grins broadly, bowing. Handshakes and laughter soon follow.

It is a good lesson for me to learn. Having the tables turned on me and being the hunted instead of the hunter will remind me to tame my trigger finger when we make our next side trip, this time to Myanmar. Where the victims are all unarmed.

Part V

BURMA – A RIDDLE WRAPPED IN A MYSTERY INSIDE AN ENIGMA VEILED IN A MYANMAR

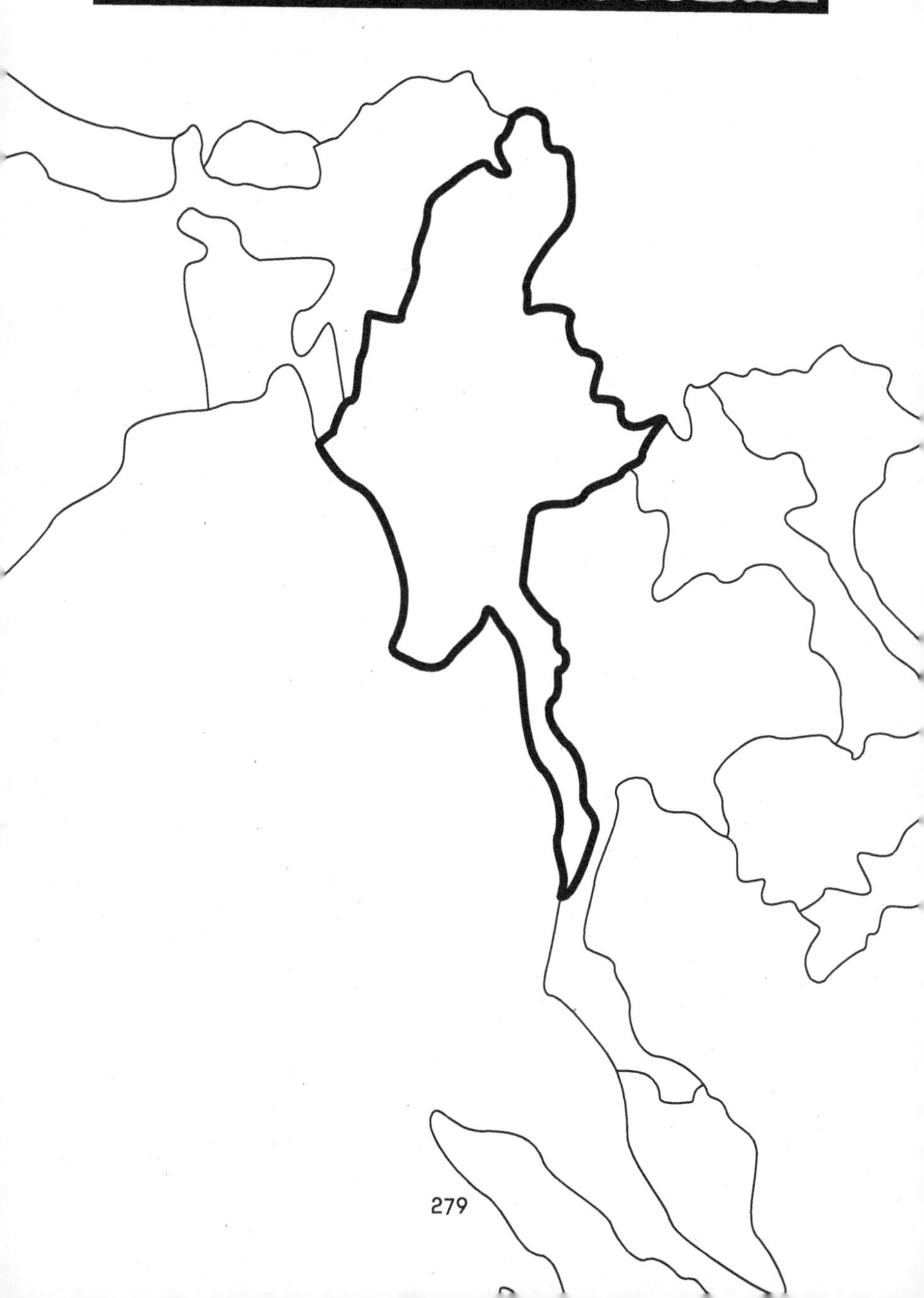

Chapter 28

Bumps in the Road

That'll be $50 for a three-month extension, please. would you rather that I wore sweatpants and flip flops?

"MYSTIQUE IS RARE NOW ISN'T IT?
THERE AREN'T MANY ENIGMAS IN THIS MODERN WORLD."
—Benedict Cumberbatch

"I LIVE ON GOOD SOUP NOT FINE WORDS."
—Molière

In the spirit of no surprises we have landed at Yangon International Airport, knowing that we have the first night of our stay reserved in a guest house and a taxi booked to take us there. If only everything could be that easy, what would be the point? We would be visiting southeast Asia's largest, poorest, and most peculiar country in a region consisting of large, poor, peculiar countries. February twenty-second brought with it a warm breeze and a whiff of apprehension.

Myanmar, a country at the time of our visit back in 2013 ranked right up there with Iran and North Korea as having one of the world's most opaque and mysterious regimes. The country has garnered more negative attention since then. The circumstances that created this complex confederacy dates back decades as you will find out.

Also known as Burma,[28] it is located at the steamy end of the Bay of Bengal, anonymously wedged between India, China, Thailand, and Bangladesh, a collection of ambitious countries with many hungry mouths to feed.

We are delivered to Yangon (Rangoon), the major city, late at night with the temperatures still in the thirties. Our twenty-eight-day visit gets off to a slow start due to a combination of jet lag, colds, and antimalarial medication.

A blowout chicken biryani dinner leads to a blowout dose of the Yangon yips later that night. I don't want to be too graphic, but if you can picture the last Space X launch with you as the payload you will understand why we hastily scrap our plan to head out of town by bus the next day. Instead, we stay put to sample a little of the country's only sizeable city. Rangoon (Yangon) is home to five-plus million inhabitants of the nation's sixty-odd million citizens. Burma is still predominantly a rural agricultural society, infrastructure is

28 https://www.riskadvisory.com/campaigns/corruption-challenges-index-2018-view

rudimentary, systems and institutions are nascent, statistics should be taken with a grain of rice.

The city has you feeling like you are in some sort of colonial time warp. Grand old Victorian buildings, with mildewed and crumbling masonry. Weird decisions based on superstition and whim have crippled a country that, prior to WWII, was one of the leading nations in Asia. The military government, which has been in place for fifty years, seems to have taken George Orwell's *1984* not so much as a cautionary tale but as a "how-to guide" to governing. George, by the way, lived here for five years; his book, *Burmese Days,* is more popular than *50 Shades of Grey* amongst the trekkers we meet.

Nothing is convenient here; it is as if there's been a deliberate attempt to make everything as confusing as possible. There are two sets of currency in simultaneous use: USD for hotels (rooms but not meals), flights, and some public transport (they like to keep you guessing), kyat for everything else. To complicate things further, you have to bring enough USD in hard cash with you for your whole trip as there's no international banking/ATMs. The use of credit cards is unimaginable. Greenbacks must be in pristine mint condition as "no antiquated or undesirable money will be taken." You can't even fold the bills in half for fear of rejection.

It's an honest country—maybe that's why there are no safety deposit boxes in the hotels. But in practical terms it means that you have to lug your money around all the time. Converting your USD into local cash doesn't help. When I exchanged US$300, I came away with over a quarter of a million kyat in 1,000 kyat bills. They gave it to me in a little bag that might as well have said "swag" on it.

All this gives rise to "The Burmese Bump," where tourists have to stash their wad. There are many none-too-discreet variations. The Smith and Wesson under the armpit style. The one overdeveloped thigh look. The rectangular stomach bulge (my own personal favourite).

The dromedarian derrière. All of these are somewhat camouflageable with a loose enough shirt. But what to do if you are a Dutch cycle tour guide who packs around US$17,000 for emergencies? Hard to figure out an anatomically believable option when fully clad in spandex. Maybe that's why he's so popular with the ladies.

Traffic volumes are low but chaotic nonetheless. Apparently one night in 1970 the "Generals" (as the locals refer to the military regime) decided that it would be a good idea for everyone to switch from driving on the left to driving on the right. As the majority of the vehicles today are still pre-1970 vintage, this, as you can imagine, still creates major problems. To name but one, when your bus makes a stop it comes as a shock not to step down onto the sidewalk but right into the path of vehicles overtaking the parked bus. It's no place for daydreamers.

Other grassroots-driven policy changes include a total ban on motorcycles in Yangon. Some poor fellow happened to dent one of the generals' cars with his moped. After many feasibility studies, much policy analysis, and public consultation conducted that same night, the edict banning motorized two-wheelers was issued the next morning—hey, it gets things done! Now if only one of those same generals would slip on a plastic bag we'd really see some improvements.

Lack of a common language is a barrier to development too—the education system is weak. Nevertheless, I try to learn a couple of Myanmarese words—it's all about building bridges. I learn a couple of menu items right away: beer, breakfast soup (excellent, by the way). Then we happen to run into an English couple who have been here for a couple of weeks, and I instantly double my vocabulary with "hello/how are you" and "thank you." I use them liberally. The reactions of the locals aren't as encouraging as I'd hoped, however.

Next morning, I peruse the dictionary, hoping to expand my repertoire further. Oh, Buddha . . . that could explain a few things. I'd switched *minglarbar* (hello/how are you) with *mohinga* (breakfast soup). I put this lapse down to antimalarial medication (may cause sunburn, hunger, dizziness, CONFUSION, etc.). Of course the trouble is I have all the symptoms, even without the drugs.

Memories from the previous day emerge no matter how I try to suppress them . . . .

Me striding through the hotel lobby with my best attempt at the Obama wave/smile combo topped off with a heartfelt "breakfast soup." The only reaction in return?? A slack-jawed vacant stare.

Me negotiating a fare with the rickshaw driver on the street, always good to do business in a dignified manner. "Breakfast soup, how much do you want to take us to the market?"

A worried frown and a crooked smile in response. Thinks. "Is this dude trying to pay me in broth?"

My countless salvos of "breakfast soup!" issued at numerous innocent bystanders earned me nothing but a few bovine looks. It's a bumpy road trying to be an ambassador.

Things are changing fast though. The generals seem to know that their days are numbered. There's little feeling of the presence of the regime for the tourist though. This is no celebrity dictatorship—not a Gaddafi-type poster in sight nor even a Saddam-like statue, it's all more insidious. Curiously, Aung San Suu Kyi, a woman who had spent the better part of twenty years under house arrest, has gained rock star status. She leads the recently recognized democracy movement, and is also known as "the lady," but more about that later. Her likeness is everywhere: tea towels, posters, mugs, calendars, etc. It's a grassroots saturation of the market without the assistance of any official media. It has all flourished through word of mouth and clandestine meetings. Until a year ago there was blanket censorship. People were sent to jail for years for having just a poster of her.

The Buddhist belief system is also a threat to the government's authority. The Buddhist monks have long been a thorn in the side of the regime and have survived due to the massive support and respect of the populace—there is no messing with the church. On the way into towns and villages it is common to see banners with pictures of the local head lamas draped across the streets, such is their influence. I'm hoping the photos don't do them justice. They certainly could do with some better PR as they look more like hoodlums on the FBI's ten-most-wanted list than the spiritual guides that they are.

The Buddha's four noble truths are:

a) Dukkha, suffering exists

b) Samudaya, there is a cause for suffering

c) Nirodha, there is an end to suffering

d) Maga, in order to end suffering you must follow the eightfold path.

Folks continue to experience number one firsthand, they have figured out who is responsible for number two, they are willing to die to create number three. The trick will be how to achieve number four, Maga, when the eightfold path prescribes things like no harm to others, no killing, no hurtful talk.

"Free" elections were planned for 2014 and the man in the street's expectations are sky high. There will be no easy solutions. There is ethnic unrest in at least five regions of the country and without some sort of a military deterrent the potential for a Yugoslavia-type meltdown is real.

To us blinkered tourists, people seem happy and content and yet, no matter where you are, every building, be it a hospital, school, residence, or hotel has razor wire and broken glass embedded in their perimeter walls. Its likely purpose is as much an insurance against the uncertainties of the future as it was for the troubles of the past.

As is usually the case, all the big player nations are lining up for a piece of the action. Obama/Clinton just happened to be passing and dropped in. The Chinese, Korean, and Indians are funding many projects. It will be a wise government that can tell the difference between what's going to be a benefit and what's going to be a problem from all this advice and assistance that is being so freely offered. As the old Burmese saying goes "never look a gift ox in the mouth, unless it looks like it's getting ready to eat your house."

Our gastrointestinal challenges put behind us, so to speak, breakfast soup a welcome remedy, we decide to make up for lost time by booking a flight to the hinterland rather than risking an ill-timed relapse on a lengthy bus trip.

This necessitates a visit to the government-administered travel agent around the corner from our guest house. Having found an English speaker amongst the clerks we make our plans understood and move to finalize the transaction. He issues us a handwritten ticket in the old red carbon paper triplicate style, which he has filled in with red pen. After some protracted negotiating, with a sigh, he assents to us using our credit card for payment. As the agent fishes out the manual card imprinter from the safe, I comment to no one in particular, "I can't even remember how inconvenient it was before we could pay with credit cards."

He nods nostalgically. "Yes, it was a different world back then."

Still is, I think to myself.

Chapter 29

Buddhists, Boats, and Backcountry

Nureyev and people who don't know how to clean their own fish.

"SUNSETS ARE GREAT. SUNRISES ARE A MIXED BAG. EITHER YOU GOT UP WAY TOO EARLY OR YOU WENT TO BED WAY TOO LATE."

—Matt Dillon

"GENEROSITY CONSISTS NOT OF THE SUM GIVEN BUT IN THE MANNER THAT IT IS BESTOWED."

—Gandhi

Inle Lake is one of the top tourism draws in Myanmar. The attractions are the variety of activities available, the cool climate at an elevation of 2,900 feet, and a rural feel. It is also the Venice of Burma, a thirty-mile lake fringed by canals, marshland, waterways, and floating vegetable gardens.

We splurge and arrive by plane to a curious protocol. We are required to put our baggage through the X-ray machines on arrival, under the sign that reads "warmly welcome and take care of tourists." If my stockbroker had gotten me into X-ray machine stocks after 9/11, I would be travelling first class by now.

After checking into our guest house, our first order of business is to venture out on the lake. It's a twenty-minute run by wood-planked canoe down the main canal from our hotel in Nyaungshwe, the largest lakeside town. We negotiate a deal with the boat manager at 18,000 kyat for a day's outing—about twenty-two dollars. We clamber aboard our canoe. Our boatman, a typically friendly Burman, however speaks no English other than the international "no worry."

He fires up the engine, which sits fully exposed in the stern of the boat about a foot behind Trixie's head. When idling, the motor has a "phut, phut, phut, phut" throbbing beat, a percussive "thud, thud, thud" like a Harley-Davidson. He manoeuvres the boat into the channel, no small feat given its length and the narrowness of the harbour. He then guns the engine, creating a blast of blue-black smoke accompanied by a roar like a dragster. We are pinned back in our seats as our thirty-foot teak torpedo surges down the waterway. Never was polluting this much fun.

At the entrance to the lake wait a small flotilla of fishermen in their double-ended canoes with single oars and ten-foot-diameter shuttlecock-shaped fishing baskets; they are the iconic symbol of the region and they know it. The most lucrative catches are to be made in this location. Tourists!

The boat preceding us stops for a photo-op. They come parallel to a fisherman. The boats are narrow—no more than three feet wide—so, the five or six tourists are seated single file. They turn as one towards their target and level their telephoto lenses at the fisher. It's an odd scene, a bit like watching a firing squad in action, but without the intimacy of a blindfold and a last cigarette being offered. Nevertheless, the fisher obliges with a series of balletic poses like Nureyev auditioning for *Swan Lake*.

Stealthily, as the photographers are changing settings, lenses, etc., the fisherman skillfully paddles over to them. He does this standing up, wrapping one leg around the only oar. If you can imagine Long John Silver standing on a skateboard propelling himself with his peg leg and crutch simultaneously, you'll get an idea of the motion involved.

He (not Long John Silver) collects his fee, and why shouldn't he? What's wrong with him being a super model for the four-month tourist season and fishing for the rest of the time? Naomi Campbell does alright being photographed in funny outfits and I bet she doesn't even know how to clean her own fish. But I digress. He poses for a few more shots then paddles over to us for more of the same.

When our turn comes, we happily participate in the pantomime, there's no denying the uniqueness of the angler's skills. When it comes time to settle up, he asks for 1,000 kyat, I proffer 300K—about forty cents. He seems happy enough. He probably thinks he's overcharged us given our pop gun camera equipment.

We spend the rest of the morning roaring around the lake visiting various little lakeshore handicraft villages, silversmiths galore, cheroot makers, weavers of lotus flower silk, and fish and fruit markets. In the afternoon we head up one of the less frequented feeder canals—a more rural way of life unfolds there. Much of the daily routine revolves around the water. Everything from scrubbing the family bullock to brushing the teeth, searching the riverbank for birds' eggs to washing the motorcycle. At times it feels a little ostentatious being ferried around semi-recumbent in our motorized palanquin but we get the impression that we are still regarded as a bit of a novelty rather than a nuisance. Later we join the Dunkirk-style armada of small boats heading back to the big town at the end of a very enjoyable day.

Nyuangshwe isn't just a centre for outdoor activity but caters to the arts too. There are several art and photograph galleries to be found. We decide to take in a live event, maybe the only show in town. Puppetry, using marionettes in particular, is big in Myanmar. We opt for the late show, 8:30 p.m., and are lucky to get in, it's nearly a full house. All eleven of us have a good view of the stage and the puppeteer's arms. It's an interesting enough art form, but I don't think Kermit and Miss Piggy have anything to worry about. The show ends at 9 p.m., and we head for our hotel down by the docks. Dusk has turned to dark. If the streets had had sidewalks they would have been rolled up by now, the traffic on Main Street, never a torrent, has dried to a trickle. There is nothing on offer for the after-theatre crowd, only a few now-familiar sights and sounds of the noisy nighttime quiet. The last of the steel shutters on the few remaining open stores being closed, the nightly squabble of the mangy street dogs arguing over territory, the odd figure emerging from the gloom, maybe singing unselfconsciously to themselves on their way home from work. The chanting of monks from the "downtown" monastery (what are they doing up so late?) are heard, over loudspeakers, no less. It all feels a bit shadowy and mysterious but not the least bit sinister or worrying.

If there's any benefit to a military dictatorship, it works wonders for the crime rate, or could it be something to do with the Buddhist chanting?

Snug in our cozy guest house, we drift off to sleep with dreams of—dun dun dun dunnn—"the back country" filling our heads.

The last component of our Inle visit is a two-night/three-day trek into the nearby hills, which rise to about 4,000 feet and surround the lake.

Our guide is Ko Ko, a twenty-four-year-old linguist (Japanese, English, and five tribal languages) and mathematician (budgets, currency conversions, statistics). What makes this all the more astonishing is that he has never learned to read or write, even in his own language, much less had any instruction in numeracy. Talk about a capacity for abstract thinking. He is also the fount of all knowledge when it comes to everything in the hills and the Shan state/culture in general. He is a go-getter and is saving to open his own tour operator business. How you can accomplish that being illiterate only he knows.

The first day is a bit of a slog, uphill all the way. The hills are only at about a third of the elevation that we have experienced on the Nepali treks, but the humid heat provides its own challenges. Ko Ko is confident that he can resource whatever we may need on the fly. Being liberated from packs, equipment, and provisions is a carefree way to travel.

On our way we pass through a fantastic variety of farming and crops at different elevations. Fertile soil and a good climate deliver quite a bounty. Wheat (83 percent for export, according to Ko Ko), tomatoes, potatoes, garlic, turmeric, sesame, peppers, sugar, bananas (thirty-seven varieties), grapefruit-sized lemons, cantaloupe-sized avocadoes, watermelon-sized papayas, and anticlimactically watermelon-sized watermelons.

If your tastes run to something more decadent, those can be satisfied too. Choose from opium (although we didn't see any of that), coffee, tobacco, grapes (there are a couple of wineries in the area), tea, and marijuana. Burma produces 90 percent of the world's rubies. Our luck is just a bit off. If we had looked a little harder we might have picked up a bargain at the market. The Cartier Sunrise ruby weighing in at a hefty finger-dislocating twenty-five carats, sold at Christie's in 2015 for a bargain $30.3 million.[29] By contrast, the country is so

29 https://www.youtube.com/watch?v=mve6wJlpruM

disconnected from the rest of the world that there is no Coca-Cola plant and they import the stuff from Singapore. I choose to take the sustainable option and drink the local rum and beer instead.

Finished our agricultural orientation class (I bet you are relieved too), we stop for lunch. Ko Ko calls in at a local villager's bamboo stilt house. We are invited in and, in a jiffy, we are sitting cross-legged on the bamboo floor watching the lady of the house whipping up a delicious soup over an open fire situated in a "sandbox" in the middle of the kitchen floor. Before long, word of our visit spreads and there are seven ladies and younger women seated in the room with us. Thanks to Ko Ko's multilingual skills we have quite a discussion with them. We cover all kinds of weighty issues, ranging to the impact that democracy will have on Burma to why do Western men have such hairy legs. Lunch over, we hit the trail for another three hours or so, arriving at our "hotel" in the late afternoon.

Our accommodation for the night is a Buddhist monastery. It sounds a bit more grand than it really is. Just a couple of ramshackle buildings inhabited by three novices (ten or twelve years old), a cheerful but ailing senior monk, and his more distant and reserved assistant. We are the only travellers there but clearly not the first. The younger monk unbidden directs us to a nearby hillock "for the best sunsets." We foreigners are nothing if not predictable in our peculiarities. We of the "sunset worshipper tribe." After a good dinner concocted from local ingredients (add chef to Ko Ko's list of accomplishments), we retire to our room, one of the aforementioned dilapidated buildings. Sleep like a log, more due to the exertions of the day than the bed, which is a mat on the concrete floor covered by a pile of blankets.

We say our goodbyes in the morning, head off on the next leg. It's easier, having gained some elevation the previous day. Ko Ko invites us to check out a kindergarten in one of the villages and make a small donation to the teacher for school supplies; we are only too happy to oblige. I guess it looked like a lot of money to her, she gets about 40,000 kyat—forty-eight dollars—a month (more Ko Ko stats). Anyway, she is so grateful that she and Ko Ko disappear to make lunch for us.

Foolishly, she leaves us in charge of the class. Mayhem soon ensues, small barefoot bodies frolic around the classroom. They get bolder by the minute. In no time they are hurtling around like dervishes, brandishing recently liberated trophies—our hats, glasses, watches, and sunglasses. This is how *Lord of the Flies* got started, isn't it?

After what seems like an eternity, Ko Ko returns to let us know that lunch is ready. One of the village mothers accompanies him, it is her job to supervise the kids as they eat their lunch. With barely a word she instantly restores order. She levelled a steady, unwavering gaze at us which seemed to say "How did these white people ever colonize anything?"

Lunch is another sumptuous affair. Such generosity is a humbling experience—embarrassing really, huge quantities, amazing attention to detail, five or six dishes, all lovingly prepared. We set off again in the afternoon having tried to eat as much as possible as a sign of appreciation.

I leave with a feeling that I somehow owe her something. The last thing she would have wanted was money—what she had given she had given from the heart. Maybe what I am in debt to her for is her lesson in generosity. My fear is that I'm not the greatest pupil.

For the final night we are going to a settlement that Ko Ko hasn't visited before. As ever, he wants to expand his horizons. There's no running water here and Ko Ko helps a young girl carry a canister of it up a hill, which leads us to one of the bigger homes in the village. Another stilt house with a bamboo seating/living area above a hard-packed earth floor, and with a sleeping loft above. The proud owners don't seem even a bit put out and we are welcomed in. I don't have to wonder what the reaction would be in Victoria if a stranger turned up on the doorstep at suppertime with two disheveled foreigners in tow and asked, "Have you ever thought about opening a B&B—like, right now?"

Another fine dinner, neighbours drop by to check out the aliens—i.e., us. More Q&As. It's getting late, about 8:30 p.m., and we're getting the signal that it's past our bedtime so we are packed off to the sleeping area—the bamboo floor on the second level. The bamboo is softer but lumpier than the concrete, but again sleep comes easily. Ko Ko wants to stay up late with our hosts, networking, explaining how the hospitality industry works (before you know it they'll be on Expedia). Apparently it was after 11:00 p.m. before Ko Ko and our hosts joined us on the floor of the sleeping loft.

A hearty breakfast the next morning followed by our last goodbyes and we are off down the hill, slip sliding on the slick trails (unseasonal rain shower to blame) like we've drunk too much of the local sugar-based hooch. By mid-afternoon we're back in civilization. At the trailhead we bump into our first aliens in three days, hire their donkey and cart, and head back to the luxuries of Nyaungshwe, a stopover en route to the south coast and a date with our tail.

Chapter 30

Heroes and Villains

"Sure, we shadowed him:
Tuesday we sit outside his house all day, but he no home.
Wednesday we went to the ball game, he fool us and no show up.
Thursday he go to the ball game, but we fool him and we no show up.
Friday it was a double header, nobody show up, so we stay home and listened to it on the radio."

—Marx Brothers

"SHOW ME A HERO AND I WILL WRITE YOU A TRAGEDY."

—F. Scott Fitzgerald

For history buffs, Burma is a fascinating destination, whether it's ancient monuments, civilizations and artifacts that float your boat or if, like me, you are more intrigued by the more recent historical events. With that in mind, Trixie and I decide to spend some time down in the southeast corner of the country and use Mawlamyine as our base.

Getting there is easy enough. On the surface everything is harmonious and downright friendly. We are treated to a coffee by the bus ticket agent, are given a candy by a passing monk, and handed some sweets by a street vendor after buying some oranges from her for the bus ride. Nice.

The bus is ramshackle but serviceable and there is a seat for each person. For some reason we have to show the driver our passports—why, I have no idea. Burma isn't a high-tech destination. As of 2013, book-ahead tourism hasn't made a breakthrough. It suits us fine.

Things though are pretty sophisticated for some. We drive by manicured golf courses and modern hospitals reserved for the military elite only. There is a duality going on that signals change is slowly happening. There are now as many right-hand drive cars as left, dual place names from both the old colonial days and the new names assigned by the military regime, signage in both Mon and English script. It is the best of times and the worst of times.

The roads are in pretty decent shape. Traffic is light and the eight-hour bus ride uneventful. It's a good introduction to the country watching the countryside slide by and the comings and goings of the passengers. It is strange sitting in our anonymous bubble cut off by lack of a common language and yet at the same time centre stage because of our colour.

We leave the city, which itself seems to be stuck somewhere in the twentieth century. I wouldn't be at all surprised if, if we came back in ten years' time, the streets will be brimming with Starbucks, Apple stores, The Gap, and SUVs. It's hard to fault this progress but you can't help wondering if another set of desires will just be replacing the existing ones. Que sera, we are happy to be here now.

The rest of the country evokes an even earlier era. Where else would you see kids manning a roadside stand hoping to get donations for a new town *stupa*? Going door to door to raise funds for your baseball tour just isn't the same. So here is hoping that they don't throw the baby out with the bath water and preserve the humanity as modernity makes its inroads.

We find the town itself to be pretty nondescript: a promenade, a harbour for the fishing boats, some restaurants, and only a few guest houses, which all seem to be full. Eventually we find a hostel, really an old colonial house on the waterfront that has gone through a metamorphosis. On the ground floor is the dorm, which I have to think was originally a stable. Each unit is the size of a horse stall, the walls made of rough-hewn, unfinished lumber that only reach about seven feet toward the ten-foot ceilings. A five-plank wooden door with its wire hasp is the token gesture to privacy.

No thanks. But not to be put off we enquire about other accommodation in the vicinity. And, lo, the master bedroom is available. The owner does warn us that it is expensive. I let him know that "I've been thrown out of better places than this."

He smiles politely but hasn't got a clue what I am talking about.

He takes us to the room, which is on the second floor. It is massive—maybe twenty-five by thirty feet—and houses two four-poster beds, two-inch-thick mattresses on a network of sagging springs, a dining table and chairs. Chic by 1910 standards, which is about the last time it was dusted.

We will take it and count our blessings we aren't sleeping in the barn. Well, this being semi-rural south Asia, you can take the barn out of the town, but you can't take the farm out of the town.

2:45 a.m.: the cats are chasing the chickens.

3:30 a.m.: the dogs are chasing the cats.

4:30 a.m.: the monks are worshipping the dogs.

5:00 a.m.: the fishing boats are putting out for the early bite.

6:00 a.m.: the gecko is stalking the bugs in the room.

6:30 a.m.: the clip-clop of pony and trap heading up main street, sleigh bells jingling, but there's nothing under the tree for Santa.

Sightseeing opportunities include a visit to Ogre Island, day trips only as the bogey men, I suppose, must come out after dark. It is hard to fathom if the various village craft industries on the circuit are actually financially viable businesses or whether it is all some sort of elaborate theme park complete with a twenty-four-seven cast of live-in characters. Not that it very much matters as it is all very quaint and charming. Long may it continue that way.

Have you ever wondered how rubber bands are made? Probably not. Here, they make them by hand. Ranks of wooden poles, three inches in diameter and three feet long, are dipped into vats of locally sourced latex, some tinted in vibrant colours to add a bit of pizzazz. The poles are then stood erect on flat ground out in the sun to dry like it's some condom showroom for Brobdingnagians. Once dry, the rubber sleeves are removed from the poles and slices of cross section are cut to form the bands.

Our multinational little tourist group is quite taken by the whole demonstration. But, and there is always a but, when folks start to try out the finished product, predictable consequences ensue. The German in the group fires first, a few exploratory salvos at a

Frenchman, who returns fire before promptly surrendering. The Swiss in the group retreat to a safe distance, the Brits are caught flat footed, the Canadians back up the Brits but nobody notices and the Americans beef up their arsenal and check to see if they have any "interests" in rubber bands before joining in.

And, like always, the locals are left to clean up the battlefield when the foreigners move on.

Which brings us to WWII. Farther east toward the Thai border are some remains of the Burma railway, also known as the "Death Railway."[30] This railway, which ran between Bangkok in neighbouring Thailand and Rangoon, was built by the Japanese during WWII using slave labour. Over a quarter of a million Allied prisoners of war and local peasants were put to work in the most atrocious conditions. Over 100,000 of them succumbed in the process. The memorial graveyard is well maintained through funding provided by Britain. The tombstones tell the familiar sad stories. Young men enlisted in their teens conceivably away from home for the first time in their lives find themselves being flogged daily in some faraway Asian jungle before dying in their twenties.

Almost all of the old track and rolling stock is gone now. Burma is always in need of cash. Sold to China as scrap to be melted down to make guns, so the story goes. A final insult to the memory of all those dead.

The next stop is Golden Rock, a Buddhist pilgrimage site. An impressive granite boulder covered in gold leaf plastered on by male-only devotees. What makes it really impressive is that the shining boulder teeters precariously on a cliff at the top of a mountain. Legend has it that the fifty-foot-wide head-shaped rock was carried up the 1,000-metre mountain by a Buddhist monk who then placed a lock of the Buddha's hair under the rock as a wedge to prevent it from rolling

---

30 https://en.wikipedia.org/wiki/Burma_Railway

off the precipice into the valley below. The village at the foot of the mountain provides access via open-air buses that shuttle up and down the mountain all day. It is a high-volume operation and the buses—more like flatbed trucks with rows and rows of benches—are designed to pack 'em in. Six abreast thigh to thigh and if you are my height your knees wedged under the bum cheeks of the passenger in front of you. If you fancy yourself as an emperor you can hire porters and a litter to carry you there in recumbent style.

Burma sits at the crossroads of Asia like a small star and has roughly the same area and population of France. It is a grab bag of ethnic groups, arbitrarily amalgamated, mixed, and mashed together during the expansion of the British Empire. It was officially colonized in 1886, and lumped with the countries currently called Pakistan, Bangladesh, and India, to form the then mega-nation known as British India. As you can imagine that didn't go down so well with the 135 or so ethnic groups who were used to running their own show. There is nothing like a common enemy to unite conflicting groups, at least temporarily. Freedom/independence was on everyone's mind.

In 1937, in an attempt at pacification, nationhood for Burma separate from British India was granted—independence, however, was not. As these machinations were unfolding, an impatient twenty-six-year-old independence militant Aung San was moved to act. Dismayed by the lack of progress toward full sovereignty, he began looking for allies outside of his country. Necessity being the mother of strange bedfellows, he threw his lot in with the Japanese. While in Japan, he received military training. The price of this support was Aung San's assistance in Japan's planning and ultimate invasion of his country.

All appeared to be going according to plan as the Japanese Imperial army swept the British and Indian regiments from Burma in 1942. The Japanese occupiers proved to be more repressive than the colonialists that had just been chased from the country.

Meet the new boss, same as the old boss. How often does history repeat that refrain?

Aung, with single-minded determination, wasn't playing any favourites. An independent nation was his goal. With that in mind, he began secret talks with the British. Sometime in 1944 it is understood that he offered to help them in their efforts to defeat the Japanese. This assistance would come at his price: full Independence for Burma. It was an offer the British couldn't refuse.

The year 1945 would see the wholesale defection of the Burmese military to the side of the allies and ultimately Japan's defeat.

After the war, Aung, as the de facto leader of Burma, set to work finalizing the terms of independence. It may have been a more complicated mess than Brexit but, by January 1947, the British and Burmese had negotiated an agreement.

Without the distraction of fighting a common foe, the colonialists, there was a real threat of civil war breaking out amongst the various ethnic groups and with the predominant Bamar (or Burman) group that makes up about two thirds of the population, the ethnic mix being more of an antipasto plate than a melting pot. Respectful compromises would be the only hope for peace.

Repairing some of the damage done by the neglect of the ethnic minorities who numbered about a third of the population was essential. These marginalized groups, who unsurprisingly tend to live on the margins—isolated by lack of infrastructure, geographically remote regions like mountainous areas or close to or overlapping neighbouring international boundaries—would and continue to present huge challenges.

In an attempt to engage these folks in shaping the future of the newly independent nation, one of Aung's first priorities was to negotiate a treaty with them. In February 1947, a bargain was reached that essentially gave the national government in Rangoon a ten-year window to institute an equitable, acceptable governance structure. If the Shan, Chin, Kachin, Mon, Rakhaing, etc., etc., etc., weren't happy with the state of affairs at that point, they would have the option to go it alone.

As part of the deal on self-rule worked out with Britain, democratic elections were held. In April of 1947, Aung San's party won a convincing 175 of a possible 225 seats. In July of that same year, Aung San was assassinated. The perpetrators escaped, the motive never conclusively established. He had made many enemies in his thirty-two years. He left a wife and three children.

Aung San continues to be revered by the Burmese as the liberator and founding father of their independent nation. Statues of him are still to be seen, even as subsequent military regimes have tried to erase his memory. The generals, even without sophisticated media to spread their propaganda, may have been able to accomplish this rewriting of history were it not for the fact that Aung San's youngest daughter is none other than Aung San Suu Kyi, "The Lady."

"The Lady," who is now recognized as the (some would say disgraced) leader of the country.

During the late 1940s, without the steady hand of Aung San to steer a middle course, the country descended into anarchy, with armed conflict erupting among ethnic groups, political parties, and bandits.

Cue the hard-line solution. Military intervention and in due course military government. Seizing power, the army took some wise steps limiting international involvement. Chinese communist agitation in the north, Western "aid" projects elsewhere, which were more about corporate exploitation than benefit for the average citizen, were stifled.

But as the generals became more convinced in their own "father knows best" superiority, a conceit that probably has its origins in observing and working with their British masters in the 1920s and 1930s, their yearning to hold onto power became all-consuming. Over the next thirty-plus years, Burma would become more and more isolated, the generals more and more paranoid and rich, the citizens poorer and poorer and more and more rebellious.

In 1988, demonstrations finally erupted, climaxing with a general strike and mass street demonstrations on the auspicious eighth day of the eighth month of 1988. The army were merciless in their suppression of these protests. They opened fire with live ammunition. The death toll was estimated at over 3,000.

During these rallies, "The Lady," as she was affectionately referred to by the people, became an icon and beacon of hope for the populace. Fearing her growing popularity and the growing civil unrest, the generals were moved to come up with a solution. Their remoteness from the people and their arrogance was so complete they thought that a general election would validate their authority and restore order. It was a colossal blunder.

The generals' hubris was so great that they didn't even think it necessary to rig the election. They thought that changing the name of the country to Myanmar and placing "The Lady" under house arrest would be enough to bamboozle the electorate.

Elections were held in 1990 and the Lady's NLD party flourished with 392 of a possible 485 seats. The generals ignored the results and acted as if the elections had never happened. NLD party leaders were rounded up, activists and dissidents disappeared, offices were raided, the dissenting press was silenced, and tighter controls than ever were instituted.

Had the generals been as naive as everyone thought they were? Or was it all a devious ploy that would flush out the identities of their opposition and give them the opportunity to ruthlessly deal with them? The debate is unresolved. The scheme, if that's what it was, backfired in one significant respect: there was now one unassailable figurehead for the opposition movement: Aung San Suu Kyi.

She had now achieved such prominence and become such a personality of esteem and adoration in the country and internationally she had become untouchable to the generals. Wherever we travelled in Burma her image was ubiquitous. Anyone who spoke English to us would at some point turn the conversation to an exaltation about the Lady and how she would transform the country. If one hair on the Lady's trademark ponytailed head was to be touched, a firestorm the military couldn't contain would erupt.

The generals hunkered down for the long haul and started opening up trade deals that would exploit Burma's rich teak forests, and gas, oil, and precious gem resources. This supplied them with much-needed foreign currency that they could then use to import weapons and military know-how. The state undercover police force burgeoned and the citizenry became more cowed and insecure.

The extensive spy networks were supposedly scaled back around 2012. But on one of our side trips we and an English couple we had met arranged an excursion to a nearby temple. A nice Toyota minivan arrived to pick us up at the appointed time, occupied by a chatty English-speaking driver and a silent front-seat passenger. The passenger was well dressed with a pressed white airline pilot-style shirt and dark aviator sunglasses. The driver didn't know who he was or why he was there, only that he was an official. I can only conclude that we were being mysteriously shadowed, not exactly secretively. He followed us around for the day like a black cloud just on the fringe of our sight. This was in 2013, so maybe he just hadn't gotten the memo. We never saw him again.

International pressure for change began to increase, and sanctions were having a bigger and bigger impact on the fragile economy. In 2010, in an effort to ease relations, the military government consented to hold the first elections in twenty years. Having learned their lesson from the abuses suffered after the 1990 election, the NLD boycotted the process. Surprise, surprise, the military-backed party, the USDP, won and one of the former generals was sworn in as president and head of Burma's first "civilian" government.

Obeying the electoral legislation that set the term of their mandate at a five-year term, elections were held again in 2015. On this occasion, the NLD did participate in the election and was rewarded with a large majority. Their leader, "the Lady," however, was banned from becoming president due to an arcane, suspiciously recent amendment to the constitution that bars any citizen with children who are foreign nationals from the office. Her two kids are British.

Since that time, the Lady's stature as Nobel Peace Prize winner, freedom fighter, and political prisoner has been tarnished by the horrors of the treatment of the Rohingya by the military in the far west of the country.

Did Aung San Suu Kyi become corrupt? Was she now a puppet of the military rolled out in an attempt to whitewash the atrocities? Or again is there a bigger game afoot here? Is she a student of her father's strategy, calculating and ruthless in pursuit of a greater goal? Tolerant and willing to make brutal sacrifices in order to win the war?

This time the dream is to rid the country of military rule, rather than the colonialists. In this case it sadly reduces the Rohingya to the status of sacrificial pawns,merely collateral damage in the bigger battle for freedom. Collateral damage being the prosaic, bureaucratic, double-speak vocabulary used to sanitize the real appalling suffering that is actually involved.

Our history makes our leaders as much as our leaders make our history, maybe more so. We may be too quick to praise our heroes and too quick to condemn them as villains when they fail. It's harder to be a hero now. We've become accustomed to too many Hollywood happy endings. We want our heroes to be infallible and immaculate. But how realistic is it for us to expect solutions without us all being willing to make compromises and sacrifice ourselves? We can't expect our leaders to have a magic wand that will solve all our problems. The issues are too intertwined and complicated.

As I write this, Aung San Suu Kyi is again under arrest and the citizens of Burma are again protesting and being shot by the military for their rebelliousness. It only confirms the poker game of compromise and confrontation that she has had to play for the last five years. My sense is that she has done the best that she can with the cards that she has been dealt, but when push comes to shove, the generals will always bring their guns to the table.

At the risk of sounding like a pompous ass (again?), I feel that the world needs hope, hope that only new heroes can supply. It is time for a changing of the guard, time to look to the young, to the women, the Malalas, the Thunbergs, the Maria Ressas, and the Suu Kyis, leaders who walk what they talk.

Apologies if this is all getting a bit long-winded. Reprieve is on its way, ironically in the form of more hot air.

Chapter 31

Around the Pagodas in Eighty Minutes

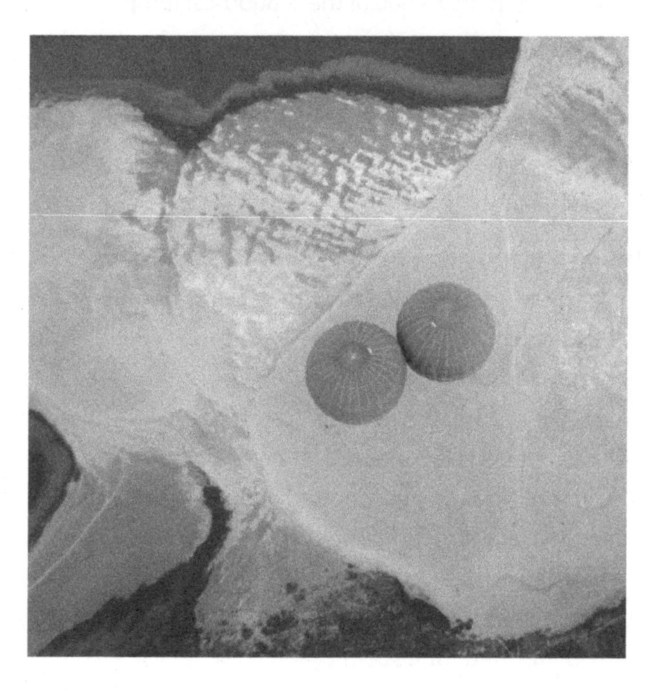

Balloons smooching over Bagan

"THIS IS MY SIMPLE RELIGION: THERE IS NO NEED FOR TEMPLES; NO NEED FOR COMPLICATED PHILOSOPHY. OUR OWN BRAIN, OUR OWN HEART IS OUR TEMPLE; THE PHILOSOPHY IS KINDNESS."

—Dalai Lama

"BECAUSE, YOU KNOW, I CAN'T WORK A BICYCLE PUMP."

—Judi Dench

Leaving the historical sites of the WWII Burma campaign in the southeast of the country, we make our way to Bagan, the one-time capital of the Burmese empire. It sits in the dry central plains of the country skirted by the Irrawaddy River to the west. It's a famed archaeological site, a Pagodas R Us sponsored by Lego, if you will. There are approximately 4,000 of these Buddhist temples constructed in a building boom that ran from the eleventh to fourteenth century. The structures commanding the landscape cover an area of about ten square miles. Numerous wars, fires, periods of abandonment, and earthquakes have taken their toll, sub-prime mortgages could be the next calamity to hit.

Restoration projects funded by organizations from all over the world have attempted reconstruction with varying degrees of success. Most of this reconstruction is done with brick, which happens to be pretty true to the original process. The soil in the area is red clay and brick kilns are still functioning to this day. The use of wood to fire the kilns has left the plains all but bereft of trees. The man-made semi-desert provides an amazing table for a Manhattan-like skyline of temples in every direction. They range in size and grandeur from village chapel to cathedrals of over 300 feet in height. The scale of the development is astounding. Where did they find all the bricklayers? Was Ireland emptied for a spell?[31]

We decide to make our first sortie out to the temples on foot. Horse hooves, actually. We hire a coachman, horse, and buggy for the day. A nice guy who spends lonely hours parked waiting for us as we explore the wonders on offer. To help pass the time he chews paan, leaves of the betel tree, which have a mildly narcotic stimulant effect. The visuals aren't so hot: ghoulish, bloodshot eyes, a blood-red mouth, and receding gums had transformed him into a daytime Dracula. While we are on the diurnal vampire theme, we clamber up one of the larger temples and join a throng of tourists to watch the sun

31 https://www.youtube.com/watch?v=Nfz9O_mSY1U?

sink behind this strangest of skylines—unforgettable—then high tail it back to the hotel before total darkness descends and the bats come out.

For a change of perspective we have booked a balloon trip for day two, our major extravagance on the holiday. We arrive for our flight in the predawn at the balloon company's launch site. Preparation for takeoff is supposed to be half of the entertainment.

Laying spread out on the ground are what appear to be massive tarps. The tarps, which are in fact the balloons, are soon transformed. Large wind fans are placed at the open ends of the balloons and cranked up. The balloons start to inflate. The technicians' job is to hold down the balloon as long as possible, which they do by holding onto ropes tethered to the sides and tops of the balloon. It's a weird sight. As the balloon swells, the "boys" take on the proportions of a crew of Lilliputians trying to hold down Gulliver as he raises his head from sleep. Dust rises from the "boys'" feet as they are dragged across the dirt field, like barefoot waterskiers. Eventually, they can hold the balloon no more and let go of the tethers. The balloon pops up vertically, half inflated, at this point looking like a giant, half-squeezed turkey baster.

The process is being repeated six other times as the other balloons in the drift (I don't know the collective noun for a collection of balloons, thought this would do) are also readied.

The eight of us passengers assigned to this balloon clamber into the basket. Yes, it is a basket made of wicker, like an oversized shopping basket (don't put all your tourists in one basket and more Lilliputian metaphors apply).

Our pilot Sandra—think Judy Dench in khakis and a bush hat, takes us through the landing drill.

"Back against the basket, look in the direction that you are coming from, crouch, bending your knees and think of England." She's clearly a veteran with a sense of humour. The pre-flight banter reveals that she is a hot air gypsy who has earned a living doing this all over the world. She exchanges professional insights with an amateur pilot who happens to be one of the passengers. At the end of the dialogue in her best jolly hockey sticks accent, she says, "It's always so much fun to do swapsies."

You have to have a certain background to get away with an utterance like that!

Pre-flight formalities concluded and, with a prolonged blast of a twelve-foot flare of naked flame into the maw of the balloon, we take off into the pre-dawn light. I am an instant convert (it's in my blood now, banana flambé for dessert tonight, fire with everything). Alas, they don't provide wieners or marshmallows during the flight. The sporadic roars from the propane burners are all Saturn 5 rocket but the motion is as gentle as being adrift in a small boat in a calm sea.

As is often the case it is an ill wind that doesn't set someone's hair on fire. I see one poor lady in her field below waving frantically and yelling, "Go away! Go away!" She must feel like Heathrow airport runway number one has been plonked down beside her house. On the plus side, the company employs as many as 200 Burmese.

The flight itself is a trip. A blood-red "Japanese" sun rises above the horizon and the whole vista slowly changes colour in sync with the sun. Sandra reels off names and legends associated with the pagodas closest to us. She needs a comprehensive knowledge of the site as no two trips are alike, all she can control is the altitude and orientation (direction, not so much). Yet she deftly manoeuvres the balloon so that the plains below us seem to rotate beneath our feet. It makes for lazy photography as each new subject conveniently spins into view.

Non-historic points of interest include the expressway built for "the generals" from the airport through the archeological site to their riverbank mansions. It's the only decent road in the area and it is for their own exclusive use. The locals have their own transitory benefits from the river. As the river recedes during the dry season they plant their crops lower and lower on the expanding riverbanks only to reverse the process in the rainy season, harvesting their crops as the swelling river chases them back.

All in all we have a spiffing wheeze of a jolly good time (I guess that I haven't quite got the accent licked yet). "Around the Pagodas in Eighty Minutes," before coming back to earth with barely a bump.

On day three we rent bikes, frequently get lost in the maze of dusty roads, stop at seemingly deserted temples. You are never alone for long. A caretaker may mysteriously appear to open the padlock and let you in. Kids show up to lead you up pitch-black staircases to the ramparts of the stupas. Trixie wonders out loud, "Do you think anyone has ever been mugged by four ten-year-olds before?" Despite the pesterings of the kids, we keep our cameras stowed. We don't want to habituate the behaviour. Better that we take only memories and leave only memories.

The whole area is a bit more commercial than Yangon. Here, there are a few semi-pushy touts hawking paintings and beautiful lacquer work but it is all pretty minor league compared to many Asian destinations. As word spreads about the wonders this will change and, before you know it . . .

In the final analysis, there's no resisting the spectacle of the selection of stupendous stupas on offer, but after a while I develop a kind of a pagoda blindness and have a bit of stupa stupification setting in. A year from now I probably won't remember the name of one of the temples, but for me it's more about the sum of the whole that makes it such an impressive sight and one that will stay with me forever. It's like the Hanging Gardens of Babylon: it's not just the one flowerbed but the whole garden.

Suitably buried in archaeological knowledge, albeit transient, it's time to sample a new mode of transport to our next destination. Rather than take the road to Mandalay, we choose to sail up the Irrawaddy River, a leisurely eleven-hour trip on an older river boat with room for about 150 passengers. It is nearing the end of the dry season so the crew have to be alive to the possibilities of running aground. Fortunately, the vessel is equipped with the latest navigational aids. They assign a young man with a bamboo pole to hang over the bow and regularly prod the bottom to test the depth like some Asian gondolier who has been given the wrong end of the stick.

It is a pleasant way to travel but concerning to see the constant convoy of barges sailing southwards all laden with enormous teak logs. One can only shudder to think what is happening to the forests in the north.

I doubt that a site is being prepared for another Bagan. Anyway, enough of the hot air for now. Happy landings. Our return to the capital for the last couple of days of our stay promise to provide more pedestrian escapades.

The visit is over all too quickly. We celebrate Trixie's birthday and our departure with dinner at the swanky "Strand" hotel, a grand, semi-restored (e.g., flat-screen TV hasn't caught on yet) British-built monster from the Victorian times. Tons of history, the Japanese used it for their HQ during their occupation of Burma during WWII. After a good dinner we head back to our hole-in-the-wall guest house. We hail a passing cycle rickshaw. It's an odd experience, lurching up the six-lane boulevard toward the Sule Paya, an impressive pagoda in the centre of downtown Yangon. It's like the Piccadilly Circus of the city, but different. Its history as a religious site supposedly goes back 2,500 years. The present incarnation of the pagoda dates back to the mid-1800s, roughly the same era as Piccadilly. But at nine o'clock on a Saturday night, the city centre and its surrounding crumbling Victorian buildings are deserted and the place is pitch black save for the few progressive entrepreneurs who have installed massive generators on the sidewalk for their own power, having long given up on the government ever providing a reliable source of electricity. This country is very rich in minerals and lumber, and has a plentiful labour supply and a potentially thriving agricultural sector that, before WWII, exported more rice than any other country in Asia. What went wrong?

Makes you think we're a bit hasty in our indignation about our own governments' shortcomings.

Our last day arrives, we drive to the airport and, like any other day in Myanmar, there is some new curiosity to take in: a monk having a sly smoke by a street vendor, a cyclist with a huge block of ice balanced on his back wheel cut us off, it's all reality TV.

Clear emigration after getting the needed three-day extension to our visa. More theatre: the visa office is a combination of filing room, staff canteen, and immigration office. We studiously avoid the big cheese in the room. He has more medals on his chest than Lord Mountbatten, first earl of Burma, and seek out a minion who good-naturedly applies the reassuring kerthunk kerthunk rubber stamp we're looking for. Pass through into the departure lounge with its smokeless, odourless, garbageless, chaosless, characterless, tasteless, surpriseless antiseptic uniformity of anywhere in the world. Spend our last few kyat on a juice, papaya only in colour, and an effigy of a chocolate brownie. We are back in the real world.

A sparrow flits by. Maybe there is hope yet.

EPILOGUE

Well after all of these stories did any of it help to answer the question why do we travel? Hopefully a few clues were to be found. Maybe they will help you answer why you travel and maybe these tales will provide a spark and your imagination will be writing the script for your next adventure and before you know it you will be away on your next jaunt.

Even now as I notice the player flags fluttering outside my bedroom window in Victoria, I find myself going back to the windswept vistas of the Langtang trek. Each trip has its own allure, a complete package with a beginning, a middle and an end. A gift, a story in a time capsule to ourselves that we can unearth and rebury as often as we like.

These are treasures that we can choose to share or not. As with all riches there is great temptation to flaunt one's good fortune and just as surely there are consequences for that vanity. The more desirable the picture painted the greater the lure for new travellers and the swifter and more dramatic the transformation of your heaven will be. It is all the more confusing that I should just be realizing this now and that maybe I don't want you to go where I have been. A bit late you might say, for me to be having a traveller's equivalent of a NIMBY moment. NIMPS- Not In My Private Shangri-La.

I would have been better to have jealously kept my favourites to myself, frozen them at a moment in time, at peak ripeness and perfection, anonymous and incorruptible, uniquely preserved not for others but just for me in case I want to go back and revisit them. A naive fantasy no doubt, given that change is inevitable. Luckily, I don't need to return to these places when I can further perfect and relive the experiences in my mind's eye refining, embellishing, sanctifying as it pleases me.

Seldom when one returns to an old haunt does one say that it has changed for the better. It is better to travel new paths. Still better to keep your favourite backwaters off the digital map which are often blind and vulnerable to the problems that visitors innocently bring with them.

With these ideas rattling around my mind, I make the fateful mistake of putting these thoughts into words and asking Trixie's opinion.

"Wouldn't it be fun to go to ….?"

Trixie doesn't need to be asked twice nor does she even need to know where we might go. Just the idea that we might change direction and travel South instead of East is reason enough to start fantasising. Africa and South America two continents new to us are just sitting there waiting for our amusement.

I am also sure that seventy isn't going to be the new sixty and as the prospects of my seventies swell somewhat foggily to fill the front windshield and my sixties rapidly shrink in significance in the rear view mirror, I am happy to have this book completed before I become raccoon 70.

Memories of trips are no small delights, especially as you approach that tipping point when you start remembering less and forgetting more. I may never become a gypsy, but I am not yet ready for the pipe and slippers yet either.

Travel?

Yes…. more please.

"South it is!"

"Now this is not the end. It is not even the beginning of the end.
But it is, perhaps, the end of the beginning."
– Winston Churchill.

About Face | APOLOGIA

"If there is anyone here whom I have not insulted
I beg his pardon." **Brahms**

I realize that as time passes what is socially acceptable changes and also as one ages time passes more quickly. So having been unable to keep up with the mores of the day I would like to apologize to everyone for everything in this book. Getting this apology out of the way up front will save us all some time later on. So here it is.

I made those decisions and they were my mistake and

I am here to say that I am sorry, I convinced myself that the normal

rules didn't apply, I was out of control and am deeply ashamed

and can only ask that you can find room in your heart to

believe in me again as I receive guidance to conquer my demons.

I have taken necessary steps to ensure my return to health,

reached out to the medical professionals for help,

to tell me why I did what I did and I will have that help.

I learned that things have happened here that never

should have happened . In the darkness we found the light.

Only 10 employees . . . are involved in making napalm

this was a big mistake on our part. Our goal has always been

to create products that our customers love.

Generally, the suicide rate in a society will increase when its GDP rises. A painful but important reminder of the progress we still need to make. I'm just very, very sorry that it's come to this, that a small personal matter has been able to be blown out of all proportion, and with such venom and such gore, I mean it's just terrible.

My behavior has caused considerable worry to my business partners. A chicken restaurant without any chicken. *It's not ideal.* ***We are not proud that happened.*** This kind of incident should **simply not happen.** **I think that the environmental impact of** this disaster is likely to have been very modest. **I want my life back.**

I have not been true to my values. I deeply regret that this is not how I meant for things ***to go I made a mistake in judgement.*** **I also let you down and I let my family down** and I've hurt myself as well. My hope is that these words can mark a new beginning.

And some more apologies if you have noticed that in preparing my mea culpa that I have borrowed a word or two from my fellow transgressors (and apologies if I am offending the trans community by using this word it was not my intent to weaponize it, nevertheless we must all be vigilant and sensitive to potential PTSD triggers) but I would be remiss if I didn't give a tip of the hat to the masters of the apologia art form, my thanks go out to: Tiger Woods, Bill Clinton, Justin Trudeau, Mark Zuccerberg, Bill Gates, Google, VW, Du Pont, Martha Stewart, Mike Tyson, BP, Kentucky Fried Chicken, Ellen DeGeneres, Dow Chemical, Harvey Weinstein, Foxconn, Apple, Mel Gibson.

https://sorrywatch.com/category/celebrity-apologies/

Health Alert

If any readers have been triggered or retraumatized by any of the content in this book they should follow the following guidelines which Boon Doggle Legal Department has developed in collaboration with The WHO. This three stage protocol is intended to stabilize readers who may be suffering from LITS (Literary Induced Trauma Syndrome). Should symptoms worsen or persist seek the advice of a health care professional immediately.

Protocol level I

Proceed immediately to the safe space on page 322 blank page.

Protocol level II

Proceed to page 323 remove calming device (cut out with scissors). Place cut outs over eyes attach with sticky tape (not included). Note–If you are using the audio book roll the paper up and stick it in your ears.

Protocol level III

Climb into a cryogenic chamber and come out a) when humanity has ceased to exist or b) even more dull when everyone shares your point of view.

PROTOCOL LEVEL I – SAFE SPACE

PROTOCOL LEVEL II

Calming Device

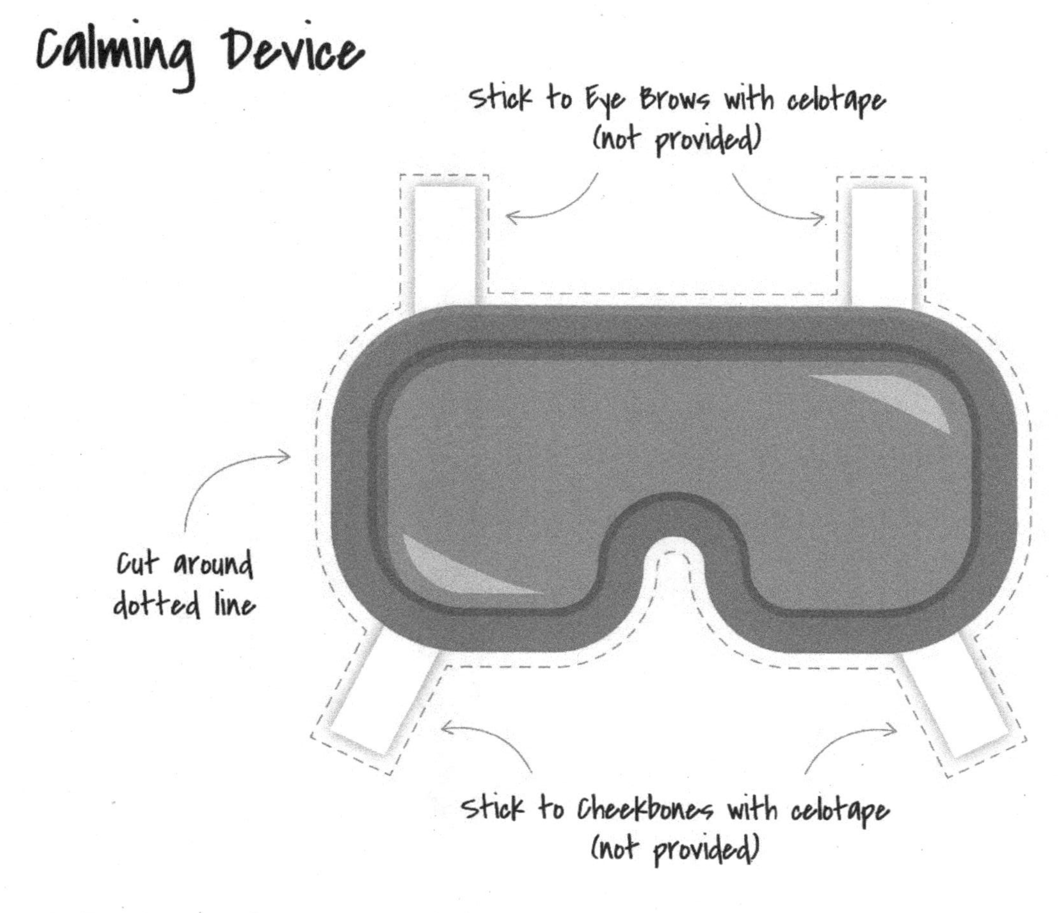

Stick to Eye Brows with celotape
(not provided)
Cut around
dotted line
Stick to Cheekbones with celotape
(not provided)

WHAT DID WE LEARN - A QUIZ

The following questions could test a variety of things.

Your general knowledge, your powers of deduction, the state of your memory, or whether you found anything of interest at all in the book

Listed below is one question per chapter, arranged in numerical sequence.

All you have to do is match the answers listed on SHEET 2 with the questions asked. Each answer may only be used once.

Hint: If you are struggling, you can refer back to the chapter in question where you should find the answer somewhere in the narrative.
(Or if you are like me, look at the solutions key on SHEET 3.)

The answer to number 1 has already been filled in to get you started

CHAPTER NUMBER	QUESTION	ANSWER	
1	Which civil war caused a diversion to India?	G	Nepalese
2	Gandhi addressed his correspondence to which infamous politician as "Dear Friend"?		
3	In which of the destinations visited would you be most likely to hear Portuguese.		
4	This metropolis was ten times more populated than London 600 years ago.		
5	God moves in mysterious ways—which one uses a Toyota?		
6	This country produces thirty-five of these every minute?		
7	This capital, founded in 380 BC, is situated where ?		
8	Where is Beckham bending it these days?		
9	How many Rolling Stones song titles are there in this mountainous episode?		
10	How many metres high is Sagarmatha?		
11	Pee turns to ice at what temperature?		

WHAT DID WE LEARN - A QUIZ

CHAPTER NUMBER	QUESTION	ANSWER	
12	This martinet brought to mind which film star?		
13	Where does this snowflake end up 1,300 kilometres later?		
14	This earthquake hit when ?		
15	*Bistari bistari* is spoken in which country (take your time)?		
16	A Kukhri is a kind of what?		
17	How many languages are in use in Nepal if you include "horn language"?		
18	What percent of its body weight does a rhino consume each day?		
19	The most dangerous airport in the world is where?		
20	Which crossing is transited up to 2.4 million times a day?		
21	A maid's work is never done. Ninety hours a week will earn you $180 US a month where?		
22	Which beer named after a dynasty became a dynasty?		
23	Which pedestrian accoutrement is being used to prevent diarrhea?		
24	What year did this pop classic hit the charts?		
25	Col. Kurtz was modelled on special ops agent Tony Poe (Hepny). Where did he operate?		
26	Brother Number One was born in 1925. What age was he in 1973?		
27	Which city still lords its superiority over its neighbours?		
28	Careless use of which word could put you in the soup?		
29	Where do Westerners go for ruby sunrises and sunsets ?		
30	Which number commemorates this modern-day revolution?		
31	Judy in the sky with tourists guided us over which historical site?		

Match these answers to the questions listed on page 324

A	Zero
B	Siem Reap
C	Mohinga
D	Burma
E	8
F	Bagan
G	Nepalese
H	Hitler
I	Goa
J	Hampi
K	Sai Baba
L	Babies
M	Sri Lanka
N	Nepal
O	17
P	8849
Q	-5
R	John Wayne
S	The Bay of Bengal
T	2015
U	Nepal
V	A knife
W	124
X	1
Y	Lukla
Z	Shibuya
AA	Phnom Penh
BB	Ankor
CC	Socks
DD	1963
EE	Laos

Solution key by chapter number and answer letter

Chapter	Answer	Chapter	Answer	Chapter	Answer	Chapter	Answer
1	G	9	O	17	W	25	EE
2	H	10	P	18	X	26	A
3	I	11	Q	19	Y	27	B
4	J	12	R	20	Z	28	C
5	K	13	S	21	AA	29	D
6	L	14	T	22	BB	30	E
7	M	15	U	23	CC	31	F
8	N	16	V	24	DD		

Its all because of the virgin

Curated selections from the time toilet aka "the internet"

Below you will find links to the Time Toilet

There is one QR code for each of the internet references included in the manuscript. These information snippets are loosely, in some cases very loosely, related to the subject matter in each chapter. They will hopefully amuse or educate you or encourage you to throw your phone away.

They are presented in chapter order with a small caption that may give a hint at as to what will be in store for you should you wish to give your thumbs some exercise.

Getting There
mumbai population

Champagne and orange
ghandi letters

Riding the Volvo U boat
head wobble

crampi in hampi
how to use and Indian toilet

from the frying pan to the ashram
indian philanthropist guru

Spitting Image
tom cruise ray bans

Serendip
kama sutra

climb every mountain
spam

satisfaction
Angie

lightening strikes the gokyo trek
tips for high altitude hiking

the 1 2 3 of A B C
family planning

true grit in mustang
kali gandaki gorge

the man in the moon
manaslu road construction

peter pan
hindi song

It Was The Best of Times It Was
octopus brain

headless in Kathmandu
hindu deities

voyage of the crammed
world's most dangerous airport

I am bat
para hawk

what to do for a 'do in kathmadu
the hippie trail

the power of the little green men
onsen etiquette

welcome to the hotel lilliputia
dame edna

white men walking
meeting jargon

put a sock in it
plastic bottles

the do ron ron
kamchatka bears

among the hmong
laos bombing

a pol potted history
even a bird needs a nest

pinnochio meets Lara croft
khmer empire

bumps in the road
corruption index

buddhists boats and back country
Burma's rubies

heroes and villains
death railway

around the pagodas in 80 mins
irish space shot

GLOSSARY

A Guide to Foreign and Obscure Words and Phrases

Acharaya - a wise and learned teacher, like Bono or Bill Gates.

Adam and Eve suits - the natural state at birth during the binary era (now obsolete).

Alphabet community - a coalition of minority groups that includes TS (trans species) as well as LGBTQ.

Alponauts - climbers who prefer capsules to tents.

Ashram - a proverbial place of reflection.

Baba, Swami, God, Clapton, Trump - givers and seers of light.

Ben Gunn - a shipwrecked character in Robert Louis Stevenson's *Treasure Island*, who dreams about being able to eat cheese again. Regarded with much empathy by hikers in the Himalaya.

Birus - post-work destresser favoured by Japanese salarymen.

Blootered - a slang term meaning somewhat intoxicated rather than entirely helpless.

Brother Number One - big brother, Pol Pot.

Bistari bistari - a desperate, if last ditch plea delivered by hikers to their Nepali porters to slow down.

Book E - hard-copy literature that contains links to the virtual world.

Brownouts - drastic measures to address an excess demand for electricity. Commonly implemented in impoverished states like Cambodia, Nepal, Rwanda, and California.

BTS - Brown Trouser Syndrome, an indicator of trauma, perhaps.

Chhanng - Himalayan beer brewed from rice. As legend would have it, catnip for Yeti.

Coonlit - prose written for, by, or about the Procyon Lotor community.

Cot case - a bed ridden person, conceivably a sufferer of the Yangon Yips.

CPP - Canada Pension Plan or Cambodia's Peoples Party. The same party has been going since 1979, but only the host is having a good time.

CUPE - Canada's largest union

Dahl Batt - K rations for Nepalese porters. A lentil or rice stew eaten for breakfast, lunch, and dinner.

Davy Crockett - boyhood hero for anyone born before 1955, anathema to all raccoons.

Eckeckeckeck - call of the woodpecker, except perhaps in Malaysia.

Foutered - a usually more affectionate than derogatory reference to inebriation.

Fructus - Latin to enjoy (see also tummy banana).

Fuji - an extinct film-making company and volcano.

Gaigin - as yet uncancelled reference to a NITNOC favoured in the birthplace of the emoji.

Gora - Indo equivalent to gringo, a relatively mild insult.

GHG - driver of climate change, escalated by Indian cuisine.

Heath Robinson - an unflattering description applied to suspect machinery.

HPM - honks per minute, a measure of safe driving.

Holi - Hindu celebration of the arrival of spring.

Horn language - a form of Nepalese especially used as a desperate attempt to avoid vehicular death.

Hindi - the most commonly used of India's more than sixty languages.

Idukki Gold - reputedly precious herbal relaxant produced in the Kerela state.

Imodium - an unblocker of the La, a hiker's best friend.

Irrawaddy dolphin - navigationally challenged mammal.

Katmandu quickstep - a desperate quest for a toilet.

Kali - Hindu goddess of ultimate power rivalled only by Serena Williams, perhaps.

Karma - destiny with a dash of metaphysical justice thrown in for good measure.

Karma yoga - oddly enough, there appears to be no equivalent.

Kip - Laotian currency currently equivalent to two thirds of four fifths of bugger all.

Kielbasa - preferred sausage of Russian anesthesiologists.

Kyat - Burmese currency; only crypto currency is less understood.

Jom jom - enthusiastic, if futile exhortation given by Nepali porters to their clients to get a move on.

Kafkaesque - dreamlike and surreal, like watching the fly on Mike Pence's head.

La - French indefinite article or a mountain pass in the Himalaya.

Langur - a grey primate found in the Himalaya, also known as Hanuman monkey, no relation to the far from languorous Hindu god Hanuman. The god of strength.

Losar - Hogmanay to the non-Scottish.

Mohinga - a Canadian form of greeting but in actuality a Burmese breakfast soup.

Momos - Tibetan dumplings (whatever they are).

Mr. Diarrhea - a fictional character created to raise awareness about the eponymous malady.

Nara - correction centre for deer, also site of Abe assassination.

Neti pot - an apparatus used for rinsing phlegm and mucilaginous deposits from nasal passages, I am afraid.

NITNOC - Non-Indigenous Traveller Not of Colour—Trixie, for example.

Om mane padme hum - Buddhist mantra ubiquitous in Tibet and yoga studios.

Pachyderms - producers of up to 200 pounds of fertilizer per day. Very large animals, typically with thick skin needed to shrug off the comments made about the amount of fertilizer they produce.

Palm Sunday - possibly a metaphor related to the weekend use of handheld devices.

Paan - chewed betel nut, which when spat out, leaves a conspicuous red stain that could easily be misidentified as the residue of a seagull with hemorrhoids.

Plekking - unsurprisingly, this verb is used mainly to refer to seniors hiking at altitude, as in plodding and not quite trekking

Quantitative easing - Argentine economic policy more recently adapted in Western countries. When all else fails, print more money.

Raksi - Nepalese beverage fermented from millet unsurprisingly very popular at Losar.

Ri - Nepalese for mountain, they should know.

Roof surfing - economy-class travel available to passengers waitlisted on Nepali bus routes. Bus companies offer a ladder up to the roof of the bus and a space to squat amongst the cargo lashed to the roof rack. In-flight entertainment includes vehement prayer and frequent sphincter clenching.

Sadhu - holy ascetic, often itinerant who survives on the charity of others. Field markings include orange robes, a staff, and ZZ Top beard. Native to the Indian subcontinent

Sagarmatha - before Everest existed, the Nepali had a name for the highest mountain in the world.

Sake - a beverage similar in flavour to raksi.

Sex tourist - a person who can't find sex at home.

Shaligram - it is of course an ammonite, a fossilized shell anything from 400 to 66 million years old.

Sherpa - originally the name of a Himalayan mountain tribe. Now commonly used to refer to anyone carrying unreasonably sized cargo on their backs for low pay.

Shihon - a capital or metropolis like Nanaimo or Basingstoke found in Japan.

Stewarddessbots - AI in heels.

Tharu - ethnic group from southern Nepal.

The East India Company - the Corporation that ruled India for roughly 100 years before the British Crown took over.

The Greek experience - possibly an early precursor to the LGBTQ movement. If not, see QE.

The holy grail - any functioning unchipped porcelain connected to a central sewage system.

The Raj - the roughly ninety years that the British Crown ruled India before independence, big tech, and call centres came along.

Twinkle cave - mysterious incubator of life.

Tourist - one who knows what they want to see.

Trans species - a person of non-homo sapiens genealogy.

Traveller - one who doesn't know what to expect.

Trilby - a narrow-brimmed hat common in the mid-twentieth century. Narrowly escaping obsolescence thanks to Leonard Cohen and Inspector Clouseau.

Tsampa - pronounced to rhyme like Tsampa. A porridge-like food eaten by Tibetans. Kilts optional.

Tummy banana - a fruit whose seed, given suitable conditions, may procreate non-fructus progeny. Possibly a euphemism for the male organ not limited to tropical locations.

Yak or dzo - in all probability left over Scrabble letters but more likely sub-species of Himalayan ox.

Yangon Yips - Kathmandu quickstep, allegedly malodorous forms of Asian exercise, not to be confused with load shedding (see also brownouts).

Zori - you need an a to z in your glossary—this is the z part. Japanese flip flops worn indoors.

BOOK CLUB QUESTIONS

1) If you could choose only one of the destinations in this book to visit, which one would it be? What appeals to you about it? How would you do your trip differently than the author?

2) In your opinion, in works of non-fiction, how strictly should authors stick to accurate descriptions of events and facts and how much leeway is justified in making the story entertaining? How well do you think the author did in finding an appropriate balance?

3) Did Trixie and Raccoon Sixty's exploits make you want to travel to more remote destinations, be more adventurous, raise raccoons, or give up air travel altogether and save the planet?

4) At various times during their travels, circumstances made Trixie and the author question their own actions and values. What event did you find the most thought-provoking? Have you experienced similarly reflective moments when travelling? What were they and what conclusions did you come to?

5) The fear of being confronted with diabolical plumbing can be a deterrent to independent travel in Third World countries. Does this book allay or confirm those fears? What has been your worst white-knuckle WC nightmare?

6) Krishna barely talks and yet his influence is palpable. How does he make his presence felt and why do you think that he converses so little?

7) What do you think compels Trixie and Raccoon Sixty to return to the mountains? Do you think the draws are the same for both of them? Discuss the pros and cons of returning to familiar destinations rather than visiting new places.

8) On more than one occasion, Trixie and Raccoon Sixty were unable to continue on their treks. How do you think they felt when they had to turn back? What would you have done, faced with similar circumstances?

9) Village life on the popular mountain treks is being transformed by the day-to-day interaction with Western travellers. What do you think are the benefits and what are the drawbacks to this transformation? Do you think that a reasonable balancing of the new ways and the old ways can be achieved?

10) "Generosity consists not of the sum given but the manner that it is bestowed." —Gandhi. Discuss this in the context of the people that the author has met during his travels. How would you compare the generosity of the schoolteacher in the Burmese backcountry with the philanthropy of a tech billionaire?

11) Au Sung Su Kyi, Burma's former leader, has been revered as a fighter for democracy, awarded a Nobel Peace Prize, and hailed as a national hero. More recently, she has been condemned as a villain for lack of action in addressing the victimization of the minority ethnic Rohingya in Burma. How do you view this now imprisoned leader? Hero or villain? What could she have done differently and what do you think would have been the consequences?

12) Quotations are used throughout the book. Are any of them familiar to you or do any of them particularly resonate with you?

13) What do you make of the relationship between Raccoon Sixty and Trixie? If you could choose anyone (alive or dead, historical, fictional, friend, or family) to accompany you on your next trip, who would it be and why?

It's All Because of the Virgin image credits

Chapters 13,17,25,27,29,31 By the author

Chapters 1,3,4,5,6,10,12,14,15,23,29 Adobe Stock

Chapters 2,7,9,11,16,19,21,24,26,30 Public Domain

Images sourced from Wikimedia commons with attribution

Chapter 17 Pearson Scott Foresman

Chapter 18 Toby Hudson

Chapter 20 Tatsuo Yamashita

Chapter 22 Zhnka

Chapter 24 Shawn Lea

Chapter 26 Casa Rosada

Chapter 28 Allan Warren

Acknowledgements

I have been fortunate to receive help and encouragement from many sources in bringing these recollections into book form. That help and encouragement has one source, generosity. People's generosity with their time. Is there anything more precious?

Some people just cannot be helped and that truism, due to a combination of my stubbornness and literary limitations, may be evident in this publication. Consequently, to protect the innocent, I have anonymized my advisors, lest any of my amateurishness reflects on them.

Many of these stories first came to life in the form of email "postcards" which I sent to friends (you know who you are) and family. I was fortunate enough to be thanked with a few words of appreciation which must have seeded some sort of notion about a travelogue (as usual I ignored the wisecracks about my sanity). Little did they know that without that kind feedback this book may never have seen the light of day. Better luck next time. Who could have predicted that a few positive words could have had such devastating results.

I should start with the marvelous Ms. EM. Who, thanks to her encouragement and perseverance, helped transform the first draft of the manuscript into something resembling a book. I was severely traumatized when other responsibilities wrested her away from the project. Why she thought that running a business, building a new house, being eight months pregnant and managing two toddlers (one of them being me) might be a bit much, I have no idea. This younger generation, no stamina, I tell you.

My mysterious designer CD has brought artistry and professionalism to my doodles. It does feel a bit odd to be praising her to you folks considering that her face I've never seen and her voice I've never heard. I don't know, for all I know she might be a chat bot. Mr. B. at the publishing house who good humoredly talked me through how to incorporate the many peculiarities inherent in producing this book. I hope that my intransigence didn't factor into his decision to change occupation. I wish him well and, if I were his counsellor, I would suggest a career in the world of diplomacy.

PF an editor par excellence and a true professional and friend whose advice I should have taken more of. It is just as well she is retired, or she could have found herself been drummed out of the business. I hope that she doesn't feel that she has brought the profession into disrepute.

To my kids Scara and Rocky who are of the TLDR (Too Long Didn't Read) generation I am especially happy that they took the time to read my words, I feel special. I am grateful that they accept me for who I am in any of my identities, humour my idiosyncrasies and encourage me to be the best version of myself that I can be. They don't even seem to mind if it causes them embarrassment anymore. They have done their best to wake me to woke.

Trixie who transforms my ruminations into realities, her implicit philosophy being "if you can think it, you can do it". Without her gung-ho impulses there would be a lot fewer stories to tell.

ABOUT THE AUTHOR

Raccoon Sixty is a retired civil servant living in Victoria, Canada. He was formerly known as the symbol for "Don't let your baby put their head in a bucket in case they might drown."

He is married with two adult children. He is a cisgendered trans-species who identifies as a raccoon but has not come out yet.

It's All Because of the Virgin was winner of the prestigious BoonDoggle Travel Book of the Year Award in 2024.

His hobbies include travel, emptying the garbage, and climbing trees.

It's All Because of the Virgin (subtitled *Twisted Tales from the East*) is his first book.